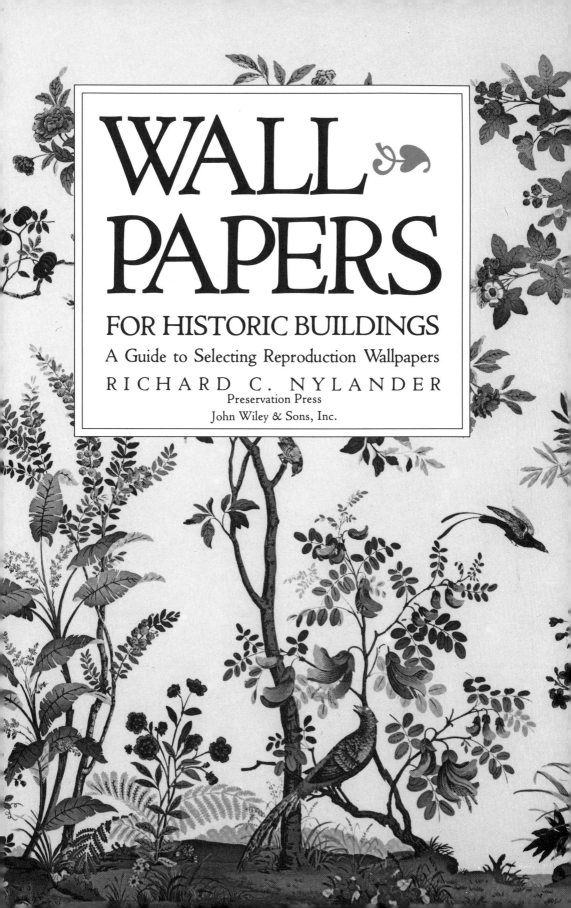

WALL PAPERS

FOR HISTORIC BUILDINGS

A Guide to Selecting Reproduction Wallpapers

R I C H A R D   C .   N Y L A N D E R

Preservation Press

John Wiley & Sons, Inc.

Printed in the United States of America
   4   3   2

Library of Congress Cataloging in Publication Data

Nylander, Richard C.
    Wallpapers for historic buildings: a guide to selecting reproduction
wallpapers / Richard C. Nylander. — [2nd ed.]
       p.   cm.
    Includes bibliographical references.
    ISBN 0-471-14431-2
    1. Wallpaper—Reproduction—Catalogs.   I. Title.
NK3399.H37   1992
747'.3'074—dc20   91-43269

Cover and endleaves: LA HAIE PANEL, 1815–25. Brunschwig & Fils. (See
page 47.)
Title pages 2–3: DECOR CHINOIS, 1832. Zuber. (See page 92.)
Page 6: Detail of a billhead, Appleton Prentiss, Boston, 1791. (Society for
the Preservation of New England Antiquities)
Pages 8–9: BOWER, c. 1910. Bradbury & Bradbury. (See page 211.)
Pages 28–29: IRIS FRIEZE, 1876, from Fenway Roomset. Bradbury &
Bradbury. (See page 175.)

Designed and typeset by Meadows & Wiser, Washington, D.C.

This revised edition of Wallpapers for Historic Buildings was made possible in part by the generous support of Brunschwig & Fils, F. Schumacher & Company, Galacar & Company, and Classic Revivals.

ACKNOWLEDGMENTS

This revised edition of *Wallpapers for Historic Buildings* would not have been possible without the interest and assistance of the following people. Special thanks goes to those who provided additional information on their collections and arranged for special photography.

Bruce Bradbury, Bradbury & Bradbury; Judy Straeten, Thomas Marshall, and Murray Douglas, Brunschwig & Fils; John Burrows and Andrew Naeve, J. R. Burrows & Company; Susan Freedman, Clarence House; John Buscemi, Paula Tomaso, Guy Evans, Patrice Mauny, Tom Helm, Robert Ness, Robert Weston, Georgina Hamilton, and Suzanne Forge, Classic Revivals; Ron Tanner, Cowtan & Tout; Whitney Lewis, Bentley Brothers; Deborah Diament, A. L. Diament & Company; Frederic Galacar, Galacar & Company; Christopher Hyland, Christopher Hyland Incorporated; Kathleen Boston and Janice Rox, Katzenbach & Warren; Martha Kazelunas, Lee Jofa; Robert Carter, Mt. Diablo Handprints; Denise Vouri and Lesley Hoskins, Sanderson & Sons; Robert Bitter and Leslie Degeorges, Scalamandré; Margot Horsey, Richard Slavin and Vivian Infante, Schumacher; Lori Reagle, Thibaut; Arthur Athas and Leah Forsman, Twigs; Florence Schroeder and Wendy Schroeder, Victorian Collectibles Limited; Bernard Scott, Waterhouse Wallhangings; Tania Bobrinskoy, Zina Studios; Gisele Chalaye, Zuber; Penny Bigmore, Essex Institute; Susan Borchardt, Gunston Hall; William Flynt, Historic Deerfield; Karin Cullity, Strawbery Banke Museum; and Robert Kelly of *Wallpaper Reproduction News*.

Additional thanks go to Andrea Gilmore for researching specific reproductions, Anne Donaghy for assisting with the production of the manuscript, and David Bohl for photographing many of the samples. Margaret Pritchard provided information on the wallpapers at Colonial Williamsburg, and Julian Hudson made it possible to include photographs of the wallpapers at Prestwould. Gretchen Smith Mui provided essential editorial support.

Special thanks to Jane Nylander, for her patience, insight, and help, and to Sarah, Tom, and Tim, who lived through the preparation of another manuscript.

7

INTRODUCTION

WALLPAPERS
FOR HISTORIC BUILDINGS

Since its earliest documented use in England, in the Master's Lodgings at Christ College in Cambridge in 1509, wallpaper has been a popular means of enhancing interior spaces in both domestic and public buildings because it fills otherwise blank walls with a wide variety of design and color. Reproduction wallpaper can be an important element in the restoration of historic buildings.

Like carpets and textiles, wallpaper was chosen to make a room fashionable, complement its architecture, and provide a unifying background for its furnishings. Once applied to the walls, however, wallpaper became a part of the structure. Unlike carpets, textiles, and other furnishings, it could not be moved and incorporated into another decorative scheme. When wallpaper became worn or unfashionable, it no longer fulfilled its purpose and was either covered or removed. Only occasionally was a fragment kept for sentimental reasons. Thus, fewer samples of historic wallpaper survive than do examples of other decorative interior elements.

Since 1983, when the first edition of *Wallpapers for Historic Buildings* was published, the interest in wallpaper as a decorative component has steadily increased. More information is now available about historic wallpaper patterns, their designers, and the technology that produced them. Many rooms of original or early wallpapers have been professionally conserved so that they can be enjoyed for years to come. Reproduction wallpapers have been introduced into countless historic houses as an integral part of the restoration process.

Interest in reproduction wallpapers has been shared by curators, historic house administrators, interior designers, and museums with wallpaper archives as well as the manufacturers themselves. The quest for accuracy in recreating period interiors has led curators, house committees, and even some private home owners to commission custom reproduction wallpapers rather than rely on what is commercially available. Manufacturers have responded by paying more attention to accurate artwork and color matching.

The stairhall, or "saloon," at Prestwould in Clarksville, Virginia,

Hanging a custom-made reproduction wallpaper at the Hamilton House, South Berwick, Maine, in 1898. The pattern copied fragments of the 18th-century pillar and arch wallpaper found in the same hallway. The pattern "Arch" on page 45 is the current reproduction. (Society for the Preservation of New England Antiquities)

provides an excellent example in one room of the various approaches to wallpaper possible in a historic building. The old photograph shows the space as it appeared around 1900. At some point after the photograph was taken, all the decorative papers in the room with the exception of the French scenic paper seen on the left wall were removed, and the walls and woodwork were painted white. Recently, the room has been restored to its former splendor. The antique scenic wallpaper has been professionally conserved. The elaborate flocked border, the only other pattern to be saved, was reproduced from a fragment. The two other designs were known only from the photograph. Research revealed that a pristine sample of the neoclassical dado was preserved in the collections of the Cooper-Hewitt Museum; it was reproduced with the museum's cooperation. No example of the sidewall pattern could be located in any wallpaper collection. Therefore the design was reproduced using the photograph for the design elements, the 1829 bill for color references, and other period wallpapers to ensure a correct approach to the design motifs.

Until the past decade, wallpaper design and its use in American buildings had not been explored as extensively as other decorative arts. The reasons are many. Foremost is that few collections of historic wallpaper samples exist. Few manufacturers had maintained a company archive in the European tradition, where samples of each pattern were retained. Major museums have not collected samples of historic wallpaper; wallpaper is not easily displayed, nor is it easily collectible unless it covers a hat box or lines a trunk. Moreover, the written records most often relied on when researching a historic house—estate inventories and probate deeds, for example—seldom document the use of wallpaper. Consequently, the importance of wallpaper in the decoration of a room had never been recognized or considered as seriously as the other elements.

This lack of interest and information changed dramatically in the 1980s both in the United States and abroad. Wallpaper finally came of age. In 1980 Catherine Lynn's *Wallpaper in America* became the first book on the subject since Nancy McClelland's study of 1924. It was followed by this author's more regional survey, *Wallpaper in New England*, in 1986. These recent publications grew out of indepth studies of the two largest repositories of historic wallpapers in the country—the collections of the Cooper-Hewitt Museum and the Society for the Preservation of New England Antiquities. In addition to these publications, special exhibitions of this rarely seen decorative art were mounted by both museums. Wallpaper collections in England and France were brought to the attention of the American public through *Wallpapers*, Charles Oman and Jean Hamilton's 1982 survey of the Victoria and Albert Museum collec-

The "Saloon" at Prestwould, Clarksville, Virginia, c. 1900 and today. The historic photograph documents the wallpapers and border that were purchased from F. Regnault, Jr., of Richmond, Virginia, in 1831. All the wallpapers except the French scenic paper seen at the left were subsequently removed. Reproduction wallpaper patterns were copied from surviving fragments of the originals and reconstructed from the historic photograph. (Prestwould Foundation)

tion, and Odile Nouvel's *Wallpapers of France* (1981).

In her introduction to *Wallpaper in America*, Lynn refers to a promotional pamphlet written in 1880 by Clarence Cook entitled "What Shall We Do with Our Walls?" The question remains a valid one that should be considered by every property owner and restoration committee dedicated to restoring a historic building accurately. A quick survey, however, reveals that little attention had been paid to this question. During the 1950s, 1960s, and 1970s the most popular solution had been to paint the walls of an 18th- or early 19th-century house white. This approach has conveyed the false impression that before the Victorian period rooms were stark, the only color coming from elaborate draperies at the windows and oriental rugs on the floors—equally false presumptions. Lynn notes that in the late 19th century, the peak period of wallpaper production and use, white walls were considered "relics of barbarism, and almost a thing of the past." In the mid-20th century, however, white walls became almost a symbol of traditional historic decoration.

Whitewash, an easy and effective treatment for walls, was used extensively in the 18th century. Wallpaper, when first produced, was a luxury. Anyone who could afford expensive furniture and textiles would also have wanted to complement this display of wealth and taste by hanging paper on the walls of the family home. As wallpaper became increasingly available and affordable, it became the typical wall treatment. In 1850 Andrew Jackson Downing wrote in his popular and useful book *The Architecture of Country Houses*: "We confess a strong partiality for the use of paperhangings for covering the walls of cottages." Downing stressed that one advantage is "in the enhanced architectural effect which may be given to a plain room, by covering the walls with a paper of suitable style."

The use of reproduction wallpaper and the choice of a particular pattern depend on the purpose of the restoration, rehabilitation, or redecoration of the historic building. The information included here is intended to serve as a guide for curators and committees of museum houses whose aim is to convey an accurate impression of a building's former appearance or create an accurate period interpretation, for homeowners who are seeking wallpapers that are appropriate to the architectural style of a historic house or that provide a sympathetic background for a collection of antiques, and for people who wish to introduce a period look to a rehabilitation or adaptive-use project.

This book presents reproductions of historic wallpapers that are currently available. The original documents from which the designs are copied date from 1700 to 1930, and the information is organized according to historical period. A short essay introducing popular patterns and technology precedes each section. The works cited in the bibliography should be consulted for their illustrations and detailed information on the history of wallpaper design and production.

Like Downing, this author confesses a strong partiality toward the appropriate use of wallpaper in restoration and rehabilitation projects, and it is hoped that the reproduction wallpaper patterns included here will help restorers of historic buildings paper their walls in a style suitable to the purpose of the restoration.

HISTORY OF REPRODUCTION WALLPAPERS

The interest in old wallpaper patterns seems to have begun in the late 19th century and coincides with a general interest in the American past that was kindled by the Centennial Exhibition of 1876 in Philadelphia. By that time architects had already begun to study early American buildings for design inspiration. In the course of the next 20 years, local groups became increasingly concerned about the fate of buildings considered historically important to their communities. Many were saved and became the repositories for collections of artifacts. Interest in the American past also was reflected in interior decoration; imitating the historical styles of European decoration was no longer the only option. The fashionable American interior acquired a certain charm and aura of stability with the inclusion of an heirloom chair found in Grandmother's attic or a piece of old china purchased during an afternoon outing of "antiquing."

Before 1900 some historical societies and occasionally even a few private owners had commissioned custom reproductions of early papers they had found on the walls of the buildings they were restoring. In her chatty book *Old Time Wall Papers*, published in 1905, Kate Sanborn indicates that wallpaper manufacturers had responded to a demand for papers appropriate for Colonial Revival houses and that wallpapers reproducing old designs were readily available. Sanborn considered wallpaper reproductions an "expensive matter," the price per roll being six to ten dollars. Expensive they were when one realizes that the cheapest paper offered in the Sears catalog of the same year cost only three cents for a double roll. These early reproductions were not as accurate as those reproduced today. More liberties were taken with the designs, and many incorporated architectural elements or motifs from old tapestries. Today, they reflect their own time more than the period they sought to represent.

During the first half of the 20th century, better reproduction wallpapers became available and were standard offerings of many wallpaper manufacturers. Firms such as Thomas Strahan Company in Chelsea, Massachusetts, and the M. H. Birge Company in Buffalo, New York, specialized in such papers. The documents from which the designs were taken dated almost exclusively before 1850, and from the 1920s to the 1940s these so-called colonial wallpapers adorned the walls of a vast number of both privately and publicly owned historic houses.

The extensive use of reproduction papers in older houses coincided with a general use of wallpaper in most American homes in the early 20th century. In the mid-20th century the preference for unadorned, white walls in modern interiors influenced the tastes of committee members in charge of the decoration of museum houses. When the wall surfaces needed to be renewed, the reproduction wallpapers that had been hung only a generation earlier were taken down and the walls painted white. Today, the pendulum has swung back. Modern designers and homeowners are incorporating wallpaper into their decorative schemes. Museum curators are no longer content to display just a small sample of antique wallpaper in a room whose walls were once covered with it; they consider the wallpaper an integral part of the room's historic decoration and are using reproduction wallpaper in an effort to present as accurate an impression of the past as possible.

RESEARCH

Paint and wallpaper are the two elements of any previous decorative scheme that are most likely to remain in a building as evidence of the tastes of the original and subsequent occupants. The probability that wallpaper was used as a decorative finish in a building should be considered from the outset of a restoration project, not toward the end, when all evidence for its use has most likely been erased. Time should be taken to examine the structure for all evidence it may yield. Often, potentially helpful wallpaper evidence is overlooked in the rush to begin structural rehabilitation of a building. Photographs should be taken before any investigation and as work proceeds. Each wallpaper remaining on the walls should be examined to determine its age; it is not inconceivable that one may be an early paper or perhaps the original paper. No wallpaper should be removed until a target date for the restoration or redecoration has been established. This includes those wallpapers that initially appear to be "too late" even to be considered because they fall within the memory of the restorers. After all the research has been done, the decision may be made to interpret the house as it was at a fairly recent time. If the decision is made to retain an existing paper, a paper conservator should be consulted about whether cleaning and readhesion are possible. Current preservation philosophy strongly favors preserving a room of original or early wallpaper rather than removing and reproducing it.

A room whose walls have been stripped to the bare plaster is not necessarily devoid of wallpaper evidence. Plaster that has never been painted can be an indication that the walls had a decorative covering from the outset, most likely a wallpaper.

Check all surfaces of the room, including the ceiling, for wallpaper evidence. Later architectural changes may obscure an early wallpaper. Often a room was divided. Occasionally a new wall was built directly in front of an old one, thereby concealing a wealth of information. Other elements, such as door and window casings, baseboards, and mantels, often were replaced in an effort to "modernize" a room. Carpenters rarely took the time to strip the wallpaper before applying the new millwork. Cupboards may have been built in, or a Victorian picture molding may have been applied just below the ceiling. Even electrical switchplates may conceal a small fragment of early wallpaper. Often, large pieces of furniture, such as bookcases or mirrors secured to the walls, were not moved when a room was repapered.

Be sure to look for samples in more than one location in any given room. Many decorative schemes made use of more than one wallpaper pattern. In the mid-19th century, for example, fresco papers, consisting of several different elements, were designed to divide the wall into a series of framed panels. In the same period many hallways were papered with columns, capitals, bases, and friezes. In the 1880s dividing the wall surface into dado, fill, and frieze was an immensely popular procedure. During the same period, ceilings were frequently papered. The wallpapers revealed during the course of investigation may range from large samples in good condition to frustratingly incomplete bits that indicate only that wallpaper was used at one time but reveal no clues as to when it was applied or what the color or pattern may have been.

When a wallpaper sample is located, it should be documented with both color and black-and-white photographs, as color photographs have a tendency to fade. The sample's location should be noted on a sketch of the wall plan. Ideally such information is included in a historic structures report.

The thickness of a paper sample removed from the walls can be deceiving. Often it contains more than one layer. Before the invention of the wallpaper steamer, removing the existing layer of paper when a new paper was applied was not common practice; only loose or damaged portions were removed so the new paper would lie flat. The layers of a wallpaper "sandwich" can be separated by careful steaming or soaking. Ideally a paper conservator should be consulted. One sandwich separated by the author contained 27 layers of paper recording the decoration of the room from which it was removed from about 1780 until a matchboard dado was installed in the 1930s.

When wallpaper is found, a record should be kept for each sample, noting the room from which it was removed and, if part of a sandwich, its place in the sequence of layers. Small fragments should not be considered worthless. They are an important part of the sequence and may be identified fully if a larger sample of the pattern exists in another wallpaper collection or the pattern is recorded in an early photograph. Interior photographs taken in the late 19th and early 20th centuries often record the design of a wallpaper that has since been removed. Many successful reproduction wallpaper patterns have been reconstructed by carefully analyzing early photographs.

If no wallpaper samples are found in the structure itself, information may be obtained from other sources related to the site. For example, objects associated with former occupants should be studied. Extra pieces of wallpaper were used for a variety of purposes, such as sealing the backs of framed pictures, covering homemade diaries and account books, and making small boxes. One should be wary of some wallpapers found in trunks or on band boxes, however. Many small-figured designs used for trunk linings were manufactured specifically for that purpose and were not used to paper rooms. The same is true for many of the large, continuous designs found on hat boxes.

All wallpaper evidence should be coordinated with a thorough search of the documents relating to the building and its occupants. Not until all the research is reviewed can a target date for the restoration be established. Although the initial idea may be to restore a building to its original appearance, complete information about all the components of its interior finishes and furnishings may not exist. Documentation about the wallpaper, textiles, and furniture used at a later date may be more extensive. A broad research project will place the building in an architectural context within the community as well as establish the socioeconomic level of its various occupants.

Once the target date for the restoration and interpretation has been established, the wallpaper samples that have been found can then be reviewed to determine whether any were used during that time. At this point the decision is made whether the sample will be duplicated in a custom-made reproduction or whether it will be used as a guide in choosing a similar pattern available as a commercial reproduction.

If no samples of wallpaper are found in a historic building, choosing an appropriate wallpaper design depends almost entirely on research into the selected historical period. This research into secondary sources is necessary to answer general questions about wallpaper: What patterns were available? What styles were fashionable? Where was wallpaper purchased? In what rooms was it most often used? These questions, asked within the framework of the documentary research on the building and its occupants, can help determine the type of wallpaper pattern to select.

In 1787, after looking at the wallpapers available for his new house, a Boston merchant wrote, "There are so great a variety of Fashions, I am totally at a loss as to what kind to get." Today, an owner of a historic building may well have the same experience when trying to choose a pattern from the variety of reproductions available. The Boston merchant concluded that a person's choice of wallpaper "principally depends on fancy." Like today's homeowner, he was trying to choose a paper that was not only fashionable but also appealing to his taste. Those responsible for a museum restoration, however, do not have the same latitude in their selection. Their choice of a reproduction wallpaper pattern should not be subject to 20th-century taste. The reproduction wallpaper should be chosen within the bounds of the prevailing taste of the period chosen for the restoration.

What to Look for in a Reproduction

The term "documentary design" is often loosely interpreted and therefore can be misleading. Many wallpaper sample books labeled "The Colonial Collection" include designs that have no relationship to the wallpapers used during the 18th century. Rather, these designs are the small-figured patterns or stenciled designs that have become associated with the traditional "Early American" look or more recently with "American Country." Many interpretive designs are created by reworking motifs from historic documents—not necessarily wallpapers—into new patterns.

Even when a wallpaper is part of a collection licensed by a museum or preservation organization, the source of the design may be another type of object in its collection, such as a printed or woven fabric, a book endpaper, or a motif from a sampler, a quilt, or a ceramic plate. These are attractive designs created to appeal to current popular taste and complement a manufacturer's collection or line. However evocative of the past, such designs have nothing to do with historic wallpaper patterns and are not recommended for use in historic buildings being restored with an eye toward accuracy. Although it has been impossible to research each reproduction wallpaper listed here, the purpose of this book is to include only those documentary designs that are derived from wallpapers.

The manufacturers listed in this book offer two types of documentary wallpapers acceptable in restoration work: exact reproductions and adaptations. An exact or accurate reproduction faithfully follows the design, scale, and color of the original document. The artwork, or an artist's rendering of the wallpaper design, should strive to reproduce the appearance of the document when it was new, not the worn, abraded look of the antique sample. A successful adaptation achieves the overall appearance of the original wallpaper but incorporates certain changes made by the manufacturer. The design and scale may have been altered; a motif may have been reworked; a design element may have been omitted or a new one introduced; the colors may vary in intensity from the original, or the number of colors may have been reduced. Often such changes are made to make the design more appealing to the contemporary market. Other times they are necessitated by production constraints. Scalamandré refers to designs where changes in scale and composition, such as embossing and flocking, have been made because of technical limitations as "historic representations."

The question to consider with adaptations is the extent to which the design of the document can be altered or reworked before it becomes a new pattern. An adaptation should not be chosen if the scale has been substantially reduced or enlarged, if a major motif has not been included or an incongruous one introduced, or if it includes a color that had not been invented when the original paper was produced. Again, always check the documentation for a paper labeled an adaptation; as noted previously, its source may not even have been a wallpaper.

The artwork of the reproduction design also should reflect the technology that produced the original wallpaper. The most successful artwork captures the variation and modulation of a hand-blocked wallpaper and the precision of machine printing. Even today's most accurate reproductions cannot exactly duplicate the appearance of the documents they are copying. The production methods, the inks that are used, and the paper stock on which the reproduction design is printed all differ substantially from those used to create the historic document. Although some reproduction papers are printed with rollers, the majority are produced with silk screens.

The silk-screen method of printing best imitates the look of a block-printed paper. When an 18th-century design is printed with a roller, the definition of line and the opacity of pigment of the original are lost, and the overall pattern appears weak. Conversely, a late Victorian roller-printed paper reproduced today by the silk-screen process often looks more substantial than the original. The running together of thin colors, which occurred in the rapid roller-printing process of the original, can best be duplicated by machine.

Both screen- and roller-printed papers use commercially available ground papers on which the design is printed. Modern ground papers do not have the texture of 18th-century handmade paper, nor are they as thin as the cheap machine-made paper on which many late Victorian designs were printed. Modern ground papers come in standard widths. These widths are wider than those of historic papers, which usually ranged from 18 to 23 inches, depending on the date and country of origin. All-over patterns with small horizontal repeats can easily be accommodated on modern widths. Although a greater number of horizontal repeats can fit on today's wider paper, the scale remains the same. Occasionally the scale of the document design has to be adjusted slightly to fill the modern width. (Such adjustment is often necessary for papers that are pretrimmed.) The horizontal repeat of a large design often cannot be adjusted to fill a modern width. The original width, therefore, is copied, leaving a wider-than-usual margin on each side. Although these margins may appear to be a waste of paper, the manufacturer compensates by increasing the length of the roll, so that the area the paper covers meets the standard of approximately 30 square feet per roll.

The visual differences created by modern production methods are most apparent when directly comparing a sample of the historic paper with a sample of the reproduction. However, the differences become less noticeable when the reproduction paper is installed and the room receives its full complement of furniture, textiles, and pictures.

The changes brought about by modern printing methods and materials are compromises that are generally accepted in restoration wallpapers today. Many curators, however, are striving to capture the visual qualities of 18th-century handmade and hand-printed wallpapers. There is renewed interest in the art of block printing. Block-printed wallpapers from England and France are being used in more and more American restorations. Colonial Williamsburg is planning to offer several of its reproduction wallpapers in block-printed as well as screen-printed versions. The colors used to print its reproductions are based on scientific pigment analysis. Others interested in historic wallpapers are pursuing sources of handmade paper so that future reproductions of early wallpapers technically will be as accurate as possible.

CUSTOM-MADE REPRODUCTION WALLPAPERS

Today's manufacturers produce reproduction wallpapers not only for use in historic buildings. They also sell to a contemporary market and, therefore, must consider current tastes when choosing patterns from historic documents. No manufacturer should be expected to include reproductions of every popular style from each historical period. Often a style most popular in a given period will simply not be appealing today and, thus, will not be found on the market.

Given the variety of patterns of historic wallpaper, the odds that the exact design of a wallpaper found in a particular historic building has already been reproduced are slim. Custom work may be the only means of obtaining an exact copy of a pattern needed for an accurate

Custom-made reproduction wallpaper ("Green Wheat" and "Green Wheat Border"), textiles, and carpets were needed to re-create the original appearance of the master bedroom in the Gardner-Pingree House (1804), Salem, Massachusetts. (Essex Institute)

restoration project. If the wallpaper samples found in a building are appropriate to the historical period of the restoration and if a complete design exists, having the paper custom-reproduced may be preferable to choosing a pattern from those commercially available. The goal of custom work is as accurate a reproduction as possible with respect to design, color, scale, and simulation of the original printing technique. It cannot be stated too strongly that neither the client nor the manufacturer should "improve" the design; unclear lines and faded colors should not be used to give the paper an "antique" look.

Most wallpaper firms will consider doing custom work, but it is an expensive and time-consuming procedure. The client is responsible for all costs incurred, including the artwork, the cost of each silk screen (one for each color of the design and often a blotch screen for the ground color), and the set-up and printing expenses. The client is responsible also for approving both the artwork before the screens are cut and the strike-offs for final color. Custom work usually requires the client to order a minimum number of rolls; it may be wise to order enough to paper a room twice in case damage occurs. Before a historic sample is sent to a manufacturer, it should be protected from possible damage by encasing it in mylar.

It is popularly believed that a wallpaper manufacturer will happily reproduce any sample of wallpaper found in a historic building, include the reproduction in a commercial line, and donate enough paper to paper one room of the building. In reality, the manufacturer rarely does any of these things. A firm may wish to add the reproduction to its line if the design is considered appealing by today's standards. In this case a royalty arrangement should be negotiated and confirmed by a written contract. The manufacturers may also wish to produce the design in other color combinations, called colorways. If a client approves such a proposal, he or she should obtain royalties on all colorways produced.

Today's Wallpaper Reproduction Market

Manufacturers approach reproduction papers from different points of view. Most firms favor a particular historic period and color pallette. Some firms reproduce the exact appearance of a historic sample, including faded colors and missing design elements. They may also reproduce a printing flaw found on the original document. Other manufacturers compensate for loss of color or design defects by making the reproduction resemble the appearance of the original when it was new. Although this book includes reproduction papers of both types, current restoration practice favors the latter approach.

This book seeks to list currently available reproduction wallpapers and establish guidelines for choosing a pattern appropriate to the project at hand. Today, as in any period in the past, there is a wide range in the quality of wallpapers on the market, both in design and execution. It behooves those making the selection to familiarize themselves with the designs that were popular during the selected period as well as the printing techniques that produced them, so that they can select from the listings in this book with an educated eye.

The reproduction wallpapers available today present an almost overwhelming array of pattern and period styles. The majority of the patterns included in commercial lines are chosen because they appeal to modern taste. Many designs that copy those in European archives may never have been available to the American consumer until the present. In addition to domestically produced reproduction wallpapers, a large number of imported ones are also available. Most are printed in England or France, although some come from as far away as Australia. Such wallpapers are included only if they are available through an American distributor.

Over the past decade dozens of custom reproductions have been commissioned by museums. Many of these wallpapers are now being made available to the public through museum shops or reproduction programs. They are listed separately at the end of the appropriate chapter. Because they are not stock items, they must be custom ordered. As in all custom work, the manufacturer may stipulate a minimum amount that must be ordered. Order information and sample availability vary with each museum. Other patterns that are not listed may be also available from a variety of museums. If you see an appealing reproduction design in a museum installation, inquire about whether it can be purchased on a custom basis.

In addition to patterns ordered through museum gift shops, other custom patterns are available directly through the manufacturers. These are on a custom only or special-order basis and are so listed in the catalog under the manufacturer's name. This type of custom order means that the pattern or document color is not carried as a stock item. The screens are already made, and the order is treated as a normal custom order by the company. Terms vary with each company. Usually a minimum number of rolls or yards of border is required; the customer is also responsible for the cost of any overruns. Other costs include set-up charges and possibly surcharges for the number of colors printed. A deposit is usually required. It is always wise to order a strike-off to make sure that the colors are correct.

PERIOD INSTALLATION

Once a reproduction wallpaper has been chosen, some attention should be paid to its installation. While the basic methods of applying paper to walls have not changed, certain period practices should be noted.

Although paste has always been the most common means of attaching paper to walls, there are references to securing some early wallpapers to the walls with small tacks. Lining paper was not commonly used during the 18th and 19th centuries. However, it is recommended when hanging modern reproduction wallpaper.

Most wallpapers today, including many of the reproduction papers, are pretrimmed. Papers produced in the 18th and 19th centuries had an unprinted margin, or selvage, on each side. Usually only one selvage was cut off and the seams were overlapped when the paper was hung. Today the preferred method of hanging an untrimmed paper is to cut off both margins and butt the edges. If, for the sake of accuracy, overlapping seams are preferred, experiment first. Because of the thickness of the modern paper stock, the seam may appear more prominently than it would have originally.

Board or sheathed walls were frequently papered instead of painted. Before paper was applied, thin strips of cloth were pasted over the joints of the boards so the paper would lie flat and not split or be punctured. Plaster dados under a chair rail were often papered rather than painted the color of the woodwork. Corner posts found in early buildings were not usually covered with paper until the late 19th century.

In the 18th and early 19th centuries fireboards used to cover the fireplace opening during the summer months were often papered.

Some papers were designed with this specific purpose in mind, although many fireboards were covered with the same paper and border used in the rest of the room.

The most important consideration when installing reproduction wallpaper, particularly when attempting an accurate restoration, is the use of a border. Borders were an important part of wallpaper design and were used to some degree in every historical period discussed. Often borders were an integral part of the overall pattern; others were designed to complement the design of the sidewall. But some found in historic buildings bear no relationship to the paper with which they were used. The extent to which borders were used in a room varies. In some cases they surrounded all the architectural elements; in other cases they were used only at the ceiling level (or just below the cornice) or at both the ceiling level and above the chair rail or baseboard. Often a border at the ceiling level was wider than the one used elsewhere in the room; also, it may have been of a completely different design. The borders in different rooms of a building may have been treated differently. The location where borders were used in a room also varied during different historical periods. During the 18th century borders were commonly used to outline the architecture of a room; each wall was treated as a separate unit, so that two widths of borders appeared in each corner. With the exception of bordering the corners, this practice continued into

A reproduction wallpaper border was used to frame the wallpaper, "Tassel," and to outline the woodwork in the north parlor of the Wells-Thorn House, Deerfield, Massachusetts. (Historic Deerfield, Inc.)

25

the early 19th century. The use of borders only around the ceiling and chair rail was also fashionable. In the mid-19th century borders were sometimes used to divide a room into a series of panels. Late 19th-century paper hangers used borders to divide the wall into three horizontal units. These general principles should be kept in mind while investigating the structure and searching for evidence that will indicate how the room was bordered.

Locating an old photograph that illustrates how the wallpaper was installed in a room can be a great help in researching an accurate restoration; it can also create a dilemma. The photograph of the parlor of the Short House, Newbury, Massachusetts, shows the best parlor of an early 18th-century house as it looked in 1911. Samples of the paper survive and date between 1800 and 1810. However, whoever hung the paper obviously did not understand the pattern. Other photographs of the room show the cornice border applied vertically in the corners and alongside the windows and doors. It was also used to outline a dado created by hanging a floral pattern horizontally. Should this evidence be precisely duplicated in hanging the reproduction wallpaper, or should the period mistake be corrected? The final decision depends on the purpose of the restoration or rehabilitation. In some cases such mistakes have been corrected.

How to Use the Catalog

The following catalog of reproduction wallpapers is arranged by historical period from 1700 to 1930. Short essays introduce the popular styles of the particular period and precede the list of available reproductions of these styles. The essays should be amplified by consulting the various books on wallpaper in particular and interior decoration in general that are cited in the bibliography.

Borders, dados, and panels are not included with sidewall papers but are listed separately at the end of each section. Other types of wallpapers, including coordinating patterns, scenic papers, ceiling papers, embossed papers, and relief decorations, are also listed separately for that historical period, as are wallpapers available through museums and types of designs that have changed little over the years, including solid stripes and nonrepeating Chinese papers.

Individual catalog entries give the following information when it is available:

Manufacturer's catalog name for the wallpaper pattern.

Country, date, and method of manufacture of the original or document, followed by the designer and original manufacturer when known.

Source of a published photograph of the document wallpaper (see bibliography for complete titles).

The photograph of the parlor at the Short House (c. 1911) in Newbury, Massachusetts, documents wallpaper that was poorly installed 100 years earlier. (Society for the Preservation of New England Antiquities)

Width, repeat, and roll content of reproduction wallpaper (listed as "yds. per s/r [single roll]" for domestically produced papers and "yds. per roll" indicating the metric roll of European imports).

Changes, if known, made by the manufacturer in the reproduction.

Organization or museum for which the wallpaper was reproduced (see sources of information for location if none is given in entry).

Information about the document and its location.

Manufacturer's catalog number or code for the reproduction wallpaper.

Manufacturer's name for the document color or description of the document color. An additional color may occasionally be listed as a period coloring; this is a colorway produced by the manufacturer that the author has selected as being an appropriate coloring for the design. The word "series" after a manufacturer's order number indicates that all colorings are acceptable.

"Block print" at the end of an entry indicates that the reproduction wallpaper itself is block printed.

Remember that American wallpaper is priced by the single roll but sold in double- or triple-roll quantities. Make sure the room being papered is measured accurately and that the repeat of the pattern is figured into the calculations to determine the number of rolls needed. Borders are sold by the yard.

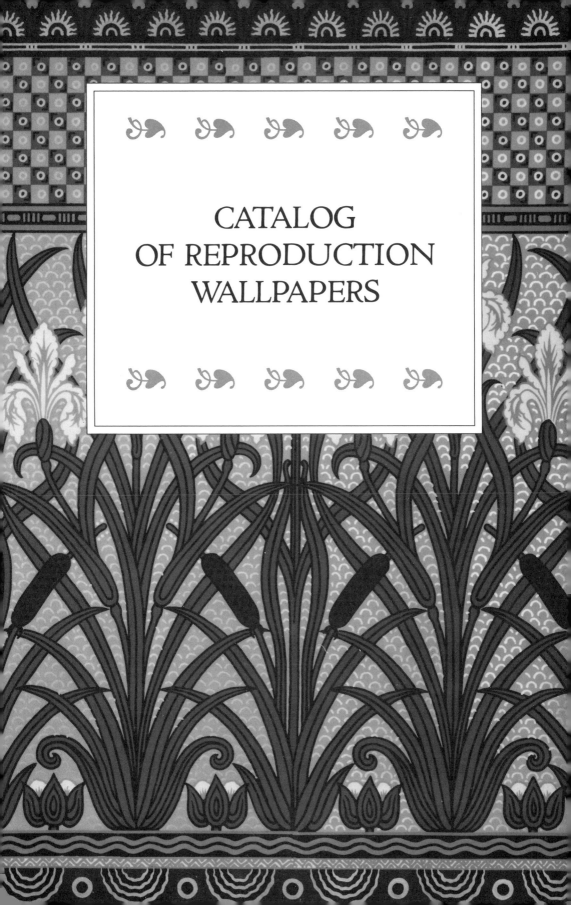

CATALOG
OF REPRODUCTION
WALLPAPERS

1700 TO 1780:
LUXURIES FOR ENGLISH
COLONISTS

The earliest reference to wallpaper in America was recorded in 1700 in the inventory of a Boston stationer. In the first half of the 18th century, painted paper hangings were found only in wealthy households in urban areas. Colonists who could afford wallpaper purchased it either from stationers or booksellers who dealt in an entire range of paper goods or from merchants as special orders. The availability and use of wallpaper increased steadily from 1750 as technology improved and demand for this new decorative commodity spread. Toward the end of the 18th century, wallpaper was purchased also from upholsterers, the equivalent of modern interior designers.

In the 18th century, wallpaper was most commonly printed with wood blocks. Occasionally, stencils were used to create large areas of color and handwork was used to create very fine lines. Individual sheets of handmade paper were pasted together to form a roll, because it was not possible to produce the continuous roll of paper we know today. Once the 12-yard roll was created, it received a ground color, which was applied with large brushes. Finally, the pattern was printed with a series of wood blocks, one for each color and unit of the design.

A roll of paper was called a "piece." This terminology, along with the use of the smaller sheets of paper to form the roll, has led to the misconception that early wallpapers were hung by pasting each separate sheet onto the wall. Although this method of application was sometimes used with the earliest "painted papers," careful examination of a large sample of 18th-century wallpaper reveals no color under the horizontal seam where the sheets are joined. Scrutiny of the design indicates that the size of the repeat (and, therefore, the size of the block used to print it) is rarely the same as the size of the individual piece of paper.

"Lambeth Saracen" (page 34), "Hogarth" (page 37), and "Hunting Scene" (page 36) are examples of the simple black-and-white wood-block prints made in England between 1690 and 1700. "Cerises" (page 33) reproduces a "domino" paper made around 1750. These early French papers are named after the group of craftsmen called

Entrance Hall of Gunston Hall, Lorton, Virginia, showing custom reproduction "Pillar and Arch," 1769. (Gunston Hall)

31

"dominotiers," who specialized in simple one-or two-color prints. All illustrate the types of patterns that may have been exported to the colonies early in the 18th century. Only "Hunting Scene" is documented as actually having been available in New England; it is preserved as the covers of three small almanacs dated 1725–27 in the collections of the Essex Institute, Salem, Massachusetts.

Most wallpapers used in American buildings before the Revolution were of English origin. The patterns available in the mid-18th century can be separated into several distinct types. Most expensive were the custom-made paper hangings—i.e., those made specifically to fit the walls of a new house. Notable examples of this type of wallpaper can be seen today in three rooms of the Jeremiah Lee Mansion (1768) in Marblehead, Massachusetts, and in the Van Rensselaer Hall (1768), installed in the American Wing of the Metropolitan Museum of Art. Designed to imitate walls hung with large framed oil paintings, they depict classical ruins copied from prints and are surrounded with large trompe l'œil frames. Wallpapers with repeating patterns simulating walls hung with smaller framed prints, such as "Lady Pepperrell House," were more readily available.

Pillar and arch designs were more popular in the 18th century than they are today. When hung, they formed a series of arcades. Their large repeats made them appropriate for rooms with high ceilings and for entries, the 18th-century term for staircase halls. "Gunston Hall" and "Arch" are two pillar and arch designs available as custom orders. "Gunston Hall" (page 30) was commissioned for the stair hall of the Virginia house of the same name. "Arch" is the pattern being installed in the 1898 photograph (page 10) depicting a paper hanger at work in South Berwick, Maine; the pattern was reproduced that year from fragments found in the same space during the course of restoration.

Textiles inspired many wallpaper designs available in the 18th century. For example, exotic chintzes and plate-printed fabrics provided the motifs used in "East India" and "Yellow Peacock" (page 39) respectively. "Pekin" (page 34) and "Green Lace" (page 37) imitate colorful silk brocades, while "Fiore" (page 36) and "Leopard" (page 36) copy the more expensive silk and wool damasks used for curtains, upholstery, and wallhangings in elaborate English houses.

Some of the large-scale damask-pattern wallpapers were made to look even more like their textile counterparts by means of flocking, a process in which small fragments of chopped wool or silk were spread over the paper, adhering where the design had been printed with a varnish instead of a color. Flocked papers were expensive; evidence of their use has been found primarily in parlors and best chambers. These large-scale flocked designs printed in bold colors are not as favored in today's decorative schemes as they were in the 18th century. Custom work may be the only way to obtain one for a restoration project.

BRUNSCHWIG & FILS

ઽꙮ CERISES. French, 1750–60, block print. 26³/₄" wide, 4¹/₄" repeat, 5 yds. per s/r. Document at Musée des Arts Décoratifs, Paris. No.12581.06 (brick and blue).

ઽꙮ CHINA FANCY. English, 1750–80, block print. 21¹/₂" wide, 43" drop repeat, 6 yds. per s/r. Adaptation: colors not reproduced exactly. Document at Winterthur Museum. Document color, no. 10771.06 (pink and jade on ivory), is a custom order.

ઽꙮ CHINOISERIE. French, 1770–90, block print. 24" wide, 36" repeat, 5 yds. per s/r. Reproduced for Museum of Early Southern Decorative Arts. Document in Brunschwig Archives. No. 610.06 (lacquer red and blue on parchment).

ઽꙮ FAMILY TREE. French, 1775–90, block print. Designed by Reveillon. Clouzot and Follot, pl. 6. 27" wide, 36" half-drop repeat, 5 yds. per s/r. Adaptation: colors softened and scale altered. Document in Brunschwig Archives. No.14450.06 (off-white).

ઽꙮ PEKIN. French, 1773–1800, block print. 20" wide, 14¹/₄" repeat, 6 yds. per s/r. Document at Musée des Arts Décoratifs. No.13442.06 (blue).

ઽꙮ REVE DU PAPILLON. French, 1770–85, hand painted. 27¹/₄" wide, 33³/₈" repeat, 5 yds. per s/r. Adapted from a hand-painted document at Corbit-Sharp House, Odessa, Del., a property of Winterthur Museum. No.12473.06 (yellow).

CLARENCE HOUSE

ઽꙮ COALPORT. English, 1770–90, block print. 20¹/₂" wide, 16¹/₈" repeat, 11 yds. per roll. Reproduced from a period design for a wallpaper. Document in Courtauld Archives, London. Period colorings: No.W9011/002 (blue); No.W9011/003 (green); No.W9011/004 (yellow).

CERISES, 1750–60.
Brunschwig & Fils.

LAMBETH SARACEN, 1690–1700. Classic Revivals (Hamilton-Weston Collection).

PEKIN, 1773–1800. Brunschwig & Fils.

ॐ TEMPLE NEWSAM. English, 1720–40, block print with flock. 21″ wide, 21″ repeat, 11 yds. per roll. Reproduction not flocked. Coles Traditional Collection. Period colorings: No.C238 (mustard); No.C242 (red on yellow).

CLASSIC REVIVALS

Hamilton-Weston Historic Handprint Collection

ॐ LAMBETH SARACEN. English, 1690–1700, block print. 20¼″ wide, 8″ repeat, 11 yds. per roll. No.8111 (black on tan).

ॐ MAYFAIR. English, 1750–80, block print. 21″ wide, 21″ repeat, 11 yds. per roll. No.405 (blue on white).

ॐ TWICKENHAM. English, 1755–80, block print. 20¾″ wide, 18½″ repeat, 11 yds. per roll. Green. Order by name.

Mauny Collection

ॐ LE CHASSEUR. French, 1770–1800, block print. 20⅞″ wide, 20″ repeat, 11 yds. per roll. No.198 (black and white on gray). Block print.

ॐ CONCERT CHAMPETRE. French, 1770–1800, block print. 21⅝″ wide, 39½″ repeat, 11 yds. per roll. No.192 (pink and gray on gray). Block print.

ॐ DANSE VILLAGEOISE. French, 1770–1800, block print. 20″ wide, 21¼″ repeat, 11 yds. per roll. No.175 (blue and orange on cream). Block print.

ॐ DENTELLE ET BOUQUETS. French, 1770–1800, block print. 21¼″ wide, 19¼″ repeat, 11 yds. per roll. No.173 (gray and white on blue-gray). Block print.

ॐ LEOPARD. French, 1760–80, block print. 20½″ wide, 21½″ repeat, 11 yds. per roll. No.1515 (green). Block print.

CHRISTOPHER HYLAND INCORPORATED

ॐ ARLESFORD. English, 1690–1700, block print. Wells-Cole, no. 30, p. 25. 21″ wide, 24½″ repeat, 11 yds. per roll. No.AB129/4 (gray, green, peach, and black).

ॐ CHINTZ. English, 1730–50, block print. 18⅝″ wide, 21⅞″ repeat, 11 yds. per roll. No.AB149/2 (blue on yellow).

ॐ FIORE. English, 1750–60, block print. 21″ wide, 44″ repeat, 11 yds. per roll. No.AB252 (black and white on blue).

ॐ HOGARTH. English, 1690–1700, block print. 15⁷⁄₁₆″ wide, 18¼″ repeat, 11 yds. per roll. No.AB151/2 (black on yellow).

ॐ HOLCOMBE. English, 1680–1700, block print. Teynac, Nolot, and Vivien, p. 56; Wells-Cole, no. 27, p. 24. 16⅜″ wide, 21″ repeat, 11 yds. per roll. No.AB144/3 (beige, blue, and black).

ॐ HUNTING SCENE. English, 1690–1710, block print. Greysmith, fig. 31, p. 46; Teynac, Nolot, and Vivien, p. 44; Wells-Cole, no. 28, p. 26. 19¾″ wide, 15¾″ repeat, 11 yds. per roll. No.AB146/4 (multi).

ॐ MELTON. English, 1720–40, block print. Wells-Cole, no. 31, p. 26.

right
HUNTING SCENE, 1690–1710. Christopher Hyland Incorporated.

below left
LEOPARD, 1760–80. Classic Revivals (Mauny Collection).

below right
FIORE, 1750–60. Christopher Hyland Incorporated.

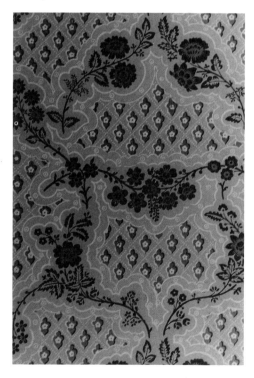

top left
HOGARTH, 1690–1700.
Christopher Hyland
Incorporated.

left and top right
Original document
and artwork for
"Green Lace," a wall-
paper of 1720–40
now reproduced by
Schumacher.

17^1/$_2$" wide, 28^1/$_2$" repeat, 11 yds. per roll. No.AB138/2 (green and white).

&❧ POMEGRANATE. English, 1750–60, block print. Wells-Cole, no. 4, p. 12. 21" wide, 20^1/$_2$" half-drop repeat, 11 yds. per roll. Document at Temple Newsam, Leeds, England. Reproduction not flocked. No.ZZ92006 (red on red).

COLEFAX & FOWLER

Available through Cowtan & Tout.

&❧ SUDBURY PARK. English, 1770–90, block print. Oman and Hamilton, no. 127, p. 128. 20^1/$_2$" wide, 3" repeat, 11 yds. per roll. No.7046/06 (gray and white).

SCHUMACHER

&❧ DAISY. English, 1770–1800, block print. Wells-Cole, no. 3, p. 10. 21" wide, 2^1/$_2$" repeat, 11 yds. per roll. Document at Temple Newsam, Leeds, England. No.TN02 (white on yellow).

&❧ DIAMONDS AND FLOWERS. English, 1750–70, block print with flocking. Wells-Cole, front cover. 21" wide, 3" half-drop repeat, 11 yds. per roll. Adaptation: flocking not reproduced. Document at Temple Newsam, Leeds, England. No.TN08 (rust on gray).

&❧ EVERARD. English, 1770–90, block print. 27^1/$_2$" wide, 11" repeat, 4^1/$_2$ yds. per s/r. Document at Colonial Williamsburg. No.513100 (document azure).

&❧ GREEN LACE. English, 1720–40, block print. Lynn, fig. 3-7, p. 74. 22^1/$_2$" wide, 20^1/$_2$" repeat, 5^1/$_2$ yds. per s/r. Document at Colonial Williamsburg. No.513060 (document emerald).

&❧ POMEGRANATE. English, 1760–70, block print with flocking. Oman and Hamilton, no. 193, p. 146; Sugden and Edmundson, pl. 30, p. 105; Wells-Cole, no. 4, p. 12. 20" wide, 20" half-drop repeat, 11 yds. per roll. Adaptation: flocking not reproduced. Document at Temple Newsam, Leeds, England. No.TN09 (red on white).

&❧ YELLOW PEACOCK. English, 1740–60, block print. Nylander, Redmond, and Sander, fig. 11-c, p. 68. 21" wide, 44" repeat, 5^1/$_2$ yds. per s/r. Document at Colonial Williamsburg. No.513070 (document flax).

WATERHOUSE WALLHANGINGS

&❧ CAPE COD FLORAL. English, 1770–90, block print. 20^3/$_4$" wide, 12^1/$_2$" repeat, 7 yds. per s/r. Document in Waterhouse Archives. No.209202 (charcoal on pale mustard).

&❧ CAPTAIN JOHN KENDRICK HOUSE. English, 1760–80, block print. 20" wide, 22" repeat, 7 yds. per s/r. Document in Waterhouse Archives. No.177269 (black and white on ochre). Period coloring: No.177248 (green on gray).

&❧ EAST INDIA. French, 1760–70, block print. Lynn, color pl. 20,

Original document for "Yellow Peacock," a wallpaper of 1740–60 now reproduced by Schumacher.

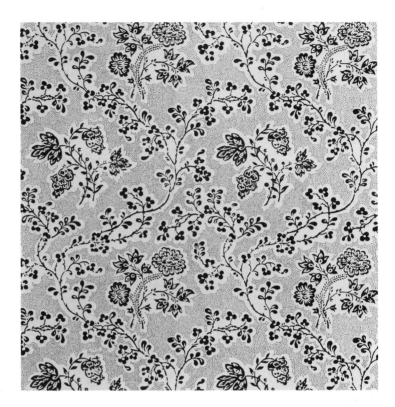

CAPE CODE FLORAL, 1770–90. Water-house Wallhangings.

p. 64. 20¹/₂" wide, 22" repeat, 7 yds. per s/r. Adaptation: colors not reproduced exactly. Document at Cooper-Hewitt Museum. No.158635 (green and orange on white).

᳁ GENERAL SAMUEL McCLELLAN. English, 1770–80, block print. 21" wide, 22¹/₂" repeat, 7 yds. per s/r. Document privately owned. No.155947 (gray ground).

᳁ LADY PEPPERRELL HOUSE. English, 1760–70, block print. Nylander, Redmond, and Sander, fig. 5.1, p. 52. 23" wide, 42" repeat, 5 yds. per s/r. Document at Society for the Preservation of New England Antiquities. No.182433 (gray on pink).

᳁ WAREHAM FLORAL. English, 1770–80, block print. 21" wide, 18¹/₂" repeat, 7 yds. per s/r. Document in Waterhouse Archives. No.176433 (pink ground).

CUSTOM PATTERNS FROM MUSEUMS

GUNSTON HALL

᳁ PILLAR AND ARCH. English, 1769–80, block print. Oman and Hamilton, color pl. p. 136; Sugden and Edmundson, frontispiece. 21" wide plus 1³/₄" border, 41¹/₄" repeat, 5 yds. per s/r. Sidewall document at Victoria and Albert Museum; border document at Society for the Preservation of New England Antiquities. Black and white on light yellow.

GENERAL SAMUEL
McCLELLAN, 1770–80.
Waterhouse Wall-
hangings.

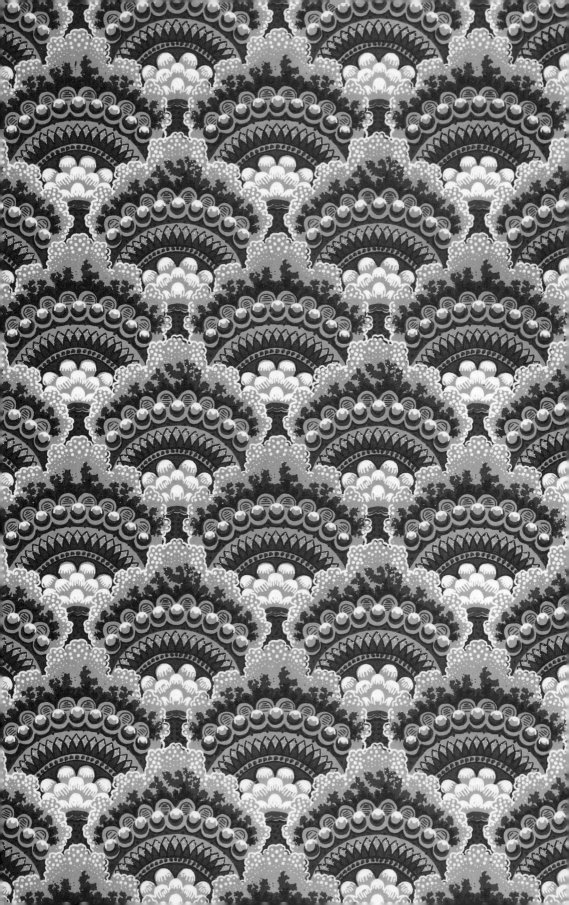

1780 TO 1840:
STYLISH IMPORTS AND
AMERICAN PATTERNS

Between 1780 and 1840 wallpaper became more commonly used in American interiors. At the same time the American consumer was confronted with a wider selection of patterns available from a greater number of sources. After the American Revolution, expanded trade opportunities enabled American merchants to import French and Chinese wallpapers directly. English wallpapers remained popular, but French imports were beginning to provide strong competition. American manufacture of wallpaper, which had been discouraged during the colonial period, was well established by 1790, especially in Boston, New York, and Philadelphia. The patterns produced by this newly founded American industry were inspired by or copied directly from imported papers; however, they were advertised as being a better buy—equal in quality and less expensive.

Because of the various sources of supply during this period, determining the origin of a paper found in the course of a restoration is often difficult. From 1714 to 1836 English wallpapers were required by law to have a stamp printed on the reverse indicating that a tax on the paper used to form the roll had been paid. This stamp usually comprises an interlace of the letters *GR* surmounted with a crown. Although the stamp indicates the origin of the paper, it is of little help in dating the sample. American and French papers, on the other hand, were rarely marked in any way. The earliest papers produced in America were not necessarily cruder than their European counterparts; in fact, the quality of inexpensive English and French papers was sometimes quite poor.

With the exception of the custom-made hangings imitating large framed paintings, the types of patterns described in the previous chapter continued to be popular during the 1780s and into the 1790s. The use of plain-colored papers with borders surrounding the architectural elements of the room increased. This type of wall treatment became fashionable in the mid-18th century; the preferred colors were blue and green, and the borders usually were made of papier-mâché. Manufacturers in the late 18th century offered a wider

ROBBINS HOUSE, 1810–25. Waterhouse Wallhangings.

43

choice of colors for the plain papers and a greater variety in the patterns and widths of printed borders.

Except when they copied an imported paper, American wallpapers from 1790 to 1820 are usually simple repeating or striped patterns, often printed in only one or two colors. These, no doubt, were the types of patterns referred to as "common papers" in one Boston manufacturer's advertisement.

Beginning in the early 19th century, the importation and use of French wallpapers increased markedly. The French manufacturers had perfected the block-printing process, and their designs and colors clearly captivated the American consumer. Until about 1870 French wallpaper styles dominated the market.

Late 18th-century and early 19th-century French papers excelled in the realistic rendering of both color and shading of flowers, fruit, drapery, lace, ribbon, marble, architectural elements, and even statuary. See, for example, "Mirage" (page 49), "La Haie Panel" (cover and endleaves), "Draperie Josephine" (page 57), "Finistere" (page 85), and "Floral Drapery Cornice" (page 79). The goal of some designs seems to have been total deception. Neoclassical designs, especially those by Reveillon, and floral patterns with arabesques seem to be as popular now as when they were first imported. They are reproduced by a number of firms. Many of these classically inspired designs were perfect complements to the new style of Federal architecture.

"Glenmoral" (page 69), "New Clarissa" (page 49), and "Wheeler House" (page 53) are reproductions of a French style of paper hanging that was popular from about 1810 until the late 1820s. The style consisted of small-figured designs, often overprinted with drapery and floral motifs and crowned by elaborate drapery borders. A similar type, called a "landscape figure," relied on the same basic formula. Vignettes of people or animals alternated with smaller floral motifs on small-figured backgrounds between stripes. An almost endless variety of motifs was plugged into this formula; see "Personnages et Oiseaux" (page 58) and "Louise" (page 72). Today, often only the stripes and small-figured grounds are copied from this style of wallpaper as these elements appeal most to modern taste. Because the principal motifs are omitted, these adaptations are unsuccessful.

"Landscape figures" should not be confused with the French scenic wallpapers often referred to as landscape papers. These continuous nonrepeating panoramas are perhaps the most widely known examples of any historic wallpapers because more examples have been preserved in historic buildings and installed in period room settings in art museums than any other type. The first scenic wallpaper, "Vue de Suisse," was produced by Zuber in 1804. Many of the titles popular during this period are available today. Most are produced by

Zuber & Cie and are still printed with the original wood blocks.

The attention given to scenic papers has often overshadowed other styles of wallpaper that were popular at the same time and used more extensively. Odile Nouvel's *Wallpapers of France, 1800–1850* presents an impressive survey of the variety of designs found in French wallpapers of the first half of the 19th century. Not all the styles illustrated actually found their way to the United States, but those that did were imitated widely by American manufacturers. Patterns composed of floral motifs, geometric designs, and medallions were popular in the 1820s and 1830s. Many French papers of the 1830s are characterized by shaded or blended backgrounds. This process, also developed by the Zuber factory, was called "irisée." These papers were referred to as "rainbow papers" in this country and are examples of a type of design that was very popular in its own day but is rarely reproduced today. A custom reproduction of an American-made rainbow paper has been installed by Historic Deerfield in a chamber of the Wells-Thorn House (page 95).

BRUNSCHWIG & FILS   WALLPAPERS

❧ ALEXANDRIA SIDEWALL. French, 1810–15, block print. 21³/₄" wide plus 4¹/₂" border, 9" repeat, 5 yds. per s/r. No. 11519.06 (clay).

❧ ANANAS. French, 1780–1800, block print. 24¹/₄" wide, 24" repeat, 6 yds. per s/r. Adaptation. Document in McClelland Collection, Brunschwig Archives. No.11606.06 (persimmon on cream).

❧ ARCH. American, c. 1787, block print and stencil. Nylander, Redmond, and Sander, fig. 9.1, p. 60, and fig. 79.2, p. 269. 21¹/₂" wide, 42¹/₄" repeat. Reproduced from an 1898 reproduction in which the background color was changed from gray to blue. Document at Hamilton House, South Berwick, Maine, a property of Society for the Preservation of New England Antiquities. No.363.6C. Custom order.

❧ AURORA. French, 1790–1800, block print. Originally printed by Reveillon. Lynn, color pl. 10, p. 57. 21" wide, 48" repeat, 6 yds. per s/r. Document at Phelps-Hatheway House, Suffield, Conn., a property of Antiquarian and Landmarks Society. No.14224.06 (green on off-white).

❧ BAGATELLE. French, 1790–1810, block print. Lynn, color pls. 4 and 5, pp. 36 and 37. 21" wide, 21" repeat, 7 yds. per s/r. Document at Cooper-Hewitt Museum. Document color, no. 12508.06 (brown), is a custom order.

❧ BOSPHORE SEMIS. French, 1790–1820, block print. 27¹/₄" wide, 19" repeat, 5 yds. per s/r. Document in McClelland Collection, Brunschwig Archives. No.11531.06 (red).

❧ BOUTONNIERE. French, 1789–1800, block print. 27" wide, 7³/₄" repeat, 5 yds. per s/r. Document at Musée des Arts Décoratifs. No.13402.06 (blue on blue).

❧ BOSQUET. French, 1798–99, block print. Originally printed by

BOUTONNIERE,
1789–1800. Brun-
schwig & Fils.

Jacquemart et Bénard. Greysmith, fig. 59, p. 86. 21¼″ wide, 20¼″
repeat, 6 yds. per s/r. Document at Musée des Arts Décoratifs, Paris.
No.12642.6C (blue). Custom order.

ঌ BULFINCH SWAG SIDEWALL AND BORDER. American, 1810–20, block
print. Nylander, Redmond, and Sander, fig. 29.6, p. 132. 27⁷⁄₁₆″ wide
including 5⁹⁄₁₆″ border, 7½″ repeat. Document at Society for the
Preservation of New England Antiquities. No.1323.6C (blue). Custom order.

ঌ CORNFLOWER RESIST. Probably American, c. 1796, block print.
Nylander, Redmond, and Sander, fig. 22.5, p. 98. 22″ wide, 9¼″ repeat. Document at Society for the Preservation of New England Antiquities. No.13202.6C (blue). Custom order.

ঌ CRISTAUX. French, 1827, block print. Designed by A. Merii. Nouvel, fig. 170, p. 61. 18½″ wide, 9¼″ repeat. Document at Musée des
Arts Décoratifs. No.12599.6C (gray). Custom order.

ঌ DEBUSSY. French, 1825–35, block print. Nouvel, fig. 201, p. 66.
24″ wide, 18¼″ repeat, 5 yds. per s/r. Document in Brunschwig
Archives. No.11579.06 (pearl gray).

ঌ DORCHESTER. Probably French, 1780–1800, block print. Nylander, Redmond, and Sander, fig. 7.3, p. 56. 21″ wide, 22½″ repeat,
6 yds. per s/r. Document at Society for the Preservation of New
England Antiquities. No.11049.06 (rose on black).

• EXETER FAN. American, 1800–20, block print. $28^{1}/_{4}$" wide, $9^{1}/_{2}$" repeat, 5 yds. per s/r. Document in Brunschwig Archives. No. 11218.6C (beige). Custom order.

• FOX AND ROOSTER. French, 1780–1800, block print. 24" wide, 21" repeat, 6 yds. per s/r. Reproduced for Museum of Early Southern Decorative Arts. Document in Brunschwig Archives. No.640.06 (rose and blue on clay beige).

• FRAMBOISE. French, 1795–1800, block print. 27" wide, $16^{1}/_{2}$" repeat, 5 yds. per s/r. Document at Musée des Arts Décoratifs. Document color, no. 12602.06 (taupe on blue), is a custom order.

• GALLIER DIAMOND. French or English, 1800–20, block print. 28" wide, $13^{3}/_{8}$" repeat, 5 yds. per s/r. Document in Brunschwig Archives. No.10410.06 (brown and green on beige).

• GEOMETRIQUE. French, 1825–35, block print. 27" wide, $4^{5}/_{8}$" repeat, 5 yds. per s/r. Document at Musée des Arts Décoratifs. Document color, no. 12569.06 (gray), is a custom order.

• LA HAIE PANEL. French, 1815–25, block print. Nouvel, fig. 39, p. 39, and fig. 262, p. 77. 21" wide, $11^{1}/_{2}$' panel. Adaptation: border motifs simplified. Document at Musée des Arts Décoratifs. No.13509.06 (forest and rose).

• IMLAY. American, c. 1794, block print. McClelland, p. 258. $20^{1}/_{2}$" wide, $21^{1}/_{2}$" repeat, 5 yds. per s/r. Document at Winterthur Museum. No.10862.6C (orange and blue on blue). Custom order.

• JARDINIERE. French, 1780–1800, block print. Probably printed by Reveillon. $21^{1}/_{2}$" wide, $21^{1}/_{4}$" repeat. Document in Brunschwig Archives. Document color, no. 12384.06 (rose on seafoam), is a custom order.

• LITCHFIELD. French, 1800–20, block print. 27" wide, $25^{1}/_{4}$" repeat, 5 yds. per s/r. Document in McClelland Collection, Brunschwig Archives. No.13713.06 (yellow).

• LOCKLIN PLANTATION. Probably English, 1780–1810, block print. $28^{1}/_{4}$" wide, 30" repeat, 5 yds. per s/r. Adaptation: pattern slightly enlarged. Reproduced for Liberty Hall, Kenansville, N.C. Document in Brunschwig Archives. No.800.06 (lacquer and blue on beige).

• MAIZE. French, 1800–20, block print. $18^{1}/_{2}$" wide plus $4^{1}/_{4}$" border, $22^{3}/_{4}$" repeat, 6 yds. per s/r. Document in McClelland Collection, Brunschwig Archives. Document color, no. 11399.06 (gray), is a custom order.

• MAYTIME. French, 1810–25, block print. 28" wide, $23^{7}/_{8}$" repeat, 5 yds. per s/r. Adaptation: width reduced by 4" between stripes. Reproduced for the Valentine Museum, Richmond, Va. Document in Brunschwig Archives. Document color, no. 10502.06 (gray and orange on blue), is a custom order.

• MIRAGE. French, 1780–1810, block print. McClelland, p. 137. 27" wide plus $5^{1}/_{4}$" border, 18" repeat, 5 yds. per s/r. Document at

Cooper-Hewitt Museum. No.12532.06 (blue).

❧ MUGUET MOUSSELINE. French, 1800–10, block print. 20¹/₂" wide, 10¹/₄" repeat, 6 yds. per s/r. Document at Musée des Arts Décoratifs. No.13391.06 (white on pink).

❧ NEW CLARISSA. French, 1823–30, block print. 18³/₄" wide, 18¹/₄" repeat, 7 yds. per s/r. Document at Society for the Preservation of New England Antiquities. No.13332.06 (yellow on azure).

❧ ONDINE. French, 1830–35, block print. 21" wide, 26⁵/₈" repeat, 6 yds. per s/r. Document at Musée des Arts Décoratifs. No.12619.6C (gray). Custom order.

❧ OSBORNE ARCADED PANEL. American, 1800–7, block print. Originally printed by Moses Grant. Nylander, Redmond, and Sander, fig. 23.1, p. 111. Panel size: 21⁵/₈" wide, 10' 2" high. Document at Society for the Preservation of New England Antiquities. No.13294.6C (green). Custom order.

❧ OTIS DAMASK. English, c. 1796, block print. Nylander, Redmond, and Sander, fig. 22.1, p. 96. 27" wide, 5¹/₄" repeat, 5 yds. per s/r. Document at Harrison Gray Otis House, Boston, a property of Society for the Preservation of New England Antiquities. No.13263.06 (gold).

❧ PASSIFLORE. French, 1825–35, block print. Originally printed by Jacquemart et Bénard, 27³/₄" wide, 4⁵/₈" repeat, 5 yds. per s/r. Document at Musée des Arts Décoratifs. No.12547.6C (dusty mauve). Custom order.

❧ PENELOPE. American or French, 1810–25, block print. 28" wide, ⁷/₈" repeat, 5 yds. per s/r. Adaptation: slight color change. Reproduced for Liberty Hall, Kenansville, N.C. Document in Brunschwig Archives. Document color, no. 792.06 (white on blue), is a custom order.

❧ PENSEES MOUSSELINE. French, 1800–10, block print. 20⁷/₈" wide, 10¹/₄" repeat, 6 yds. per s/r. Document at Musées des Arts Décoratifs. No.13412.06 (violet on blue).

❧ POMMIER. French, 1830–40, block print. 28" wide, 18" repeat, 5 yds. per s/r. Document in McClelland Collection, Brunschwig Archives. No.11408.06 (vanilla).

❧ RAYURES MOUSSELINE. French, 1801–10, block print. 20¹/₂" wide, 10¹/₄" repeat, 6 yds. per s/r. Document at Musée des Arts Décoratifs. Period coloring: No.13452.06 (aqua on blue).

❧ REVEILLON TULIPS. French, 1790–95, block print. Originally printed by Jacquemart et Bénard. Clouzot and Follot, p. 193. 27³/₄" wide, 18⁵/₈" repeat, 5 yds. per s/r. Document in McClelland Collection, Brunschwig Archives. Period coloring: No.11593.06 (red on yellow).

❧ ROYAL DOLPHIN. English, 1817–25, block print. Designed by Robert Jones; originally printed by Frederick Crace. Greysmith, fig. 52, p. 74; Oman and Hamilton, fig. 1024, p. 353. 25³/₈" wide, 40" half-drop repeat, 5 yds. per s/r. Document at Royal Pavilion, Brighton, England. Document color, no. 13024.6 (jade), is a custom order. Period color-

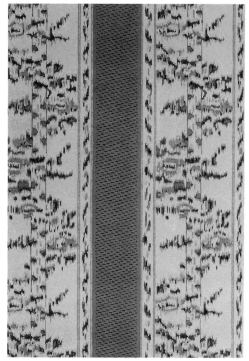

left
NEW CLARISSA
and
NEW CLARISSA
FESTOON BORDERS,
1823–30.
Brunschwig & Fils.

top
MIRAGE, 1780–1810.
Brunschwig & Fils.

above
OTIS DAMASK, c. 1796.
Brunschwig & Fils.

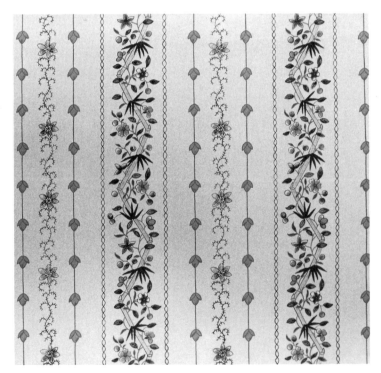

above left
POMMIER, 1830–40.
Brunschwig & Fils.

above right
RAYURES MOUSSELINE,
1801–10. Brun-
schwig & Fils.

right
SHIRLEY PLACE
FLORAL, 1790–1810.
Brunschwig & Fils.

ings: No.13021.06 (pomegranate); No.13023.06 (mandarin yellow).

❧ ROYAL PROMENADE PANELS. English, 1800–20, hand painted. Adaptations of hand-painted panels in entrance of Royal Pavilion, Brighton, England. Nos.13065.06, 13075.06, 13085.06, 13095.06, 13105.06, 13115.06 (all blue on pink).

❧ ROYALTON VINE. American, 1790–1810, block print. Nylander, Redmond, and Sander, fig. 12.3, p. 71. 28" wide, 18³⁄₄" repeat. Document at Society for the Preservation of New England Antiquities. No.13192.6C (blue on aqua). Custom order.

❧ SHIRLEY PLACE FLORAL. Chinese, 1790–1810, hand painted. Nylander, Redmond, and Sander, fig. 21.3, p. 94. 27" wide, 11¹⁄₂" repeat, 5 yds. per s/r. Document at Society for the Preservation of New England Antiquities. No.13240.06 (white).

❧ SPATTERWARE. Probably English or French, 1790–1820, block print. 27" wide, 5 yds. per s/r. Document in Brunschwig Archives. No.11702.06 (blue).

❧ LES SYLPHIDES. French, 1790–1800, block print. Originally printed by Reveillon. *Bulletin*, p. 121; Clouzot and Follot, p. 93; Lynn, color pl. 9, p. 40, and fig. 4.3, p. 95. 21" wide, 48" repeat, 6 yds. per s/r. Adaptation: not all motifs reproduced. Document at Phelps-Hatheway House, Suffield, Conn., a property of Antiquarian and Landmarks Society. No.14234.06 (green).

❧ TALAVERA. American, 1810–25, block print. 27" wide, 25" repeat, 5 yds. per s/r. Adaptation: colors not reproduced exactly. Document in Brunschwig Archives. No.14346.06 (bisque).

❧ TENTURE FLOTTANTE. French, c. 1812, block print. 20³⁄₄" wide, 21¹⁄₄" repeat, 6 yds. per s/r. Adaptation. Document in McClelland Collection, Brunschwig Archives. No.11569.06 (gray).

❧ TRELLIS. French, 1800–5, block print. Designed by Ebert & Buffard; printed by Jacquemart et Bénard. Nouvel, fig. 166, p. 61. 27" wide, 3¹⁄₂" repeat, 5 yds. per s/r. Document at Musée des Arts Décoratifs. No.12579.6C (gray). Custom order.

❧ VOLGER HOUSE. Probably French, 1815–25, block print. Nylander, Redmond, and Sander, color pl. 16, p. 107 (pattern shown reversed). 21¹⁄₂" wide, 20³⁄₄" repeat. Document at Old Salem, Winston-Salem, N.C. No.367.6C. Custom order.

❧ WHEELER HOUSE SIDEWALL. French, 1810–25, block print. 21³⁄₈" wide, 21" repeat. Reproduced for John Wheeler House, Murfreesboro, N.C. No.12899.06 (grisaille). Custom order.

CLARENCE HOUSE

❧ GARDEN VINE. English, 1815–25, block print. 20¹⁄₂" wide, 10¹⁄₂" repeat, 11 yds. per roll. Document in Courtauld Archives, London. No.W9007/048 (sage green).

❧ GOTHIK FRETWORK. English, 1835–45, block print. For a similar

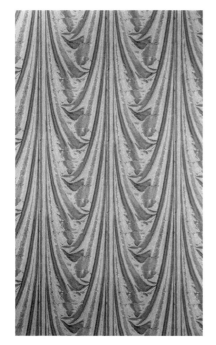

top
TENTURE FLOTTANTE, c. 1812.
Brunschwig & Fils.

above
TALAVERA, 1810–25. Brunschwig
& Fils.

right
LES SYLPHIDES, 1790–1800.
Brunschwig & Fils.

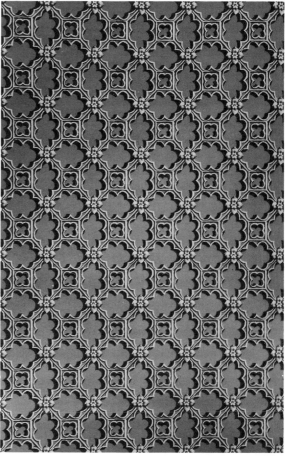

pattern, see Oman and Hamilton, no. 692A, color pl. p. 261. 27″ wide, 3½″ repeat, 5 yds. per s/r. Document in Clarence House Archives. No.9400/6 (red).

☙ OAK LEAF. English, 1810–20, block print. 27″ wide, 3¼″ repeat, 5 yds. per s/r. Adaptation. Document in Clarence House Archives. No.9430/3 (green).

☙ REGENCY MEDALLION. English, 1820–30, block print. 27″ wide, 5½″ repeat, 5 yds. per s/r. Document in Clarence House Archives. No.9290/1 (white).

CLASSIC REVIVALS

Hamilton-Weston Historic Handprint Collection

☙ BEDFORD STRIPE. English, 1780–90, block print. 21″ wide, 5¼″ repeat, 11 yds. per roll. No.301 (blue and tan).

☙ BLOOMSBURY SQUARE. English, 1800–10, block print. 21″ wide, 1½″ repeat, 11 yds. per roll. No.507 (green and black).

above left
WHEELER HOUSE SIDEWALL and border, 1810–25. Brunschwig & Fils.

above right
GOTHIK FRETWORK, 1835–45. Clarence House.

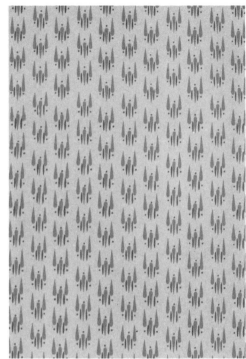

above left

ROYAL CRESCENT,
1780–1810. Classic
Revivals (Hamilton-
Weston Collection).

above right

STRAND TEARDROP,
1790–1810. Classic
Revivals (Hamilton-
Weston Collection).

ᗷ COVENT GARDEN FLORAL. English, 1830–40, block print. 21"
wide, 11¼" repeat, 11 yds. per roll. No.8141 (red on yellow).

ᗷ FUCHSIA ST. JAMES. English, 1830–40, block print. 21" wide,
10¾" repeat, 11 yds. per roll. No.8151 (red and green on gray).

ᗷ KINGSTON MARKET. English, 1810–20, block print. 21" wide,
10½" repeat, 11 yds. per roll. No.8131 (blue and white).

ᗷ RICHMOND TRELLIS. English, 1830–40, block print. 21" wide,
7¾" repeat, 11 yds. per roll. No.8161 (green on ivory).

ᗷ ROYAL CRESCENT. English, 1780–1810, block print. 21" wide, 21"
repeat, 11 yds. per roll. Gray on blue. Order by name.

ᗷ STRAND TEARDROP. English, 1790–1810, block print. 20½" wide,
1½" repeat, 11 yds. per roll. No.8121 (blue and white).

Mauny Collection

ᗷ ALLEGORIES. French, 1790–1810, block print. McClelland, p. 174.
18¼" wide, 20⅞" repeat, 11 yds. per roll. No.239 (green and tan on
white). Block print.

ᗷ AMOUR AVEUGLE. French, 1815–25, block print. 19¼" wide,
25¼" repeat, 11 yds. per roll. No.171 (grays on gray). Block print.

ᗷ LES AMOURS. French, 1780–1800, block print. McClelland, p. 133.
21⅝" wide, 46" repeat, 11 yds. per roll. No.203 (multi on gray).
Block print.

ᗷ AMOURS ET OISEAUX. French, 1780–1800, block print. 21¼" wide,

54

21$^{1}/_{4}$" repeat, 11 yds. per roll. No.134 (multi on yellow). Block print.

ᲒᲔ ANANAS. French, 1780–1800, block print. 21$^{5}/_{8}$" wide, 20$^{7}/_{8}$" repeat, 11 yds. per roll. No.197 (multi on cream). Block print.

ᲒᲔ ARC DE TRIOMPHE. French, 1780–1800, block print. 20$^{1}/_{2}$" wide, 19$^{5}/_{8}$" repeat, 11 yds. per roll. No.105 (tan on blue). Block print.

ᲒᲔ LE BAL DE SCEAUX. French, 1815–25, block print. 18$^{7}/_{8}$" wide, 26$^{3}/_{4}$" repeat, 11 yds. per roll. No.1512 (green on tan). Block print.

ᲒᲔ BARABAN. French, 1800–30, block print. 21$^{1}/_{4}$" wide, 5$^{1}/_{4}$" repeat, 11 yds. per roll. No.161 (white on yellow). Block print.

ᲒᲔ BLUET. French, 1835–45, block print. 19" wide, 9" repeat, 11 yds. per roll. No.223 (tan on ochre). Block print.

ᲒᲔ BOSQUET DE LUNAN. French, 1790–1810, block print. 21$^{1}/_{4}$" wide, 34$^{1}/_{2}$" repeat, 11 yds. per roll. No.1503 (multi on cream). Block print.

ᲒᲔ BOUQUET ET AQUEDUC. French, 1780–1800, block print. McClelland, p. 77. 23$^{1}/_{4}$" wide, 32$^{5}/_{8}$" repeat, 11 yds. per roll. No.119 (multi on white). Block print.

ᲒᲔ BOUQUET TRANSITION. French, 1780–90, block print. Originally printed by Reveillon. Clouzot and Follot, p. 39. 23$^{1}/_{2}$" wide, 37" repeat, 11 yds. per roll. No.180.

ᲒᲔ BRANCHE D'EGLANTIER. French, 1800–50, block print. 21$^{1}/_{4}$" wide, 21$^{5}/_{8}$" repeat, 11 yds. per roll. No.296 (multi on dark brown). Block print.

ᲒᲔ BRIGHTON. French, 1830–60, block print. 18$^{7}/_{8}$" wide, 5$^{1}/_{2}$" repeat, 11 yds. per roll. No.2014 (green on cream). Block print.

ᲒᲔ LE CAMEE. French, 1790–1800, block print. 21$^{1}/_{4}$" wide, 21$^{1}/_{4}$" repeat, 11 yds. per roll. No.214 (gray and blue on gray). Block print.

ᲒᲔ CAMPAGNE FLEURIE. French, 1800–20, block print. 21$^{1}/_{4}$" wide, 21$^{1}/_{4}$" repeat, 11 yds. per roll. No.186 (multi on cream). Block print.

ᲒᲔ CENELLE. French, 1815–25, block print. 19$^{7}/_{8}$" wide, 19$^{7}/_{8}$" repeat, 11 yds. per roll. No.262 (pink and green on yellow). Block print.

ᲒᲔ CHASSE AU CANARD. French, 1790–1800, block print. 20" wide, 21$^{5}/_{8}$" repeat, 11 yds. per roll. No.187 (mauve on yellow). Block print.

ᲒᲔ CHAR ET COLOMBES. French, 1780–1800, block print. 21$^{5}/_{8}$" wide, 21$^{5}/_{8}$" repeat, 11 yds. per roll. No.137 (pink and white on blue). Block print.

ᲒᲔ CHIEN COURANT. French, 1780–1800, block print. 21$^{5}/_{8}$" wide, 21$^{5}/_{8}$" repeat, 11 yds. per roll. No.189 (orange and blue on light blue). Block print.

ᲒᲔ CLOCHETTES. French, 1780–1800, block print. 21$^{1}/_{4}$" wide, 21$^{1}/_{4}$" repeat, 11 yds. per roll. No.127 (multi on yellow). Block print.

ᲒᲔ LES COLOMBES. French, 1780–1800, block print. 22" wide, 21$^{1}/_{4}$" repeat, 11 yds. per roll. No.110 (blue and red on blue). Block print.

❧ COLONNADES. French, 1780–1800, block print. 21⅝" wide, 21⅝" repeat, 11 yds. per roll. No.114 (pinks and green on light blue). Block print.

❧ COMBAT AERIEN. French, 1780–90, block print. Olligs, vol. 1, fig. 165, p. 244. 20½" wide, 24¾" repeat, 11 yds. per roll. No.199. Block print.

❧ LE COQ. French, 1780–1800, block print. Olligs, vol. 1, fig. 166, p. 244. 21⅝" wide, 42½" repeat, 11 yds. per roll. No.116 (multi on tan). Block print.

❧ CORBEILLE ET TREILLAGE. French, 1820–30, block print. 22" wide, 18½" repeat, 11 yds. per roll. No.174 (rust on yellow). Block print.

❧ COUPE DE PIERRE. French, 1830–50, block print. 11 yds. per roll. No.229 (gray and tan). Block print.

❧ LES CYGNES. French, 1780–1800, block print. McClelland, p. 130. 21¼" wide, 21¼" repeat, 11 yds. per roll. No.135 (gray and white on light gray). Block print.

❧ DAMAS CHARLES X. French, 1825–40, block print. 18½" wide, 15¾" repeat, 11 yds. per roll. No.297 (gray on gray). Block print.

❧ DAMAS DE MARSAN. French, 1825–40, block print. 18⅞" wide, 18⅛" repeat, 11 yds. per roll. No.235 (cream on red). Block print.

❧ DAMAS LOUIS XV. French, 1825–40, block print. 21¼" wide, 21⅝" repeat, 11 yds. per roll. No.221 (ochre on yellow). Block print.

❧ DAMAS MEDAILLON LOUIS XVI. French, 1825–90, block print. 21¼" wide, 13⅜" repeat, 11 yds. per roll. No.226 (gold on gold). Block print.

❧ DAMAS RIVIERE. French, 1835–60, block print. 23⅝" wide, 15¾" repeat, 11 yds. per roll. No.233 (cream on red). Block print.

❧ DAMAS VITRIAL. French, 1835–50, block print. 18½" wide, 20½" repeat, 11 yds. per roll. No.222 (gold on gray). Block print.

❧ DRAPERIE JOSEPHINE. French, 1810–25, block print. Nylander, Redmond, and Sander, fig. 25b, p. 117; Olligs, vol. 1, fig. 231, p. 325. 20½" wide, 15⅜" repeat, 11 yds. per roll. Fragments and samples at Old Manse, Concord, Mass., and Society for the Preservation of New England Antiquities. No.245 (white and gray on gold). Block print.

❧ DRAPERIE MARIE LOUISE. French, 1815–25, block print. 20⅞" wide, 21¼" repeat, 11 yds. per roll. No.227 (blue-gray). Block print.

❧ ECUREUIL. French, 1790–1810, block print. 21¼" wide, 19⅝" repeat, 11 yds. per roll. No.126 (white on blue). Block print.

❧ ECUREUIL POLYCHROME. French, 1790–1810, block print. 21¼" wide, 17" repeat, 11 yds. per roll. No.208 (multi on cream). Block print.

❧ ELYSEE. French, 1830–40, block print. 20½" wide, 10½" repeat, 11 yds. per roll. No.283 (gray on white). Block print.

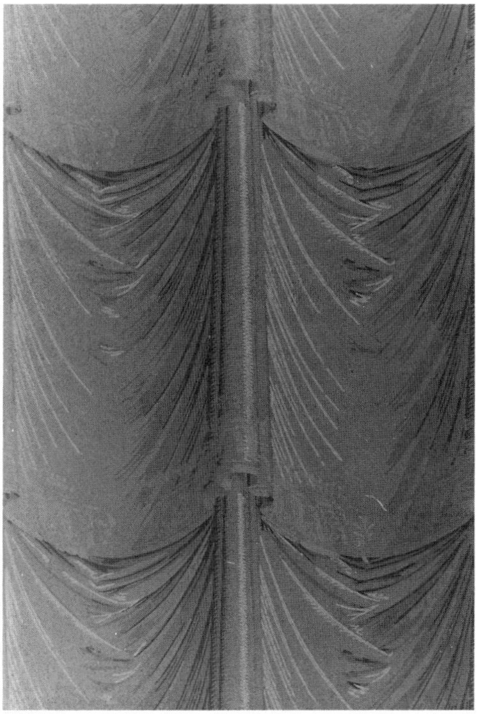
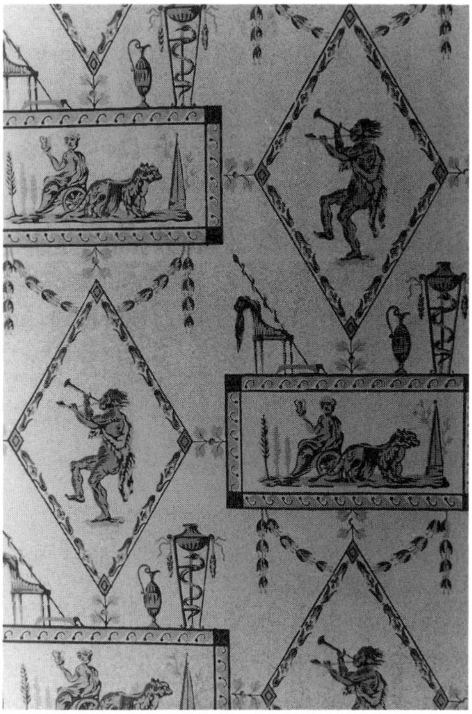

above left
DRAPERIE JOSEPHINE, 1810–25. Classic Revivals (Mauny Collection).

above right
FAUNE DANSANT, 1790–1810. Classic Revivals (Mauny Collection).

EMPIRE MAIS. French, 1800–20, block print. Olligs, vol. 1, fig. 227, p. 322. 18½" wide, 23¼" repeat, 11 yds. per roll. No.104. Block print.

EMPIRE POLYCHROME. French, 1815–25, block print. 21⅝" wide, 9½" repeat, 11 yds. per roll. No.177 (multi on cream). Block print.

ESCARGOT. French, 1830–60, block print. 18½" wide, 1¾" repeat, 11 yds. per roll. No.864 (gold on cream). Block print.

FAUNE DANSANT. French, 1790–1810, block print. 18⅛" wide, 19" repeat, 11 yds. per roll. No.107 (black and mauve on yellow). Block print.

FELICITE. French, 1790–1810, block print. 21¼" wide, 21¼" repeat, 11 yds. per roll. No.170 (multi on yellow). Block print.

FEUILLE JAUNE. French, 1810–25, block print. McClelland, p. 178. 18" wide, 18⅞" repeat, 11 yds. per roll. No.1502 (yellow on rose). Block print.

FRANKLIN. French, 1815–30, block print. 19¼" wide, 14" repeat, 11 yds. per roll. No.1510 (red, white, and blue on tan). Block print.

LA GLORIETTE. French, 1780–1800, block print. 22½" wide, 43" repeat, 11 yds. per roll. No.133 (pinks and greens on blue). Block print.

GRAND CHINOIS ET VASES. French, 1780–1800, block print. 21¼" wide, 42½" repeat, 11 yds. per roll. No.136 (tans). Block print.

above left

PERSONNAGES ET
OISEAUX, 1815–25.
Classic Revivals
(Mauny Collection).

above right

PLUMES DE PAON,
1790–1810. Classic
Revivals (Mauny
Collection).

☙ GRENADE. French, 1780–1800, block print. McClelland, p. 77. 22" wide, 16⅛" repeat, 11 yds. per roll. No.122 (multi on white). Block print.

☙ HORTENSIA. French, 1800–30, block print. 19¼" wide, 19¼" repeat, 11 yds. per roll. No.147 (green and pink on yellow). Block print.

☙ LES IFS. French, 1790–1810, block print. 21¼" wide, 9½" repeat, 11 yds. per roll. No.146 (orange and blue on buff). Block print.

☙ LANTERNE MAGIQUE. French, 1790–1800, block print. McClelland, p. 134; Olligs, vol. 1, fig. 219, p. 317. 20⅛" wide, 21⅝" repeat, 11 yds. per roll. No.115 (pinks and green on light blue). Block print.

☙ LYS ET PERDRIX. French, 1780–1800, block print. McClelland, p. 138. 21¼" wide, 45¼" repeat, 11 yds. per roll. No.121 (pink and white on blue). Block print.

☙ MA NORMANDIE. French, 1780–1800, block print. 20½" wide, 21¼" repeat, 11 yds. per roll. No.206 (blue and orange on yellow). Block print.

☙ MARBRE. French, 1820–40, block print. 18½" wide, 19¾" repeat, 11 yds. per roll. No.163 (gray on gray). Block print.

☙ MINERVE. French, 1795–1810, block print. 21¼" wide, 21¼" repeat, 11 yds. per roll. No.1511 (multi). Block print.

☙ MOIRE ANCIENNE. French, 1835–50, block print. 19⅞" wide,

20$\frac{1}{2}$" repeat, 11 yds. per roll. No.270 (white on gray). Block print.

❧ LES MOUTONS. French, 1780–1800, block print. Olligs, vol. 1, fig. 177, p. 253 (variant). 21$\frac{1}{4}$" wide, 21$\frac{1}{4}$" repeat, 11 yds. per roll. No.194 (multi on gray). Block print.

❧ OEUILLER ET NARCISSE. French, 1790–1810, block print. 21$\frac{5}{8}$" wide, 21$\frac{5}{8}$" repeat, 11 yds. per roll. No.191 (multi on yellow). Block print.

❧ OFFRANDE A CERES. French, 1815–30, block print. McClelland, p. 174. 17$\frac{3}{4}$" wide, 18$\frac{1}{2}$" repeat, 11 yds. per roll. No.1509 (black and white on tan). Block print.

❧ PALMETTE. French, 1800–20, block print. 20$\frac{7}{8}$" wide, 4" repeat, 11 yds. per roll. No.100 (gray and black). Block print.

❧ PALMIERS ET BOUQUETS. French, 1780–1800, block print. 21$\frac{1}{4}$" wide, 21$\frac{1}{4}$" repeat, 11 yds. per roll. No.145 (multi on light blue). Block print.

❧ PAPIER FLEURETTE. French, 1810–25, block print. 18$\frac{7}{8}$" wide, 3$\frac{1}{4}$" repeat, 11 yds. per roll. No.1513 (tan). Block print.

❧ PARASOL. French, 1790–1800, block print. 21$\frac{5}{8}$" wide, 43" repeat, 11 yds. per roll. No.168 (multi on gray). Block print.

❧ LE PECHEUR. French, 1780–1800, block print. 19$\frac{3}{4}$" wide, 18$\frac{7}{8}$" repeat, 11 yds. per roll. No.117 (mauve on light blue). Block print.

❧ LA PENSEE. French, 1825–35, block print. 21$\frac{1}{4}$" wide, 2$\frac{3}{8}$" repeat, 11 yds. per roll. No.202 (tan on off-white). Block print.

❧ PERSONNAGES ET OISEAUX. French, 1815–25, block print. 19$\frac{1}{4}$" wide, 20$\frac{7}{8}$" repeat, 11 yds. per roll. No.164 (blue on gray). Block print.

❧ PETITS PONTS CHINOIS. French, 1780–1800, block print. 22$\frac{1}{2}$" wide, 22$\frac{1}{2}$" repeat, 11 yds. per roll. No.124 (multi on off-white). Block print.

❧ PILLEMENT. French, 1790–1810, block print. 21$\frac{5}{8}$" wide, 20$\frac{7}{8}$" repeat, 11 yds. per roll. No.156 (multi on cream). Block print.

❧ LES PLUMES. French, 1825–40, block print. 26$\frac{3}{4}$" wide, 22$\frac{7}{8}$" repeat, 11 yds. per roll. No.225 (white on blue). Block print.

❧ PLUMES DE PAON. French, 1790–1810, block print. 19$\frac{1}{4}$" wide, 21$\frac{1}{4}$" repeat, 11 yds. per roll. No.118 (blue and lavender on yellow). Block print.

❧ POMETTES. French, 1780–1800, block print. 20$\frac{7}{8}$" wide, 16$\frac{1}{2}$" repeat, 11 yds. per roll. No.181 (green). Block print.

❧ POUPETTE. French, 1815–25, block print. 18$\frac{1}{2}$" wide, 18$\frac{7}{8}$" repeat, 11 yds. per roll. No.207 (pink and green on blue). Block print.

❧ RAYURE CYGNE. French, 1785–1800, block print. 21$\frac{5}{8}$" wide, 20" repeat, 11 yds. per roll. No.182 (tans). Block print.

❧ RAYURE ET CORAIL. French, 1815–30, block print. 20$\frac{7}{8}$" wide, 26$\frac{3}{8}$" repeat, 11 yds. per roll. No.279. Block print.

❧ RAYURE FEUGERE. French, 1810–25, block print. 18$\frac{1}{2}$" wide,

9½" repeat, 11 yds. per roll. No.246 (white on buff). Block print.

&❧ REVEILLOND. French, 1790–1810, block print. 21¼" wide, 21⅝" repeat, 11 yds. per roll. No.228 (multi on cream). Block print.

&❧ REVOLUTION. French, 1790–1810, block print. 20½" wide, 22" repeat, 11 yds. per roll. No.143 (blue on off–white). Block print.

&❧ ROBESPIERRE. French, 1815–25, block print. 24" wide, 9⅞" repeat, 11 yds. per roll. No.149 (blue and orange). Also available with flocked border; No.608. Block print.

&❧ ROSACE ET CANARD. French, 1790–1810, block print. 19" wide, 12⅝" repeat, 11 yds. per roll. No.101 (black on yellow). Block print.

&❧ ROSE DE NOEL. French, 1780–85, block print. Probably originally printed by Reveillon. Clouzot and Follot, p. 38 (pattern shown reversed). 20½" wide, 40⅛" repeat, 11 yds. per roll. No.184 (multi on cream). Block print.

&❧ ROSES FRANCE. French, 1780–1800, block print. Lynn, color pls. 4 and 5, pp. 36 and 37. 21¼" wide, 22" repeat, 11 yds. per roll. No.210 (multi on blue). Block print.

&❧ ROSE LAQUE. French, 1790–1810, block print. 22¾" wide, 34¼" repeat, 11 yds. per roll. No.195 (yellow). Block print.

&❧ LE SALON DE MUSIQUE. French, 1780–1800, block print. 21¼" wide, 11" repeat, 11 yds. per roll. No.292 (multi on buff). Block print.

&❧ SATIN BLANC REGENCY. French, 1830–60, block print. 18⅞" wide, 8¼" repeat, 11 yds. per roll. No.244 (gold on cream). Block print.

&❧ SEMIS BOSPHORE. French, 1790–1820, block print. 19⅞" wide, 19⅞" repeat, 11 yds. per roll. No.273 (green on white). Block print.

&❧ SEMIS ETOILE. French, 1835–60, block print. 18½" wide, 3¼" repeat, 11 yds. per roll. No.255 (buff on gray). Block print.

&❧ SEMIS PILASTRE. French, 1815–25, block print. 26¾" wide, 1⅜" repeat, 11 yds. per roll. No.285 (brick). Block print.

&❧ LA STATUE. French, 1790–1810, block print. 20⅞" wide, 21¼" repeat, 11 yds. per roll. No.112 (blue and green on light blue). Block print.

&❧ TEMPLE DE L'AMOUR. French, 1780–1800, block print. 22⅞" wide, 21¼" repeat, 11 yds. per roll. No.132 (mauve and black on light blue). Block print.

&❧ TENTURE FLOTANTE. French, 1812–40, block print. 26¾" wide, 23⅝" repeat, 11 yds. per roll. No.220 (gray). Block print.

&❧ LES TULIPES. French, 1790–95, block print. Originally printed by Jacquemart et Bénard. Clouzot and Follot, p. 23. 21⅝" wide, 21¼" repeat, 11 yds. per roll. No.190 (multi on gray). Block print.

&❧ VASE ET BOUQUET. French, 1790–1810, block print. 21¼" wide, 21¼" repeat, 11 yds. per roll. No.106 (multi on gray). Block print.

Silvergate Collection

ᔥ MISTLETOE. English, 1780–90, block print. 21" wide, 7⁷/₈" repeat, 11 yds. per roll. Document at Rosehill House, Ironbridge, England. No.CS053. Block print.

ᔥ NEWMAN HOUSE. English, 1780–90, block print. 21" wide, 11 yds. per roll. Document at Newman House, Dublin, Ireland. No.AS081. Block print.

COLE & SON

Available through Clarence House as custom order only.

ᔥ CHINESE TRELLIS. English, 1830–60, block print. Oman and Hamilton, no. 265, p. 159. 21" wide, 11 yds. per roll. Coles Book. No.98846 (gold on white). Block print.

ᔥ CLANDON. English, 1810–20, block print with flocking. Oman and Hamilton, no. 128, p. 128. 21" wide, 11 yds. per roll. Adaptation: flocking not reproduced. Coles Book. No.98880 (red). Block print.

ᔥ FLOWER SPRAY. English, 1790–1810, block print. 21" wide, 10¹/₂" repeat, 11 yds. per roll. Coles Book. No.98883 (tan on white). Block print.

ᔥ HADDON HALL. English, 1780–1810, block print. 21" wide, 13" repeat, 11 yds. per roll. Coles Book. No.98840 (brown on white). Block print.

ᔥ WHICKHAM. English, 1780–1800, block print. 21" wide, 30" repeat, 11 yds. per roll. Coles Book. No.98831 (green on blue). Block print.

COLEFAX & FOWLER

Available through Cowtan & Tout.

ᔥ ALBANY DAMASK. English, 1800–10, block print. 20¹/₂" wide, 5¹/₂" repeat, 11 yds. per roll. No.7073-03 (taupe); No.7073-04 (yellow).

ᔥ BERKELEY SPRIG. English, 1780–1800, block print. Oman and Hamilton, no. 126, p. 127, and endpapers. 20³/₄" wide, 11³/₄" repeat, 11 yds. per roll. No.7010/01 (navy blue); No.7010/03 (blue on off-white).

ᔥ CAMROSE. English, 1800–20, block print. 20¹/₂" wide, 3" repeat, 11 yds. per roll. No.7107-4 (yellow).

ᔥ HUNTINGTON. English, 1790–1815, block print. 20¹/₂" wide, 6" repeat, 11 yds. per roll. No.7025/6 (green); No.7025/11 (blue).

ᔥ SACKVILLE. English, 1800–10, block print. 20¹/₂" wide, 2¹/₂" repeat, 11 yds. per roll. No.7071-03 (stone); No.7071-07 (yellow); No.7071-08 (red).

COWTAN & TOUT

ᔥ BRAMDEAN. English, 1790–1815, block print. 20¹/₂" wide, 3¹/₂" repeat, 11 yds. per roll. No.8020-04 (beige and blue).

A. L. DIAMENT & COMPANY

ॐ LES ABEILLES. French, 1825–35, block print. 27″ wide, 26³/₄″ half-drop repeat, 5 yds. per roll. No.151-10 (green, rose, and tan on blue).

ॐ DECOR LOUIS XVI CABLE DOVES. French, 1785–95, block print. 21¹/₂″ wide, 50¹/₂″ repeat. Multi on beige.

ॐ HERMITAGE SIDEWALL. French, 1830–50, block print. 21³/₄″ wide, 18¹/₂″ repeat, 6 yds. per s/r. No.111-03 (green and copper).

ॐ LE JOUEUR DE FLUTE. French, 1780–1800, block print. 19¹/₄″ wide, 21″ repeat. No.175-04 (buff on ochre).

ॐ MENTON. French, 1815–25, block print. 27″ wide, 18¹/₂″ repeat, 5 yds. per s/r. No.80211-07 (gray).

GALACAR & COMPANY

ॐ LA FALAISE. French, 1799, block print. Originally printed by Jacquemart et Bénard. 27¹/₄″ wide, 13¹/₄″ repeat, 5 yds. per s/r. Document at Musée des Arts Décoratifs. No.GP-2801 (blues and greens).

ॐ FIGARO. French, 1805, block print. Originally printed by Jacquemart et Bénard. 27¹/₂″ wide, 27¹/₂″ repeat, 5 yds. per s/r. Document at Musée des Arts Décoratifs. No.GP-3101 (greens and orange).

ॐ FINISTERE. French, 1798, block print. Originally printed by Jacquemart et Bénard. 25″ wide, 25¹/₄″ half-drop repeat, 5 yds. per s/r. Document at Musée des Arts Décoratifs. No.GP-1701 (document colors on white).

CHRISTOPER HYLAND INCORPORATED

ॐ AMBOISE. English, 1835–50, block or machine print. 20¹/₂″ wide, 20¹/₂″ repeat, 11 yd. per roll. No.ZZCHC03 (multi on creme).

ॐ BLOIS. English, 1800–20, block print. 20¹/₂″ wide, 3¹/₂″ repeat, 11 yds. per roll. No.ZZCHB01 (white on tan).

ॐ BOUQUET TRANSITION. French, 1780–90, block print. Originally printed by Reveillon. Clouzot and Follot, p. 39. 23¹/₂″ wide, 37″ repeat, 11 yds. per roll. No.MN180. Block print.

ॐ BRANCHE D'EGLANTIER. French, 1800–50, block print. 21¹/₂″ wide, 21¹/₂″ repeat, 11 yds. per roll. No.MN296. Block print.

ॐ CHAUMONT. French, 1820–40, block print. 20¹/₂″ wide, 3¹/₂″ repeat, 11 yds. per roll. No.ZZCHEO2 (blue ground).

ॐ CHENONCEAU. English or French, 1810–40, block print. 20¹/₂″ wide, 4¹/₂″ repeat, 11 yds. per roll. No.ZZCHF series.

ॐ CHINON. French, 1815–20, block print. 20¹/₂″ wide, 5¹/₃″ repeat, 11 yds. per roll. No.ZZCHA10 (blue ground).

ॐ DUFOUR. French, 1805–20, block print. 21″ wide, 34⁵/₈″ repeat, 11 yds. per roll. No.ZZ0404 (creme).

ॐ HYDRANGEA. French, 1815–25, block print. 18⁷/₈″ wide, 9³/₈″ repeat, 11 yds. per roll. No.ZZ1103 (gray and white).

ॐ LILY. French, 1810–25, block print. 21″ wide, 14⁵/₈″ repeat, 11

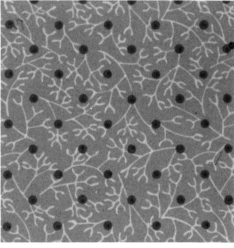

above left
LE JOUEUR DE FLUTE,
1780–1800.
A. L. Diament &
Company.

above right
MISTLETOE, 1780–90.
Classic Revivals (Sil-
vergate Collection).

left
AMBOISE, 1835–50.
Christopher Hyland
Incorporated.

top left

REVEILLON, 1785–1800. Christopher Hyland Incorporated.

top right

LILY, 1810–25. Christopher Hyland Incorporated.

yds. per roll. No.ZZ0704 (blue base, multi).

&❧ OAK GARLAND. English, 1790–1800, block print. Greysmith, fig. 48, p. 70; Wells-Cole, no. 10, p. 14. 21" wide, 18⅝" repeat, 11 yds. per roll. Document at Temple Newsam, Leeds, England. No.ZZ94007 (gold on pink).

&❧ REVEILLON. French, 1785–1800, block print. 21" wide, 21¾" repeat, 11 yds. per roll. No.ZZ0205 (blue base).

&❧ ROBESPIERRE. French, 1815–25, block print. 25½" wide, 9½" repeat, 11 yds. per roll. No.MN149. Block print.

&❧ ST. JAMES PLACE. English, 1790–1810, block print. 21" wide, 5" repeat, 11 yds. per roll. No.ZZ1301 (rust red, black, and white).

&❧ TRIANON. French, 1810–20, block print. 21" wide, 21" repeat, 11 yds. per roll. No.ZZ061 (ivory, steel gray, and red).

&❧ VALENCAY. English, 1800–30, block print. 20½" wide, 3¾" repeat, 11 yds. per roll. No.ZZCHD02 (terra cotta and white).

KATZENBACH & WARREN

&❧ MARBLE ASHLAR. French, 1800–50, block print. 27" wide, 32¼" half-drop repeat, 4½ yds. per s/r. Adaptation. Document at The Athenaeum of Philadelphia. No.AE1024 (sienna).

SCALAMANDRE

&❧ BLAKESLEE HOUSE. American or French, 1830–40, block print. 27⅛" wide, 22" repeat, 5 yds. per s/r. Historic representation. Reproduced for Old Economy Village, Ambridge, Pa. No.WP8820 (white and brown on blue). Special order.

❦ THE CEDARS. French, 1833, block print. Designed by A. Merii. Nouvel, fig. 13, p. 35. 18^1/$_2$" wide, 18^1/$_2$" repeat, 8 yds. per s/r. Reproduced from an English copy of the French pattern. Reproduced for Bliss Nash Davis House, Danville, Vt. No.WP81221-001 (pearl gray on ivory). Special order.

❦ CHESTERFIELD. American, 1800–20, block print. 28^1/$_2$" wide, 6^7/$_8$" repeat, 5 yds. per s/r. Reproduced for Hayes Tavern, Brattleboro, Vt. No.WP8640 (brown and white on tan). Special order.

❦ CHLOE. French, 1810–30, block print. Printed by Dufour et Leroy. Guibert, fig. 459, p. 68. 27" wide, 19" repeat, 5 yds. per s/r. Adaptation: floral motifs omitted. Document at Bibliothèque Forney, Paris. No.WP81402-001 (multi peaches on emerald).

❦ CHRISTOPHER MURPHY HOUSE. Probably American, 1820–30, block print. 27" wide, 13^1/$_2$" repeat. Historic Savannah Foundation. No.WP81125 (green and white on yellow). Special order.

❦ DERBY HOUSE. American, 1810–25, block print. 26^3/$_4$" wide, 8^3/$_4$" repeat, 5 yds. per s/r. Document at Shelburne Museum, Shelburne, Vt. No.WP8931 (yellow and green on white). Special order.

❦ FARRINGTON HOUSE. American, 1815–30, block print. 28" wide, 10" repeat, 5 yds. per s/r. Adaptation. Old Deerfield Collection. No.8902 (white and green on light blue). Special order.

❦ 48 LAURENS STREET. English, 1800–10, block print. 27" wide, 36" repeat, 5 yds. per s/r. Adaptation. Historic Charleston Reproductions. No.WP81274 (blue ground). Special order.

❦ HAYES TAVERN. French or English, 1810–25, block print. 28^1/$_2$" wide, 8" repeat, 5 yds. per s/r. Reproduced for Hayes Tavern, Brattleboro, Vt. No.WP8642 (blue and white on gray). Special order.

❦ MIDDLETON'S PLANTATION PARLOR. French or American, 1830–50, block print. 21" wide, 21" half-drop repeat, 7 yds. per s/r. See borders (page 80) for companion frieze and base border. Reproduced for Middleton's Plantation, Edisto Island, S.C. No. WP81416-001 (aquas and mahogany on pearl gray). Special order.

❦ MONIQUE. French, 1820–30, block print. Guibert, fig. 228, p. 29. 27" wide, 27" repeat, 5 yds. per s/r. Historic representation. Reproduced from a period design for a wallpaper; scale enlarged. Document at Bibliothèque Forney, Paris. No.WP81396-001 (multi roses and lilacs on ivory).

❦ MUIR'S MEDALLION. French or American, 1825–35, block print. 27" wide, 15" repeat, 5 yds. per s/r. Historic representation. Old Deerfield Collection. No.WP8913 (blue on gold). Special order.

❦ NANCY. French, 1800–15, block print. Guibert, fig. 583, p. 89. 21" wide, 21" repeat, 5 yds. per s/r. Adaptation: sprig motif omitted.

right
MONIQUE, 1820–30.
Scalamandré.

right and above
MIDDLETON'S
PLANTATION PARLOR
and frieze, 1830–50.
Scalamandré.

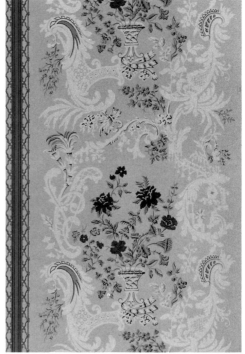

Document at Bibliothèque Forney, Paris. No.WP81397-001 (multi terragons and lilacs on nude).

&❧ PRESTWOULD SALOON SIDE PAPER. French, 1820–30, block print. 18¾" wide, 19½" repeat, 7 yds. per s/r. Historic representation. Reproduced from a photograph for Prestwould, Clarksville, Va., operated by Prestwould Foundation. No.WP81502-001 (multi greens on pearl gray). Special order.

&❧ PRINCESS LACE. American, 1810–25, block print. 27½" wide, 20" repeat. Old Deerfield Collection. No.WP8905 (cream on beige). Special order.

SCHUMACHER

&❧ BERNARDSTON. American, 1790–1810, block print. Document at Colonial Williamsburg. 20" wide, 18¾" repeat. No.513080 (document gold).

&❧ BLUEBELLS. English, 1790–1820, block print. 21" wide, 9" half-drop repeat, 11 yds. per roll. Document at Temple Newsam, Leeds, England. No.TN04 (blue on white).

&❧ CARNATION. English, 1820–40, block print. Wells-Cole, no. 17, p. 18. 21" wide, 15" half-drop repeat, 11 yds. per roll. Document at Temple Newsam, Leeds, England. No.TN06 (blue on buff).

&❧ FLORALESQUE. French, 1835–50, block print. 27" wide, 12⅞" repeat, 4½ yds. per s/r. Document in Schumacher Archive. No.505244 (pumice).

&❧ FOX GRAPE. English or French, 1780–1810, block print. 27" wide, 18" repeat, 4½ yds. per s/r. Document at Colonial Williamsburg. No.513050 (document ivory).

&❧ GWENDOLYN SWAG. French, 1835–60, block print. 20½" wide, 25¼" repeat, 5½ yds. per s/r. Document in Hobe Erwin Collection, Schumacher Archive. No.506185 (opal).

&❧ HOBE BLOCK. American or French, 1815–30, block print. 19" wide, 18¼" repeat, 6 yds. per s/r. Document in Hobe Erwin Collection, Schumacher Archive. No.506234 (delft).

&❧ LONG GALLERY. English, c. 1827, block print. Sugden and Edmundson, pl. 31. 20" wide, 40" half-drop repeat, 11 yds. per roll. Document at Temple Newsam, Leeds, England. No.TN10 (red).

&❧ LONG GALLERY. English, c. 1827, block print. Wells-Cole, no. 8, p. 13. 21" wide, 42" repeat, 11 yds. per roll. Document at Temple Newsam, Leeds, England. No.TN12 (green).

&❧ OAK GARLAND. English, c. 1796, block print. Greysmith, fig. 48, p. 70; Wells-Cole, no. 10, p. 14. 21" wide, 18½" half-drop repeat, 11 yds. per roll. Document at Temple Newsam, Leeds, England. No.TN05 (gold on pink).

&❧ PARLOR PORTIERES. French, 1815–20, block print. 27" wide, 19" repeat, 4½ yds. per s/r. Document in Schumacher Archive. No.505274 (document moss).

ᴥ PENNYWEATHER BLOCKS. French, 1825–35, block print. 18" wide, 15¾" repeat, 6 yds. per s/r. Document in Hobe Erwin Collection, Schumacher Archive. No.506121 (cafe au lait).

ᴥ REDOUBTE'S WREATH. French, 1820–35, block print. 27" wide, 19" repeat, 4½ yds. per s/r. Reproduced from a period design for a wallpaper. Document in Schumacher Archive. No.512890 (aqua).

ᴥ STENCIL SQUARE. American, 1815–25, block print. Nylander, Redmond, and Sander, fig. 30.1, p. 133. 19¼" wide, 19" repeat, 5½ yds. per s/r. Document at Colonial Williamsburg. No.513040 (document indigo).

THE TWIGS

ᴥ BIRDS OF PARADISE. French, 1780–1810, block print. Originally printed by Jacquemart et Bénard. McClelland, p. 244. 18½" wide plus 7½" border, 37" half-drop repeat, 5 yds. per s/r. Adaptation. Reproduced for Gore Place, Waltham, Mass. No.6504 (multi on meringue).

ᴥ BRIGHTON LATTICE. English, 1830–40, block print. 27¼" wide, 14" repeat, 5 yds. per s/r. No.7501 (green on meringue).

ᴥ CAPRICCIO. French, 1800–20, block print. 25" wide plus 2¾" border, 10" repeat, 5 yds. per s/r. No.4509 (coral and green on white).

ᴥ CHENONCEAUX. French, 1780–1800, block print. 21" wide plus 3" border, 21" half-drop repeat, 5 yds. per s/r. No.6492 (documentary on bone).

ᴥ DRAPERY SIDEWALL. French, 1810–25, block print. 27½" wide, 23½" repeat, 5 yds. per s/r. No.5501 (gray); No.5502 (taupe).

ᴥ DUTTON HOUSE. American, 1810–25, block print. 27" wide, 5" repeat, 5 yds. per s/r. No.A2210/007 (white on custard).

ᴥ FAUX MARBRE. English, 1820–40, block print. 27" wide, 36" repeat, 5 yds. per s/r. No.66250/002 (cream).

ᴥ FOLSOM TAVERN. French, 1835–45, block print. 27" wide, 12" repeat. Custom order.

ᴥ GLENMORAL SIDEWALL. French, 1810–20, block print. 19" wide plus 4¾" border, 2½" repeat, 6 yds. per s/r. No.63600/004 (green and salmon); No.63600/007 (green and gold).

ᴥ JAFFREY ROOM. French, 1780–90, block print. 22½" wide, 42½" half-drop repeat. Document at Museum of Fine Arts, Boston, Mass. No.4010 (multi on melon).

ᴥ LA NANCY. French, 1810–20, block print. 19¼" wide, 22½" half-drop repeat. No.A2290/004 (coral and green on white).

ᴥ LA NANCY FILLER. French, 1810–20, block print. 19¼" wide, 23" repeat. No.FA229/004 (green and kraft on white).

ᴥ ORLEANS. French, 1815–20, block print. 26½" wide, 26¼" repeat, 5 yds. per s/r. No.6511 (multi).

๖๖ OSIER. French, 1830–40, block print. 24¹/₄" wide plus 1³/₄" border, 3" repeat, 5 yds. per s/r. No.63100/001 (tan on custard).

๖๖ PINGREE HOUSE. French, 1800–15, block print. 27" wide, 24" repeat, 5 yds. per s/r. No.A1220/009 (camel on meringue).

๖๖ RED ANCHOR. French, 1830–40, block print. Guibert, fig. 234, p. 30. 19" wide, 18" one third–drop repeat. Reproduced from a period design for a wallpaper. No.99800/003 (burgundy and cerulean blue on almost white).

WATERHOUSE WALLHANGINGS

๖๖ BREWSTER FLORAL. Probably American, 1800–20, block print. 20¹/₂" wide, 15¹/₂" repeat, 7 yds. per s/r. Document in Waterhouse Archives. No.194635 (slate blue on white).

๖๖ CHATHAM LACE. Probably American, 1825–35, block print. 20" wide, 9¹/₂" repeat, 7 yds. per s/r. Document in Waterhouse Archives. No.190312 (blue). Period colorings: No.190335 (pink); No.190519 (gray); No.190518 (yellow).

๖๖ CHRISTMAS ROSE. Probably American, 1790–1810, block print. 24" wide, 2¹/₂" repeat, 6 yds. per s/r. Document in Waterhouse Archives. Document color not reproduced. Period coloring: No.161258 (green on light blue).

๖๖ COYLE HOUSE. American, 1822–28, block print. Lynn, figs. 12-19

above left
Original document for "Stencil Square," 1815–25, a wallpaper reproduced by Schumacher.

above right
GLENMORAL SIDEWALL with border, 1810–20. The Twigs.

and 12-20, p. 283. 26½″ wide, 5 yds. per s/r. Document at Old Sturbridge Village, Sturbridge, Mass., and the Coyle House, Natchez, Miss. No.168190 (pink and white on yellow). Period coloring: No.168579 (green and orange on light green).

◈ DANDELION STRIPE. American, 1810–25, block print. 18″ wide, 7 yds. per s/r. Document in Waterhouse Archives. No.128512 (blue and orange). Period colorings: No.128622 (mustard); No.128518 (yellow).

◈ DEVIL PAPER. French, 1820–40, block print. 26½″ wide, 5 yds. per s/r. Document at Gore Place, Waltham, Mass. No.138576 (black on white). Special order.

◈ EAGLE HILL. English, 1790–1810, block print. 26″ wide, 4½″ repeat, 5 yds. per s/r. Adaptation: color not reproduced exactly. Document in Waterhouse Archives. No.106335 (gray on white).

◈ EDGARTOWN. American, 1800–15, block print. 23¾″ wide, 9½″ repeat, 6 yds. per s/r. Document in Waterhouse Archives. No.163618 (brown ground).

◈ ENOCH FRYE. Probably American, 1790–1810, block print. Nylander, Redmond, and Sander, fig. 30.2, p. 134 (variant). 24″ wide, 9½″ repeat, 7 yds. per s/r. Document in Waterhouse Archives. Additional sample at Society for the Preservation of New England Antiquities. No.112815 (ochre on gray-green). Period coloring: No.112496 (white on blue).

◈ FRENCH TASSEL. French or American, 1810–25, block print. 21½″ wide, 15½″ repeat, 7 yds. per s/r. Document in Waterhouse Archives; additional sample at Society for the Preservation of New England Antiquities. No.123437 (blue ground).

◈ THE GAZEBO. French, 1790–1800, block print. 20½″ wide, 22″ repeat, 7 yds. per s/r. Document in Waterhouse Archives. No.186613 (red and blue on gray). Period coloring: No.186444 (pink and green on blue).

◈ GENERAL JOHN WALKER. American, 1790–1810, block print. 20½″ wide, 5½″ repeat, 7 yds. per s/r. Document in Waterhouse Archives. No.188437 (white and black on blue).

◈ GENERAL THAYER. American, 1780–1810, block print. 19″ wide, 7 yds. per s/r. Reproduced for Sylvanus Thayer House, Braintree, Mass. Document at Sylvanus Thayer House; additional sample at Society for the Preservation of New England Antiquities. No.117840 (red ground).

◈ GORE PLACE. French, 1780–1810, block print. 18¾″ wide, 19″ repeat, 7 yds. per s/r. Document at Gore Place, Waltham, Mass. No.139506 (multi on beige).

◈ GOVERNOR BADGER. American or French, 1815–30, block print. 18″ wide, 19″ repeat, 7 yds. per s/r. Document in Waterhouse Archives. No.113426 (red on brown). Period coloring: No.113496 (orange on blue).

LOUISE. French or American, 1810–30, block print. 27" wide, 18½" repeat, 5 yds. per s/r. Document in Waterhouse Archives. No.141447 (pink and green on ochre). Period coloring: No.141581 (green on gray).

MARY LYON. French or American, 1810–20, block print. 28" wide, 5 yds. per s/r. Document in Waterhouse Archives. No.136632 (pink). Special order.

MEDALLION. French, 1820–30, block print. 28¼" wide, 7" repeat, 5 yds. per s/r. Document in Waterhouse Archives. No.104613 (yellow on gray).

NORWELL STRIPE. American, 1810–20, block print. 26" wide, 5½" repeat, 5 yds. per s/r. Document in Waterhouse Archives. No.108463 (rust on tan).

NYE HOMESTEAD. American, 1790–1810, block print. 26½" wide, 5 yds. per s/r. Document in Waterhouse Archives. No.118496 (white on blue).

OLD OAKEN BUCKET. American or French, 1810–25, block print. 28" wide, 18" repeat, 5 yd. per s/r. Document in Waterhouse Archives. No.197437 (white on blue).

PARKER HILL. American, 1825–35, block print. 19" wide, 18½" repeat. Document in Waterhouse Archives. Period coloring: No.114650 (tan ground).

LE PECHEUR. French, 1790–1810, block print. 18¾" wide, 18¾" repeat, 7 yds. per s/r. Document in Waterhouse Archives. No.175206 (blue and orange on white).

PLYMOUTH STENCIL. American, 1815–35, block print. 20" wide, 9½" repeat, 7 yds. per s/r. Document in Waterhouse Archives. No.191613 (blue on light gray).

POMEGRANATE. American, 1780–1800, block print. 28" wide, 10¾" repeat, 5 yds. per s/r. Document in Waterhouse Archives. No.208496 (white on blue).

REVEILLON. French, 1785–1810, block print. 27¼" wide, 44½" repeat, 5 yds. per s/r. Document in Waterhouse Archives. No.195707 (multi on white).

ROBBINS HOUSE. American, 1810–25, block print. 27½" wide, 9¼" repeat, 5 yds. per s/r. Document in Waterhouse Archives. No.213840 (gray and blue).

SALEM STRIPE. Probably American, 1790–1815, block print. 26½" wide, 5 yds. per s/r. Document in Waterhouse Archives. No.169437 (white on blue).

STRAWBERY BANKE STENCIL. American, 1815–25, block print. 24¼" wide, 21" repeat, 7 yds. per s/r. Document at Strawbery Banke Museum, Portsmouth, N.H. No.145158 (blue on mustard).

STRAWBERRY STRIPE. French or American, 1810–25, block print.

above left
RED ANCHOR,
1830–40. The Twigs.

above right
LE PECHEUR,
1790–1810. Water-
house Wallhangings.

right
LOUISE, 1810–30.
Waterhouse Wall-
hangings.

above left
REVEILLON,
1785–1810. Water-
house Wallhangings.

above right
STRAWBERRY STRIPE,
1810–25. Water-
house Wallhangings

left
POMEGRANATE,
1780–1800. Water-
house Wallhangings.

24" wide, 9¼" repeat, 6 yds. per s/r. Document in Waterhouse Archives. No.143447 (mustard).

ᕹ WHEAT DAMASK. American, 1810–25, block print. 24" wide, 24" repeat, 7 yds. per s/r. Document in Waterhouse Archives. No.154621 (white on mustard).

BORDERS

An asterisk (*) at the end of an entry indicates that the border was designed to go with a sidewall listed in the previous section.

LOUIS W. BOWEN

ᕹ VERSAILLES BORDERS (architectural elements). French, 1800–25, block prints. Charcoal tones, gray, and white.

> GUILLOCHE. 3½" wide, 9" repeat. No.87004-A.
> DOUBLE GREEK WAVE. 3" wide, 9¼" repeat. No.87004-B.
> EGG AND DART. 4⁷/₁₆" wide, 9" repeat. No.87004-C.
> COLUMN. 3¼" wide, 16¾" repeat. No.87004-D.
> SPIRAL. 5¼" wide, 36" repeat. No.87004-E.
> LEAF AND SPIRAL. 2½" wide, 17¾" repeat. No.87004-F.
> CORNICE. 12½" wide, 19" repeat. No.87004-G.

BRUNSCHWIG & FILS

ᕹ ACANTHUS. French, 1805–20, block print. 8½" wide, 8¾" repeat. Document in Brunschwig Archives. No.14441.06 (red and saffron).

ᕹ ALEXANDRIA BORDER. French, 1810–15, block print. 13½" wide, 18¾" repeat. Document in McClelland Collection, Brunschwig Archives. No.11529.06 (sand on clay).

ᕹ BOSPHORE BORDER. French, 1810–25, block print. 9¾" wide, 18⅛" repeat. Document in McClelland Collection, Brunschwig Archives. No.11541.06 (red and green).

ᕹ BOSPHORE TASSEL BORDER. French, 1810–25, block print. 3¾" wide, 18⅛" repeat. Document in McClelland Collection, Brunschwig Archives. No.11551.06 (red and green).

ᕹ BRAINTREE ACORN BORDER. American, 1800–10, block print. Nylander, Redmond, and Sander, fig. 14.2, p. 76. 2" wide, 1⅛" repeat. Document at Society for the Preservation of New England Antiquities. No.11076.6C. Custom order (minimum 300 yards).

ᕹ ENTRELACS ET PIROUETTES. French, 1810–20, block print. 2¾" wide, 3½" repeat. No.11850.06 (multi on gray). Block print.

ᕹ MARGUERITE BORDER. French, 1810–25, block print. 4½" wide, 10½" repeat. Document in McClelland Collection, Brunschwig Archives. No.14439.06 (black).

ᕹ NEW CLARISSA FESTOON BORDER. French, 1825–30, block print. Nouvel, fig. 423, p. 100. Top: 10½" wide; bottom: 7½" wide; 18⅞" repeat. Adaptation: motifs simplified. Document at Society for the Preservation of New England Antiquities. No.13342.06 (yellow on azure).*

❧ OTIS GARLAND BORDERS. English or French, c. 1796, block print. Nylander, Redmond, and Sander, fig 22.1, p. 96. Top: 5⅜" wide; bottom: 2¹¹/₁₆" wide; 21" repeat. Document at Harrison Gray Otis House, Boston, a property of Society for the Preservation of New England Antiquities. No.13283.06 (gold on gray).

❧ PATCHWORK BORDER. French, 1800–20, block print. Lynn, p. 131. 4⅝" wide, 4⅝" repeat. Document at Cooper-Hewitt Museum. No.12442.06 (multi with pink and sky blue).

❧ PEONY SCROLL BORDER. English or French, 1790–1810, block print. 4¾" wide, 9⅛" repeat. Document at Society for the Preservation of New England Antiquities. No.13323.06 (banana).

❧ POMPEIAN BORDER. French, c. 1795, block print. 7½" wide, 38½" repeat. Adaptation: complete repeat not reproduced. Document at Society for the Preservation of New England Antiquities. No. 13359.06 (black and orange).

❧ PORTSMOUTH DAISY BORDER. Probably French, c. 1807, block print

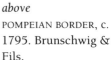

above

POMPEIAN BORDER, C. 1795. Brunschwig & Fils.

left

OTIS GARLAND BORDERS, c. 1796. Brunschwig & Fils.

left

PEONY SCROLL BORDER, 1790–1810. Brunschwig & Fils.

with flocking. Nylander, Redmond, and Sander, color pl. 11, p. 106. 5½" wide, 20" repeat. Adaptation: reproduction not flocked. Document at Rundlet-May House, Portsmouth, N.H., a property of Society for the Preservation of New England Antiquities. No.11086.6C (terra cotta). Custom order (minimum 150 yards).

❧ NEW SALEM FEATHER BORDER. American, 1790–1810, block print. 2⅜" wide, 10" repeat. Document at Society for the Preservation of New England Antiquities. Period coloring: No.13279.06 (taupe and blue).

❧ SUDBURY PINEAPPLE BORDER. American, 1790–1810, block print. Nylander, Redmond, and Sander, fig. 14.1, p. 75. 3¾" wide, 20" repeat. Document at Society for the Preservation of New England Antiquities. No.11066.6C (terra cotta). Custom order (minimum 150 yards).

❧ WHEELER HOUSE BORDER. French, 1810–25, block print. 20¼" wide plus two 3" borders, 27¾" repeat. Reproduced for John Wheeler House, Murfreesboro, N.C. No.12889.06 (gray and brown). Custom order.*

CLARENCE HOUSE

❧ BORDURE DIRECTOIRE. French, 1820–40, block print. 4½" wide, 9" repeat. No.F30 (orange and yellow).

CLASSIC REVIVALS

Hamilton-Weston Collection

❧ ANTHEMION BORDER. English, 1800–20, block print. 1⅝" wide, 1¾" repeat. No.BD11 (black on green).

❧ EMBROIDERY BORDER. English, 1800–10, block print. 1⅝" wide, 5½" repeat. No.BD22 (rose on white).

❧ GUILLOCHE BORDER. English, 1790–1810, block print. 1⅝" wide, 1½" repeat. No.BD42 (black and white on ochre).

❧ PEARL BORDER. English, 1790–1810, block print. 1¼" wide, ½" repeat. No.BD31 (green and brown).

Mauny Collection

❧ ACANTHE ET TORSADE. French, 1810–40, block print. Top: 9¼" wide; bottom: 4½" wide; 5" repeat. No.638C (grays); No.638G (orange and gray). Block print.

❧ AMOUR AVEUGLE. French, 1820–30, block print. Top: 11¾" wide; bottom: 7½" wide. No.611B (pink, green, and gray). Block print.

❧ AMOUR AVEUGLE. French, 1810–25, block print. 1⅜" wide. No.554F (rose on gray); No.554H (black on pink); No.554Q (black on yellow). Block print.

❧ BORDURE ANTIQUE. French, 1820–40, block print. 2½" wide. No.568B (blue and gray); No.568D (green and yellow); No.568F (rust and yellow). Block print.

&❧ LES BELIERS. French, 1810–25, block print. 15$\frac{1}{2}$" wide. No.632A (gray and pink). Block print.

&❧ BORDURE SAINT CLOUD. French, 1810–30, block print. 1$\frac{1}{2}$" wide. No.5002B (green and gray); No.5002D (red and green); No.5002P (dark green and yellow). Block print.

&❧ BOSPHORE. French, 1810–25, block print. 9$\frac{3}{4}$" wide. No.637A (red and green); No.637D (blue). Block print.

&❧ CHEVREFEUILLE. French, 1790–1810, block print. 4$\frac{7}{8}$" wide. No.2604D (multi on blue); 2604E (multi on white). Block print.

&❧ LES DEUX PIGEONS. French, 1790–1810, block print. 12$\frac{1}{2}$" wide. No.617E (light green on gray). Block print.

&❧ DIRECTOIRE RINCEAUX. French, 1800–25, block print. 3" wide. No.511A (black and white on green). Block print.

&❧ DRAPERIE ET GLAND. French, 1800–15, block print. 18$\frac{3}{4}$" wide. No.625A (gray). Block print.

&❧ ETRUSQUE. French, 1790–1810, block print. 3$\frac{1}{8}$" wide. No.512F (brown and rust on tan). Block print.

&❧ FABLE. French, 1800–30, block print. 9" wide. No.603G (green on yellow). Block print.

&❧ FEUILLES ET GRAPPES. French, 1800–15, block print. 4$\frac{3}{4}$" wide. No.526A (blue and tan on black). Block print.

&❧ FLEURETTE. French, 1810–15, block print. Top: 8$\frac{1}{2}$" wide; bottom: 4$\frac{3}{4}$" wide. No.1507E (blue, green, and gray). Block print.

&❧ FLOREAL. French, 1800–30, block print. 3$\frac{7}{8}$" wide. No.565D (rose, green, and gray). Block print.

&❧ GISORS. French, 1815–40, block print. 3$\frac{1}{2}$" wide. No.544D (pink on gray); No.544F (grays); No.544G (tans). Block print.

&❧ GREQUE. French, 1825–40, block print. 2" wide. No.506K (brown and orange); No.506L (grays). Block print.

&❧ GUIRLANDE ET TULLE. French, 1800–20, block print. 21" wide, 21$\frac{1}{2}$" repeat. No.639A (blue and orange). Block print.

&❧ LES LIONS. French, 1800–20, block print. 5$\frac{1}{2}$" wide. No.612C (gray on gray); No.612D (gray on yellow); No.612G (lavender on yellow). Block print.

&❧ LOSANGE ET GREQUE. French, 1790–1815, block print. 3$\frac{3}{8}$" wide. No.509B (orange and gray on black). Block print.

&❧ MALMAISON. French, 1790–1810, block print. 9" wide. No.601A (brown on orange); No.601B (gray on brown); 601D (gray on yellow). Block print.

&❧ PANIER. French, 1810–20, block print. Top: 13$\frac{1}{2}$" wide; bottom: 2" wide. No.629C (green and orange); No.629N (yellow and lavender). Block print.

&❧ PERLES ET FILLETS. French, 1800–40, block print. 1$\frac{3}{8}$" wide. No.5020 (gray). Block print.

ᐧᑆ POINTE YACKS. French, 1800–15, block print. 4³/₄" wide. No.558D (green, black, and mauve). Block print.

ᐧᑆ REGENCY. French, 1810–25, block print. Top: 12" wide; bottom: 6¹/₂" wide. No.621 (red and green). Block print.

ᐧᑆ ROMANTIQUE. French, 1800–15, block print. 4¹/₂" wide. No.2606D (blue and peach on yellow). Block print.

ᐧᑆ ROSACES ET FEUILLES. French, 1815–25, block print. 5" wide. No.530. Block print.

ᐧᑆ SALOME. French, 1790–1810, block print. 4³/₄" wide. No.574C (yellow and blue on black); 574F (pink and green on light blue). Block print.

ᐧᑆ TORE. French, 1800–40, block print. 1⁵/₈" wide. No.559H (grays). Block print.

A. L. DIAMENT & COMPANY

ᐧᑆ HERMITAGE LION BORDER. French, 1830–50, block print. 9³/₄" wide, 21¹/₂" repeat. No.110-03 (green and copper).

KATZENBACH & WARREN

ᐧᑆ ACANTHUS FRIEZE. French, 1800–40, block print. 8¹/₂" wide, 3¹/₄" repeat. Document at The Athenaeum of Philadelphia. No.AE 1004B (gray and gold). Period coloring: No.AE1005B (gray).

ᐧᑆ EGG AND DART BORDER. French, 1800–20, block print. 2¹/₂" wide, 1¹/₂" repeat. Document at The Athenaeum of Philadelphia. No.AE1014B (gold). Period coloring: No.AE1015B (gray).

ᐧᑆ FLORAL DRAPERY CORNICE. French, 1810–20, block print. 20³/₄" wide, 21" repeat. Document at The Athenaeum of Philadelphia. No.AE1181B (blue). Period coloring: No.AE1183B (green).

LEE JOFA

ᐧᑆ JOSEPHINE BORDER. French, 1800–20, block print. 12" wide, 20¹/₄" repeat. Document in a museum archive. No.P902154 (blue mist and brick).

ᐧᑆ NAPOLEON BORDER. French, 1790–1815, block print. 7 ¹/₄" wide, 13" repeat. Document in a museum archive. Document color not re-produced. Period coloring: No.P902003 (red and green).

SCALAMANDRE

ᐧᑆ CHARLESTON FRIEZE. French, 1800–25, block print. 6¹/₂" wide, 18" repeat. Reproduced for Historic Charleston Reproductions. No. WB81268-001 (light peach, pinks, and teal on sorrel). Special order.

ᐧᑆ CHLOE BORDER. French, 1810–20, block print. Designed by Xavier Mader; originally printed by Dufour. Guibert, fig. 341, p. 48. 12" wide, 18" repeat. Adaptation. Document at Bibliothèque Forney, Paris. No.WB81403-001 (multi peaches on emerald).

ᐧᑆ CLASSICAL BORDER. French, 1810–25, block print. 14³/₄" wide,

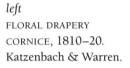

above
SALOME, 1790–1810.
Classic Revivals
(Mauny Collection).

left
FLORAL DRAPERY
CORNICE, 1810–20.
Katzenbach & Warren.

left
CHLOE BORDER,
1810–20. Scalamandré.

19″ repeat. Historic representation. Reproduced for Rosehill, Geneva, N.Y. No.WB81205-001 (blues, tans, browns, and rust on smoke blue). Period coloring: No.WB81205-004 (olives, golds, and teal on smoke).

❧ CONSTANTINE DADO. French, 1835–50, block print. 27¹/₂″ wide, 21″ repeat, 5 yds. per s/r. Historic representation. Reproduced from a period design for a wallpaper. Document in Scalamandré Archive. No.WP81462-001 (multi on plum).

❧ 48 LAURENS STREET FRET. Probably English, 1800–10, block print. 1³/₈″ wide, ³/₄″ repeat. Historic representation. Reproduced for Historic Charleston Reproductions. No.WB81275-001 (grays and midnight blue on deep blue).

❧ LINDENWALD BALUSTRADE. French, 1830, block print. Originally printed by Jacquemart et Bénard. Lynn, fig. 10-2, p. 232; McClelland, p. 169; Nouvel, fig. 346, p. 89. 19″ wide, 5¹³/₁₆″ repeat. Reproduced

LINDENWALD
BALUSTRADE, 1830.
Scalamandré.

for Martin Van Buren National Historic Site, Kinderhook, N.Y. Additional sample at Cooper-Hewitt Museum. No.WP81338-001 (grays, greens, and black on marble white).

ᘐ MEZZA MAJOLICA. French, 1800–20, block print. 10" wide, 9" repeat. Historic representation. No.WB81494-1 (gold and redwood on ivory).

ᘐ MIDDLETON'S PLANTATION BASEBOARD. French or American, 1830–50, block print. 5¼" wide, 21" repeat. Companion border to "Middleton's Plantation Parlor" wallpaper. Adaptation. Reproduced for Middleton's Plantation, Edisto Island, S.C. No.WB81426-001 (aquas and mahogany on pearl gray). Special order.*

ᘐ MIDDLETON'S PLANTATION FRIEZE. French or American, 1830–50, block print. 10½" wide, 42" repeat. Companion frieze to "Middleton's Plantation Parlor" wallpaper. Reproduced for Middleton's Plantation, Edisto Island, S.C. No.WB81415-001 (aquas and mahogany on pearl gray). Special order.*

ᘐ PRESTWOULD DRAWING ROOM TOP BORDER. French, 1820–35, block print. 10½" wide, 18¾" repeat. Reproduced for Prestwould, Clarksville, Va., operated by Prestwould Foundation. No.WB81505-001 (bronze and slate on cranberry).

ᘐ PRESTWOULD SALOON DADO. French, 1810–35, block print. De-

opposite
AURORA, 1790–1800.
Brunschwig & Fils.
Page 45.

MINERVE, 1795–1810.
Classic Revivals
(Mauny Collection).
Page 58.

LA FALAISE, 1799.
Galacar & Company.
Page 62.

right
FIGARO, 1805.
Galacar & Company.
Page 62.

opposite
FINISTERE, 1798.
Galacar & Company.
Page 62.

top
PRESTWOULD SALOON
TOP BORDER, 1810–35.
Scalamandré.
Page 89.

above
PRESTWOULD SALOON
DADO, 1810–35.
Scalamandré.
Page 80.

BERNARDSTON and BERNARDSTON BORDER, 1790–1810. Schumacher. Pages 67 and 89.

FOX GRAPE, 1780–
1810. Schumacher.
Page 67.

signed by Xavier Mader; originally printed by Dufour. Guibert, color pl. 2; Lynn, fig. 9-20, p. 214, and color pl. 41, p. 241; Nouvel, fig. 457, p. 107. 22″ wide, 43¼″ repeat. Reproduced for Prestwould, Clarksville, Va., operated by Prestwould Foundation. Document at Cooper-Hewitt Museum. No.WB81504-002 (royal and gold on gray).

ॐ PRESTWOULD SALOON TOP BORDER. French, 1820–35, block print with flocking. 9⅛″ wide, 18¾″ repeat. Reproduced for Prestwould, Clarksville, Va., operated by Prestwould Foundation. No.WB81508-001 (teals and taupe). Also available unflocked; No.WP81508A.

ॐ STROBEL FRIEZE. French, 1810–30, block print. 6¼″ wide, 18″ repeat. Historic representation. Reproduced for Historic Charleston Reproductions. No.WB81271-001 (grays, yellow, and browns on dark teal).

SCHUMACHER

ॐ BERNARDSTON BORDER. Possibly American, 1790–1810, block print. Nylander, Redmond, and Sander, color pl. 8, p. 105. 2¼″ wide, 12⅜″ repeat. Document at Colonial Williamsburg. No.513230 (document gold).

ॐ CORNUCOPIA SCROLL BORDER. French, 1810–25, block print. 8½″ wide, 13½″ repeat. No.509501 (sepia).

ॐ LANETTE'S LILAC BORDER. French, 1815–25, block print. Nouvel, fig. 263, p. 77. 13⅝″ wide, 21″ repeat. No.509510 (document).

ॐ LAUREL BOUQUET BORDER. French, 1835–50, block print. 13½″ wide, 12″ repeat. Document in Schumacher Archive. No.505312 (lake and sand).

ॐ LONG GALLERY BORDER. English, c. 1827, block print. 2½″ wide. Document at Temple Newsam, Leeds, England. No.TN11 (green).

ॐ PARLOR PORTIERE BASE. French, 1815–20, block print. 13″ wide, 13½″ repeat. Document in Schumacher Archive. No.505344 (document moss).*

ॐ PARLOR PORTIERE BORDER. French, 1815–20, block print. 15″ wide, 13½″ repeat. Document in Schumacher Archive. No.505334 (document moss).*

RICHARD E. THIBAUT

ॐ BOXWOOD BORDER. Possibly French, 1830–40, block print. 6″ wide, 18½″ repeat. Historic Homes of America Collection, produced in collaboration with the National Preservation Institute. Document at Boxwood, Yanceyville, N.C. No.839-T-790059 (multi).

THE TWIGS

ॐ ACANTHUS BORDER. French, 1790–1810, block print. 2¼″ wide, 10″ repeat. No.6716 (gray).

ॐ ARCHITECTURAL BORDER. French, 1800–10, block print. 9¼″ wide, 20¾″ repeat. No.6721 (gray and beige); No.6725 (gold and green).

THE MONUMENTS OF PARIS, 1814. The Twigs.

᎒ CONCORD BORDER. American, 1811–17, block print. Originally printed by Moses Grant, Jr., & Company, Boston. Nylander, Redmond, and Sander, fig. 1-12, p. 13. 5½" wide, 5½" repeat. Adaptation: original color not reproduced. Period coloring: No.6604 (Pompeiian red and white).

᎒ ERECHTHEUM DADO. English, 1790–1815, block print. 21¼" wide plus 4¾" border, 42½" repeat. No.66150/001 (green); No. 66150/002 (gray on cream).

᎒ FEDERAL BORDER. French, 1800–10, block print. 2½" wide, 21⅝" repeat. No.67300/005 (red).

᎒ FLEURETTE FRIEZE. French, 1810–15, block print. 9" wide, 19" repeat. No.A1650/009 (coral and green).

᎒ GLENMORAL BORDER. French, 1810–20, block print. 19" wide, 18¾" repeat. No.63700/004 (green and salmon); No.63700/007 (green and gold).*

᎒ L'ENFANT BORDER. French, 1800–10, block print. 2" wide, 8⅝" repeat. Period colorings: No.67400/002 (beige); No.67400/004 (navy); No.67400/005 (gray); No.67400/006 (terra cotta); No.67400/007 (coral).

᎒ MALMAISON. French, 1810–25, block print. 21⅛" wide, 21⅛" repeat. No.66500/004 (blue).

᎒ LA NANCY FRIEZE AND BASE BORDER. French, 1810–20, block print. Frieze: 13½"; bottom: 5¼"; 19¼" repeat. No.A2310/004 (coral and green on white).*

᎒ PINGREE HOUSE BORDER. French, 1800–10, block print. 6" wide, 19½" repeat. No.A1230/009 (camel on meringue).*

᎒ VENDOME BORDER. French, 1800–10, block print. 2½" wide, 10" repeat. No.67000/001 (rose and gray).

WATERHOUSE WALLHANGINGS

⁊ ROBBINS HOUSE BORDER. English or French, 1790–1810, block print. Nylander, Redmond, and Sander, color pl. 8, p. 105. 2¼" wide, 2¼" repeat. Document in Waterhouse Archives; additional samples at Society for the Preservation of New England Antiquities and the Essex Institute. No.215634 (multi on dark brown).

SCALAMANDRE

PLAIN PAPERS

Plain papers that approximate the popular colors of the late 18th and early 19th centuries include the following ground papers. All are 30" wide. No.WG115-000 (pink); No.WG119-000 (Pompeiian red); No.WG357-000 (pastel citron); No.WG396-000 (empire blue); No.WG410-000 (sage); No.WG513-000 (soft yellow); No.WG524-000 (sunflower); No.WG536-000 (peach); No.WG1852-000 (blue sky).

THE TWIGS

SCENIC WALLPAPERS

⁊ THE MONUMENTS OF PARIS. French, 1814, block print in 80 colors from 2,062 blocks. Designed by Dufour et Leroy after designs by Jean Broc. Greysmith, fig. 69, p. 96; Lynn, color pl. 34, p. 173, and fig. 9-14, p. 210; McClelland, p. 337; Oman and Hamilton, color pl. p. 274 and pp. 286–87. Total width: 48'; total height: 8½'; 17"–28" per panel; 22 panels per set. Reproduced in cooperation with Metropolitan Museum of Art, New York; installed in American Wing. No.MP-22 (full set); No.MP-11 (half set).

ZUBER

⁊ LES COURSES DE CHEVAUX (THE RACES). French, 1837, block print. Designed by Jean-Julien Deltil. McClelland, p. 293. Total width: 50'

LES VUES DE
L'AMERIQUE DU NORD
(detail, "Military
Review at West
Point"), 1834. Zuber.

4"; total height: 12' 10"; 18⅞" per panel; 32 panels per set. Block printed in 18 colors from 767 wood blocks.

ઠ➧ DECOR CHINOIS. French, 1832, block print. Designed by Eugene Ehrmann and Hermann Zipelius. Greysmith, color pl. 13, p. 99; Lynn, color pl. 35, pp. 174–75; Nylander, Redmond, and Sander, color pl. 37, p. 162; fig. 52-a, p. 206; Teynac, Nolot, and Vivien, p. 69. Total width: 17' 6"; total height: 12' 10"; 21" per panel; 10 panels per set. Block printed in 57 colors from 387 wood blocks.

ઠ➧ L'HINDOUSTAN. French, 1808, block print. Designed by Antoine Pierre Mongin. *Bulletin*, color pl. 13, no. 1. Total width: 43' 11½"; total height: 12' 10"; 26⅜" per panel; 20 panels per set. Block printed in 85 colors from 1,265 wood blocks.

ઠ➧ LES LOINTAINS (CLASSIC LANDSCAPE). French, 1822, block print. Designed by Antoine Pierre Mongin. Total width: 10' 6"; total height: 12' 10"; 21" per panel; 6 panels per set. Printed in 11 colors from 149 wood blocks.

ઠ➧ LE PAYSAGE A CHASSES (LANDSCAPE OF THE CHASE). French, 1832, block print. Designed by Jean-Julien Deltil. McClelland, pp. 169–70. Total width: 49' 4"; total height: 12' 10"; 18½" per panel; 32 panels per set. Block printed in 142 colors from 1,253 wood blocks.

ઠ➧ PSYCHE. French, 1816, block print. Designed by Mery Joseph

Blondel and Louis Lafitte; originally printed by Dufour. Clouzot and Follot, p. 166; McClelland, pp. 283–86; Oman and Hamilton, no. 1040, p. 358. Four scenes: "Psyche au bain," 85" wide by 72" high (4 panels); "Psyche aux enfers," 21¼" wide by 72" high (single panel); "Psyche recueille par un pecheur," 42½" wide by 72" high (2 panels); and "Hymen de Psyche et de Cupidon," 21¼" wide by 72" high (single panel). Block printed en grisaille (shades of gray).

ᐛ LES VUES DE L'AMERIQUE DU NORD (SCENIC AMERICA). French, 1834, block print. Designed by Jean-Julien Deltil. *Bulletin*, color pl. 14, no. 4; Clouzot and Follot, p. 190; Lynn, color pl. 33, p. 172; fig. 9-8, p. 193; McClelland, p. 387; Teynac, Nolot, and Vivien, p. 116. Total width: 49' 4"; total height: 12' 10"; 18½" per panel; 32 panels per set. Block printed in 223 colors from 1,690 wood blocks.

ᐛ LES VUES DE SUISSE. French, 1804, block print. Designed by Antoine Pierre Mongin. Guibert, fig. 695, p. 105; Teynac, Nolot, and Vivien, p. 108. Total width: 36' 2"; total height: 12' 10"; 27½" per panel; 16 panels per set. Block printed in 95 colors from 1,024 wood blocks. This was the first scenic wallpaper.

Zuber also prints a wide variety of wallpapers and borders. The company prefers that inquiries concerning these additional patterns be made directly to its New York showroom.

ESSEX INSTITUTE

CUSTOM
PATTERNS FROM
MUSEUMS

All patterns were reproduced for the Gardner-Pingree House, Salem, Mass. Documents are at Essex Institute. For color illustrations, see Dean Lahikainen, "The Gardner-Pingree House, Salem, Massachusetts," *Antiques*, March 1990, pp. 718–29.

ᐛ DERBY BLOCK. American, 1800–10, block print. 21" wide, 5½" repeat, 7 yds. per roll. No.GP 101 (green, black, and white).

ᐛ GARDNER BLOCK. American, 1800–15, block print. 21" wide, 11" repeat, 7 yds. per roll. No.GP 102 (gray, green, blue, black, and white).

ᐛ GREEN WHEAT. English, 1800–10, block print. 21" wide, 5½" repeat, 7 yds. per roll. No.GP 103 (greens, black, gray, and white on light green).

ᐛ GREEN WHEAT BORDER. English, 1800–10, block print. 3⅞" wide, 11¾" repeat. No.GP 104 (greens, brown, gold, and gray on white).

ᐛ ORANGE TWIG. English, 1800–10, block print. 20⅛" wide, 20½" repeat, 7 yds. per roll. No.GP 105 (orange, red, blue, and green on light blue).

HISTORIC DEERFIELD

ᐛ BURRINGTON HOUSE. American, c. 1818, block print. 21" wide, 31½" repeat, 7 yds. per s/r. Reproduced for E. H. Williams House,

Deerfield, Mass. Document at Burrington House, Charlemont, Mass. No.145102 (green, dark green, and black on light blue).

&❧ CELESTIAL SWAG. American, 1810–25, block print. 21³/₄" wide, 5³/₄" repeat, 7 yds. per s/r. Reproduced for E. H. Williams House, Deerfield, Mass. Document at Historic Deerfield. No.145094 (green, black, white, and pink on blue-gray).

&❧ E. H. WILLIAMS FLORAL. American, 1815–25, block print. 21⁵/₈" wide, 10¹/₄" repeat, 7 yds. per s/r. Reproduced for E. H. Williams House, Deerfield, Mass. Document at Historic Deerfield. No.145093 (greens, red, and pink on tan).

&❧ FLORAL STRIPE. American, 1810–25, block print. 19⁵/₈" wide, 11³/₄" repeat, 7 yds. per s/r. Reproduced for E. H. Williams House, Deerfield, Mass. Document at Historic Deerfield. No.145103 (red on white).

&❧ HOIT HOUSE. American, 1810–25, block print. 18¹/₂" wide, 9¹/₄" repeat, 7 yds. per s/r. Reproduced for E. H. Williams House, Deerfield, Mass. Document at Historic Deerfield. No.145105 (gray on light gray).

&❧ PARSONAGE. American, 1815–30, block print. 19¹/₄" wide, 2³/₈" repeat, 7 yds. per s/r. Reproduced for E. H. Williams House and Wells-Thorn House, Deerfield, Mass. Document at Historic Deerfield. No.145061 (burgundy on ochre or blue on white).

&❧ SPRIGS. American, 1810–25, block print. 19" wide, 2¹/₂" repeat, 7 yds. per s/r. Reproduced for E. H. Williams House, Deerfield, Mass. Document at Historic Deerfield. No.145104 (dark blue and white on blue).

&❧ SWAN AND URN. American, 1810–25, block print. 21¹/₂" wide, 19" repeat, 7 yds. per s/r. Reproduced for E. H. Williams House, Deerfield, Mass. Document at Historic Deerfield. No.145095 (brown, ocher, and white on beige).

&❧ TASSEL. American, 1790–1810, block print. 21¹/₄" wide plus 1³/₄" border, 20³/₄" repeat, 7 yds. per s/r. Reproduced for Wells-Thorn House, Deerfield, Mass. Document at Historic Deerfield. No.145053 (green, black, and white on gray).

POCUMTUCK VALLEY MEMORIAL ASSOCIATION

&❧ P.V.M.A. GEOMETRIC. American, 1825–35, block print. 19¹/₄" wide, 7¹/₄" repeat, 7 yds. per s/r. Reproduced for E. H. Williams House, Deerfield, Mass. Document at Pocumtuck Valley Memorial Association. Yellow and white on gray.

&❧ P.V.M.A. RAINBOW. American, 1830–40, block print. 19" wide, 19¹/₈" repeat, 7 yds. per s/r. Reproduced for Wells-Thorn House, Deerfield, Mass. Document at Pocumtuck Valley Memorial Association. Blue, yellow, and white on ungrounded paper.

P.V.M.A. RAINBOW, 1830–40, as installed in the Wells-Thorn House, Deerfield, Massachusetts. Pocumtuck Valley Memorial Association. (Historic Deerfield Inc.)

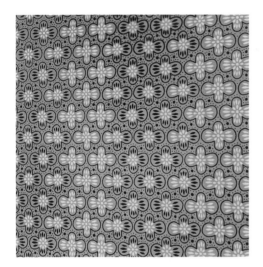

above left
RIDER-WOOD CHAM-
BER, 1810–25. Straw-
bery Banke Museum.

above right
RIDER-WOOD HALL,
1810–25. Strawbery
Banke Museum.

right
RIDER-WOOD PARLOR,
1815–30. Strawbery
Banke Museum.

SOCIETY FOR THE PRESERVATION OF NEW ENGLAND ANTIQUITIES

ঙ SARAH ORNE JEWETT HOUSE—GUEST ROOM PAPER. French, 1829,
block print. Probably printed by Zuber. See Nouvel, fig. 180, p. 63,
for variant. 18¹/₂" wide, 18¹/₂" repeat, 7 yds. per roll. Reproduced
from a photograph for Sarah Orne Jewett House, South Berwick,
Maine, a property of Society for the Preservation of New England
Antiquities. Gray on gray.

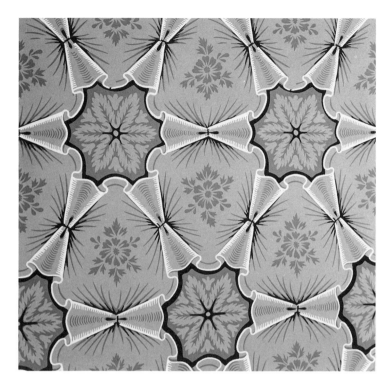

JACOB WENDELL, 1811–17. Strawbery Banke Museum.

STRAWBERY BANKE MUSEUM

❧ JACOB WENDELL. American, 1811–17, block print. Originally printed by Moses Grant, Jr., & Company, Boston. 21¼" wide, 20¼" repeat, 7 yds. per roll. Reproduced for Chase House, Portsmouth, N.H. Document at Strawbery Banke Museum. Rose and mustard.

❧ RIDER-WOOD HALL. American, 1810–25, block print. 18³⁄₈" wide, 18³⁄₈" repeat, 7 yds. per roll. Reproduced for Rider-Wood House, Portsmouth, N.H. Document at Strawbery Banke Museum. Brown and tan on tan.

❧ RIDER-WOOD CHAMBER. American, 1810–25, block print. 19" wide, 3" repeat, 7 yds. per roll. Reproduced for Rider-Wood House, Portsmouth, N.H. Document at Strawbery Banke Museum; additional sample at Society for the Preservation of New England Antiquities. Dark blue and white on blue.

❧ RIDER-WOOD PARLOR. American, 1815–30, block print. Nylander, Redmond, and Sander, fig. 33.2, p. 139. 19½" wide, 2³⁄₈" repeat, 7 yds. per roll. Reproduced for Rider-Wood House, Portsmouth, N.H. Document at Strawbery Banke Museum; additional sample at Society for the Preservation of New England Antiquities. Brown and white on rose.

1840 TO 1870:
REVIVAL STYLES AND
MACHINE PRINTING

The changes brought on by the Industrial Revolution were clearly evident in the wallpaper industry after 1840. The Four-driner machine, invented in 1799, and other similar machines enabled manufacturers to produce continuous rolls of paper. The use of continuous paper increased steadily in American wallpaper production after 1830. American manufacturers also began experimenting with cylinder printing soon after 1839, when the firm of C.,H. & E. Potter of Darwen, Lancashire, developed the first successful machine to print from rollers with raised surfaces. The output of early machine production was very uneven, and the number of colors was limited to only a few. Block printing continued to be the preferred method for printing high quality wallpapers.

Once perfected, machine production of wallpaper had an impact on the product itself as well as on the appearance of American interiors. The colors used in machine printing were thinner than those used in block printing, thus giving the design a different visual effect. The circumference of the printing roller restricted the size of the repeat. Paper width became standardized. The machine enabled manufacturers to produce larger quantities of wallpaper, making it less expensive and more within the reach of the general population. The latest styles were as readily available to consumers in rural country stores as they were in the large wallpaper warehouses in urban areas.

During this period an increasing number of books and magazines on how to decorate and manage the home were published. They promoted the use of wallpaper and began to suggest the appropriateness of specific types of patterns for certain rooms. For example, papers imitating stone, such as "Whidden Marble" (page 131) and "Thomas Sulley Ashlar" (page 112), were recommended for hallways. More elaborate schemes for the same space could be created by the paper hanger from the numerous available sets of columns, capitols, cornices, and marble papers.

The mid-19th century marked the beginning of an age of revival styles. Wallpaper manufacturers were quick to create designs that would be compatible with any style or whim of fashion. The two

FLOREAL, 1865–75.
Zina Studios.

most prevalent styles during the period 1840–70 were the Gothic Revival and the Rococo Revival. Andrew Jackson Downing, a great promoter of the Gothic style in architecture, approved of wallpaper as an appropriate treatment for the walls. However, he preferred rococo florals, Elizabethan strapwork (small pieces of wood applied decoratively to walls), and even papers in imitation wood grain to Gothic Revival papers with designs imitating pointed pinnacles and carved stone arches. Evidence suggests that the latter were used to lend an air of fashion in redecorating an older home.

Bold scrolls and combinations of flowers and scrolls epitomize Rococo Revival papers. These were produced in an endless variety of design and quality, making them affordable for use in almost any building. A representative example is "Rebecca" (page 124). Striped papers and those with small repeating patterns often incorporated Gothic or rococo elements.

French imports continued to set the style throughout this period. However, by the early 1870s a reaction was building against these elaborate and over-ornamented designs that had been so popular. In the previous decade, English designers had begun to criticize French wallpapers for their flamboyant naturalism and trompe l'œil patterns. These reformers advocated two-dimensional, stylized designs as a more "honest" approach to the decoration of flat walls. These contrasting principles of design are illustrated by comparing "Roses Pompon" (page 121), an illusionistic French wallpaper, and "Isis" (page 125), a stylized design in the neo-Grec taste.

Late 20th-century infatuation with lush all-over patterning has revived many of the elaborate and illusionistic wallpaper patterns of the mid-19th century. Not all the designs favored during the mid-19th century, however, hold the same appeal. This is especially true of the inexpensive, almost ubiquitous one- and two-color wallpapers printed on ungrounded paper stock that were advertised by one Boston manufacturer as "Good-looking and Tasty as well as Cheap."

WALLPAPERS

BRADBURY & BRADBURY

ঽ◉ CARPENTER GOTHIC. American, 1860–70, machine print. 27″ wide, 19″ repeat, 5 yds. per s/r. Reproduced for Lathrop House, Redwood City, Calif. Code CGW. Crimson and vert on buff. Special order.

ঽ◉ FLEUR DE LYS. English, 1840–50, block print. Designed by Augustus W. N. Pugin. 27″ wide, 7″ repeat, 5 yds. per s/r. Adaptation: one-fourth scale. Document at Victoria and Albert Museum. Code FLW. Gold on buff. Special order.

BRUNSCHWIG & FILS

ঽ◉ ASHENDON. English, 1855, block print. Originally printed by Holmes and Aubert. $20^{1}/_{4}$″ wide, $11^{3}/_{4}$″ repeat, 11 yds. per roll. Reproduced from a gouache design. Document privately owned. No.14701.06 (red).

❧ CHALFONT. English, 1844, block print. Originally printed by William Cooper Boyle. 20½" wide, 20½" repeat, 11 yds. per roll. Reproduced from a gouache design. Document privately owned. No.14735.06 (pink and blue).

❧ COOMBE. English, 1855, block print. Originally printed by Holmes and Aubert. 21½" wide, 18½" repeat, 11 yds. per roll. Adaptation: satin finish in stripe not reproduced. Document privately owned. No.14775.06 (shell and cream).

❧ CRESHAM. English, 1854, block print. 20½" wide, 10¼" repeat, 11 yds. per roll. Adaptation: background stripe not reproduced. Document privately owned. No.14741.06 (red and mauve).

❧ ELVIRE SIDEWALL. French, 1840–60, block print. Greysmith, fig. 89, p. 120. 27" wide, 3½" repeat, 5 yds. per s/r. Adaptation: colors softened. No.10260.06 (red and blue). Period coloring: No.10262.06 (blue and brown).

❧ LATIMER. English, 1846, block print. Originally printed by Henry Noel Turner & Company. 20½" wide, 11⅛" repeat, 11 yds. per roll. Reproduced from a gouache design. Document privately owned. Document color not reproduced. Period coloring: No.14682.06 (blue).

❧ MARLOW. English, 1857, block print. Originally printed by Henry Noel Turner & Company. 20½" wide, 8" repeat, 11 yds. per roll. Adaptation: not all motifs reproduced. Document privately owned. Document color not reproduced. Period coloring: No.14720.06 (stone).

❧ MIGNONNE. French, 1850–60, block print. Nouvel, fig. 222, p. 69. 24" wide, 24" repeat, 5 yds. per s/r. Document at Musée des Arts Décoratifs. No.12639.06 (gray).

❧ MONCEAU. French, 1855–60, block print. 17¾" wide, 21½" repeat, 7 yds. per s/r. Adaptation. Document at Musée des Arts Décoratifs. No.12677.06 (aubergine).

❧ OAKLEY. English, 1856, block print. Originally printed by C. E. & J. G. Potter. 20½" wide, 10¼" repeat, 11 yds. per roll. Adaptation: spacing between motifs slightly enlarged. Design derived from a gouache design. Document privately owned. No.14664.06 (green).

❧ ROSES POMPON. French, 1850–65, block print. Greysmith, fig. 71, p. 100; Nouvel, fig. 217, p. 68. 20¼" wide, 23¼" repeat, 6 yds. per s/r. Document at Musée des Arts Décoratifs. No.13468.06 (taupe).

❧ SOPHIE. English, 1840–70, block print. Oman and Hamilton, fig. 318, p. 167. 24" wide, 15½" repeat, 5 yds. per s/r. Adaptation: pin dot ground not reproduced. Document in Brunschwig Archives. Document color not reproduced. Period coloring: No.12322.06 (blues).

❧ TAFT SIDEWALL. American, 1850–70, block or machine print.

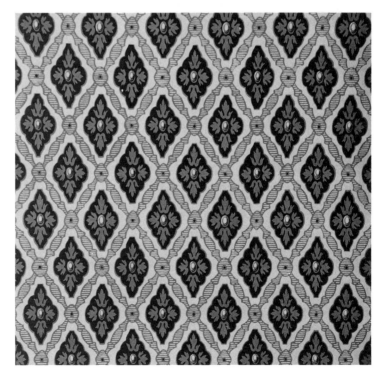

above left
OAKLEY, 1856. Brun-
schwig & Fils.

above right
MIGNONNE, 1850–60.
Brunschwig & Fils.

right
DEMSCENE, 1850–70.
Classic Revivals
(Authentic Interiors
Collection).

18½" wide, 6⅛" repeat. Reproduced for William Howard Taft National Historic Site, Cincinnati. No.365.6C. Custom order.

🌣 TRING. English, 1849, block print. Originally printed by Casper Melchior Schick. 20½" wide, 23½" repeat, 11 yds. per roll. Adaptation: colors changed slightly; background floral stripe not reproduced. Document privately owned. No.14792.06 (blue).

🌣 WENDOVER. English, 1845, block print. Originally printed by Henry Noel Turner & Company. 20½" wide, 16½" repeat, 11 yds. per roll. Reproduced from a gouache design. Document privately owned. No.14715.06 (pink).

CLARENCE HOUSE

🌣 GRAN CRU. English, 1850–60, machine print. 20½" wide, 5¼" repeat, 11 yds. per roll. Document in Courtauld Archives, London. No.W9001/003 (green).

🌣 PARLIAMENT HOUSE. English, 1850–60, block print. 27" wide, 14½" repeat, 5 yds. per s/r. Document in Clarence House Archives. No.9460/4 (red).

CLASSIC REVIVALS

Authentic Interiors Collection

🌣 BIANCA. English, 1850–60, block print. 21" wide, 16" repeat, 11 yds. per roll. Price Collection. No.W-203-2A (black on green).

🌣 DEMSCENE. English, 1850–70, machine print. 21½" wide, 21½" repeat, 11 yds. per roll. Archival Collection. No.W-208-2A (blue and tan).

🌣 JUNIPER HALL. English, 1850–65, block print. 20½" wide, 15¼" repeat, 11 yds. per roll. Archival Collection. No.W-204-4A (light gray on gray).

🌣 LACE. Possibly American, 1840–60, block print. 28" wide, 18½" repeat, 11 yds. per roll. Archival Collection. No.W-157-1A (gray on white).

🌣 SKINNER FLORAL. English or French, 1845–60, block print. 20½" wide, 15½" repeat, 11 yds. per roll. Archival Collection. No.W-199-4A (brown and green).

Mauny Collection

🌣 CAPITON CORDE. French, 1845–75, block print. 18½" wide, 6¼" repeat, 11 yds. per roll. No.218 (blue on gray). Block print.

🌣 CAPITON RUBAN. French, 1845–70, block print. 18½" wide, 10⅝" repeat, 11 yds. per roll. No.219 (gray on tan). Block print.

🌣 CHEVREFEUILLE. French, 1860–80, block print. 18½" wide, 22⅝" repeat, 11 yds. per roll. No.287 (multi on white). Block print.

🌣 DAMAS AUGUSTE COMPTE. French, 1845–60, block print. 18⅞" wide, 26¾" repeat, 11 yds. per roll. No.234 (taupe on tan). Block print.

☙ DAMAS LOUIS XIV. French, 1840–50, block print. 21⅝" wide, 20½" repeat, 11 yds. per roll. No.269 (gold on buff). Block print.

☙ DAMAS SAINT LOUIS. French, 1840–70, block print. 18½" wide, 4¾" repeat, 11 yds. per roll. No.150. Block print.

☙ DAMAS VERSAILLES. French, 1840–60, block print. 21¼" wide, 23⅝" repeat, 11 yds. per roll. No.274 (brown and tan). Block print.

☙ DAMAS VOLUTE. French, 1845–60, block print. 19¼" wide, 19¼" repeat, 11 yds. per roll. No.232 (gold on gold). Block print.

☙ DRAPERIE VICTORIA. French, 1840–60, block print. Olligs, vol. 1, fig. 230, p. 324. 26⅜" wide, 21⅝" repeat, 11 yds. per roll. No.241 (cream on rose). Block print.

☙ FLEURS COUPEES. French, 1860–80, block print. 20⅞" wide, 20⅞" repeat, 11 yds. per roll. No.128 (pinks on gray). Block print.

☙ GRAND CAPITON. French, 1845–60, block print. 18½" wide, 9⅞" repeat, 11 yds. per roll. No.277 (tans). Block print.

☙ HOUBLON. French, 1840–60, block print. 18½" wide, 16½" repeat, 11 yds. per roll. No.123 (grays). Block print.

☙ PAQUERETTES. French, 1860–70, block print. 18½" wide, 9⅞" repeat, 11 yds. per roll. No.238 (gray on cream). Block print.

☙ LES PAVOTS. French, 1850–70, block print. 18½" wide, 24⅝" repeat, 11 yds. per roll. No.290 (red and green on white). Block print.

☙ PETITES FLEURS. French, 1840–60, block print. 20½" wide, 23¼"

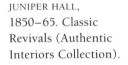

JUNIPER HALL, 1850–65. Classic Revivals (Authentic Interiors Collection).

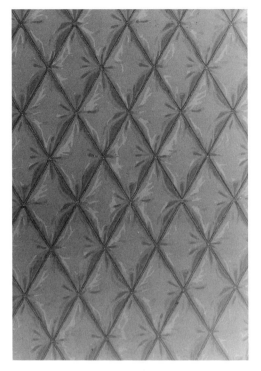

above left
CAPITON CORDE,
1845–75. Classic
Revivals (Mauny
Collection).

above right
LES PAVOTS, 1850–70.
Classic Revivals
(Mauny Collection).

left
SKINNER FLORAL,
1845–60. Classic
Revivals (Authentic
Interiors Collection).

repeat, 11 yds. per roll. No.200 (blue on taupe). Also available with pin dot ground. Block print.

❧ PETITES MAISONS. French, 1850–70, block print. 21⅝" wide, 2⅝" repeat, 11 yds. per roll. No.165 (brown and green on pink). Block print.

❧ PETIT SEMIS. French, 1840–60, block print. 21¼" wide, 12¼" repeat, 11 yds. per roll. No.151 (multi on cream). Also available with pin dot ground. Block print.

❧ RAYURES BOURGOURAIS. French, 1860–70, block print. 19¾" wide, 11 yds. per roll. No.854 (gold on cream). Block print.

❧ LES ROSES. French, 1850–70, block print. 21⅝" wide, 21¼" repeat, 11 yds. per roll. No.153 (multi on white). Block print.

❧ SEMIS MUGUET. French, 1850–70, block print. 18½" wide, 4¾" repeat, 11 yds. per roll. No.263 (white on gold). Block print.

❧ SEMIS POULETTE. French, 1840–60, block print. 18½" wide, 1⅜" repeat, 11 yds. per roll. No.857 (gold on cream). Block print.

❧ VELOURS DE GENES. French, 1830–50, block print. 19¼" wide, 16½" repeat, 11 yds. per roll. No.205 (gray on blue). Block print.

❧ VIZELLE. French, 1840–60, block print. 18⅞" wide, 9½" repeat, 11 yds. per roll. No.2012 (rust and yellow on cream). Block print.

Silvergate Collection

❧ BEECH LEAF. English, c. 1840, block print. 21" wide, 10½" repeat, 11 yds. per roll. Document at Oxburgh Hall, Norfolk, England. No.CS013. Block print.

❧ BURGES SNAIL. English, 1860–70, block print. Designed by William Burges. 21" wide, 10½" repeat, 11 yds. per roll. Document in collection of Royal Institute of British Architects, London. No.CS293. Block print.

❧ CHIRK. English, c. 1860, block print. Designed by J. G. Crace. 21" wide, 42" drop repeat, 11 yds. per roll. Document at Chirk Castle, Wales. No.AS 26 1. Block print.

❧ HANBURY HALL. English, 1840–60, block print. 20¾" wide, 15" repeat, 11 yds. per roll. Order by name. Block print.

❧ OXBOROUGH FLEUR DE LIS. English, 1850–60, block print. 16¼" wide, 8⅜" repeat, 11 yds. per roll. Document at Oxburgh Hall, Norfolk, England. No.BS102. Block print.

❧ TABLEY FLOCK. English, 1850–60, block print. 21" wide, 51¾" repeat, 11 yds. per roll. Document at Tabley Hall, England. No.AS251. Block print.

COLE & SON

Available through Clarence House as custom orders only.

❧ BUTTERFIELD TILE. English, 1860–70, block print. 21" wide, 11 yds. per roll. Coles Book. No.98859 (tan and brown). Block print.

❧ CHINESE FRET. English, 1850–60, block print. 21" wide, 11 yds.

per roll. Coles Book. No.98849 (white on green). Block print.

❧ CRACE DIAPER. English, c. 1848, block print. Designed by Augustus W. N. Pugin for J. G. Crace. Oman and Hamilton, no. 1116, p. 403. 21" wide, 11 yds. per roll. Coles Book. No.98855 (light olive on white). Block print.

❧ CRACE TILE. English, 1850–60, block print. Originally printed by J. G. Crace. 21" wide, 10½" repeat, 11 yds. per roll. Coles Book. No.98860 (terra cotta and brown). Block print.

❧ GOTHIC LILY. English, c. 1850, block print. Designed by Augustus W. N. Pugin for J. G. Crace. 21" wide, 16" repeat, 11 yds. per roll. No.98862 (white ground). Period coloring: Coles Book. No.98863 (brown ground). Block print.

❧ NOWTON COURT. English, 1840–50, block print with flocking. Oman and Hamilton, no. 533, p. 204. 21" wide, 10½" repeat, 11 yds. per roll. Adaptation: flocking not reproduced. Coles Book. No.98866 (rose and brown). Block print.

❧ QUATREFOIL. English, 1850–60, block print, 21" wide, 11 yds. per roll. Coles Book. No.98853 (tan on white). Block print.

❧ SMALL GOTHIC SCREEN. English, 1840–60, block print. 21" wide, 7" repeat, 11 yds. per roll. No.98851 (brown on red). Period coloring: Coles Book. No.98852 (brown on blue). Block print.

❧ STRAWBERRY. English, c. 1850, block print. 21" wide, 15" repeat, 11 yds. per roll. Coles Book. No.98864 (white ground). Block print.

❧ VAUGHAN DESIGN. English, 1860–70, block print. 21" wide, 5" repeat, 11 yds. per roll. Coles Book. No.OEW166 (gold and brown). Block print.

COWTAN & TOUT

❧ EUGENIE. American or French, 1840–60, block print. 27" wide, 21" repeat, 5 yds. per s/r. No.16033 (green and beige).

❧ FERN TRELLIS. English, 1860–70, block print. 21" wide, 21" repeat, 11 yds. per roll. No.20530 (greens). Block print.

❧ FUSCIA. English, 1860–70, block print. 21" wide, 21" repeat, 11 yds. per roll. No.20100 (multi with gold stripe). Block print.

❧ MAGIQUE. French, 1840–60, block print. 25" wide, 26½" repeat, 5 yds. per s/r. No.13027 (blue). Period colorings: No.13026 (green); No.13025 (red).

❧ ROSE AND LABURNUM. English, 1850–80, block print. 24" wide, 30" repeat, 5 yds. per s/r. No.97301-02 (red and lilac on figured ground).

❧ SEA CORAL. English or American, 1840–60, block print. 26" wide, 4" repeat, 5 yds. per s/r. Period colorings: No.60360 (green); No.60220 (brown).

❧ WOOD TRELLIS. English, 1850–80, block print. 27" wide, 9" repeat, 5 yds. per s/r. No.94001 (green and tan).

above left
BURGES SNAIL,
1860–70. Classic
Revivals (Silvergate
Collection).

above right
REGENCE, 1840–60.
A. L. Diament &
Company.

right
EUGENIE, 1840–60.
Cowtan & Tout.

A. L. DIAMENT & COMPANY

ঙ৯ REGENCE. French, 1840–60, block print. 18³/₄" wide plus 4" and 1¹/₂" borders, 43¹/₄" half-drop repeat. No.137-03 (dark green on cream).

GALACAR & COMPANY

ঙ৯ LA DAUPHINE. French, 1869, block print. Originally printed by Desfossé et Karth. 27" wide, 35¹/₂" half-drop repeat, 5 yds. per s/r. Document at Musée des Arts Décoratifs. No.GP-1301 (document colors on white).

ঙ৯ PASSERELLE. French, 1869, block print. Originally printed by Desfossé et Karth. 27¹/₂" wide, 54" repeat, 5 yds. per s/r. Document at Musée des Arts Décoratifs. No.GP-2002 (greens with cinnabar).

ঙ৯ LA TOSCA. French, 1869, block print. Originally printed by Desfossé et Karth. 27" wide, 35¹/₂" half-drop repeat, 5 yds. per s/r. Document at Musée des Arts Décoratifs. No.GP-1401 (document colors on white).

CHRISTOPHER HYLAND INCORPORATED

ঙ৯ ANDOVER. English, 1850–70, block print. 21" wide, 6¹/₂" repeat, 11 yds. per roll. No.WTGAAND (creme, blue, and white).

ঙ৯ ASHLAR MARBLE BLOCKS. English or French, 1840–60, block print.

above left
FUSCIA and FUSCIA CROWN, 1860–70. Cowtan & Tout.

above right
SEA CORAL, 1840–60. Cowtan & Tout.

18" wide, 21" repeat, 11 yds. per roll. No.AB111/4B (gray, light gray, and dark gray).

❧ BELLINI. English, 1860–90, block print. 21" wide, 7" repeat, 11 yds. per roll. No.WTSTBL.

❧ BRANDILLES. English, 1860–80, block print. 20" wide, 12" repeat, 11 yds. per roll. No.WTBR01 (brown, dark brown, gold, and maroon).

❧ ENFIELD. English, 1840–60, block print. 21" wide, 38¹/₂" repeat, 11 yds. per roll. No.WTGAENF (white, silver, and gray).

❧ FLORAL BOUQUET. English, 1840–70, block print. 21" wide, 10" repeat, 11 yds. per roll. No.AB143/9 (white, gray, green, and pink).

❧ IMPERIUM. English, 1865–90, block print. 18¹/₂" wide, 18¹/₂" repeat, 11 yds. per roll. No.AB407. Can be custom colored. Minimum order 10 rolls.

❧ KIRBY. English, 1840–70, block print. 21" wide, 15⅛" repeat, 11 yds. per roll. No.AB116/4 (putty, beige, and red).

❧ MANCHESTER. English, 1865–75, block print. 21" wide, 14" repeat, 11 yds. per roll. No.WTGAMAN (gold on gray).

❧ NAPOLIAN. English, 1850–80, block print. 18" wide, 21" repeat, 11 yds. per roll. No.WTN101 (forest, black, gold, and rust).

❧ OSBOURNE HOUSE. English, 1840–60, block print. 21" wide, 11 yds. per roll. No.AB153/9 (pink and purple on white ground).

❧ OSCAR. English, 1850–70, block print. 18¹/₂" wide, 11 yds. per roll. No.WTOSCAR (green, tan, and putty).

❧ OWEN JONES. English, 1855–80, block print. 20¹/₂" wide, 8¹/₂" half-drop repeat, 11 yds. per roll. No.ZZBLX. Period colorings.

❧ PUGIN SHREWSBURY. English, c. 1850, block print. 21" wide, 18¹/₂" repeat, 11 yds. per roll. No.WTC5B.

❧ PUGIN TRELLIS. English, c. 1850, block print. 21" wide, 7" repeat, 11 yds. per roll. No.WTHTR5. Block print.

❧ RIALTO. English or French, 1845–65, block print. 21" wide, 21¹/₄" repeat, 11 yds. per roll. No.ZZ1203 (olive green and burgundy).

❧ SOMMES. English, 1840–60, block print. 21" wide, 21" repeat, 11 yds. per roll. No.WTGASOM01 (French yellow). Block print.

❧ STONE BLOCK. English, 1840–60, block print. 21" wide, 11 yds. per roll. No.AB180/3.

❧ TRIAD. English, 1851, block print. Designed by Augustus W. N. Pugin. Oman and Hamilton, no. 1125, p. 405. 21" wide, 31¹/₂" repeat, 11 yds. per roll. No.WTCTD1 (red on creme).

❧ VERNON. English, 1850–75, block print. 21" wide, 7¹/₂" repeat, 11 yds. per roll. No.WTGAVER (tan and light blue).

KATZENBACH & WARREN

❧ CORDED SATIN. French, 1840–60, block print. 20¹/₂" wide, 25¹/₄" repeat, 6 yds. per s/r. Document at The Athenaeum of Philadelphia. No.AE1241 (gray and mauve). Period colorings: No.AE1242 (gray

FLORAL BOUQUET, 1840–70. Christopher Hyland Incorporated.

OSCAR, 1850–70. Christopher Hyland Incorporated.

above left
THOMAS SULLEY
ASHLAR, 1840–50.
Katzenbach &
Warren.

above right
LINCOLN'S PARLOR,
1850–60. Mt. Diablo
Handprints.

and blue); No.AE1243 (gold); No.AE1245 (beige and green).

❧ THOMAS SULLEY ASHLAR. English or American, 1840–50, block print. 20$^{1}/_{2}$" wide, 18" repeat, 6 yds. per s/r. Document at The Athenaeum of Philadelphia. No.AE1083 (tan and green). Period coloring: No.AE1082 (tan and red).

LEE JOFA

❧ BOWOOD DAMASK. French, 1840–60, block print. 26$^{3}/_{4}$" wide, 13$^{1}/_{2}$" repeat, 5 yds. per s/r. Document in a museum archive. Original color not reproduced. Period colorings: No.P902102 (taupe); No.P902103 (pale gray).

❧ REBECCA. French, 1840–60, block print. 27" wide, 20" repeat, 5 yds. per s/r. Document in a museum archive. No.P902200 (dove).

❧ HOLLYHOCK MINOR. French, 1840–50, block print. 24" wide plus 3$^{1}/_{2}$" border, 23$^{1}/_{2}$" repeat, 5 yds. per s/r. Adaptation. No.P9394-0 (ivory). Period coloring: No.P9395-0 (light green).

MT. DIABLO HANDPRINTS

Order by name unless pattern number is listed.

❧ BARBER HOUSE FOLIAGE WITH BORDER. American or French, 1850–60, block print. 19" wide, 11$^{1}/_{8}$" repeat. Reproduced for Eliel Barber House, Bloomington, Ill. Dark gray on light gray.

ঌ CARR HOUSE FLORAL. Canadian or American, c. 1860, machine print. 21" wide, 11⅞" repeat. Reproduced for Richard Carr House, Canada. Gold and pale blues on gray.

ঌ THE CEVERA. French or American, 1850–60, block or machine print. 18½" wide, 22" repeat. Copy of a c. 1930 reproduction by Thomas Strahan Company, Chelsea, Mass. Mauves and greens on cream.

ঌ CHINESE LATTICE. American, 1840–60, machine print. 19" wide, 6¼" repeat. Reproduced for Santa Cruz Mission Adobe, operated by California Department of Parks and Recreation. No.SCW-001 (documentary blue and gray on eggshell).

ঌ EDSEL STRIPE. American, 1860–90, block or machine print. 18½" wide, 1⅛" repeat. Reproduced for Henry Ford Museum & Greenfield Village, Dearborn, Mich. Ultramarine blue, yellow, gray, and black.

ঌ FARNSWORTH FLORAL. American, 1850–70, machine print. 18¾" wide, 20½" repeat. Reproduced for Farnsworth Museum, Rockland, Maine. Gray, green, and chocolate on cream.

ঌ GREVENBERG LATTICE. American, c. 1860, machine print. 27½" wide, 4⅛" repeat. Reproduced for Grevenberg House, Franklin, La. Document at Chicago Historical Society. Maroon and blue on parchment.

ঌ GREVENBERG SCENIC. American, 1860–70, machine print. 18⅞" wide, 19½" repeat. Reproduced for Grevenberg House, Franklin, La. Document at Chicago Historical Society. Gray, green, and umber on off-white.

ঌ HENRY FORD PANEL STRIPE. American, 1860–70, block or machine print. 19⅝" wide, 3¼" repeat. Reproduced for Henry Ford Museum & Greenfield Village, Dearborn, Mich. Burnt orange, white, and grays.

ঌ LINCOLN'S BEDROOM. French, 1850–60, block print. 19" wide, 21½" repeat. Reproduced for Lincoln Home National Historic Site, Springfield, Ill. Ultramarine blue, white, and browns.

ঌ LINCOLN'S PARLOR. French, 1850–60, block print. 18½" wide, 20¼" repeat. Reproduced for Lincoln Home National Historic Site, Springfield, Ill. Document at Society for Preservation of New England Antiquities. No.LPW-001 (document taupes and gold on cream).

ঌ NETZLEY-YENDER STRIPE. American, 1850–60, machine print. 18¾" wide, 9¼" repeat. Reproduced for Netzley-Yender House, Lisle, Ill. Maroon, aqua, and cream.

ঌ WIDOW CLARKE STRIPE. French or American, 1850–60, block or machine print. 18½" wide, 18⅝" repeat. Reproduced for Widow Clarke House, Chicago, Ill., a property of Chicago Architecture Foundation. Document at Chicago Historical Society. Gray and blue on bone.

ॐ WIDOW CLARKE VERTICAL STRIPE WITH OVERLAY. American, 1850–60, machine print. 18" wide, 19¹/₂" repeat. Adaptation. Reproduced for Widow Clarke House, Chicago, Ill., a property of Chicago Architecture Foundation. Gray and green on bone.

ॐ WIDOW CLARKE WALLPAPER. American, 1850–60, machine print. 18" wide, 18" repeat. Reproduced for Widow Clarke House, Chicago, Ill., a property of Chicago Architecture Foundation. Blue-grays on bone.

ॐ WILLIAM TAFT DIAMOND WALL. American, 1840–70, machine print. 21" wide, 1³/₈" repeat. Reproduced for William Howard Taft National Historic Site, Cincinnati. Red and cream on gray-green.

ॐ WILLIAM TAFT TILE. American, 1860–80, machine print. 18¹/₂" wide, 9¹/₂" repeat. Reproduced for William Taft National Historic Site, Cincinnati. Red and cream on gray-green.

ARTHUR SANDERSON & SONS

ॐ AVON. English, 1850–1900, block print. 20¹/₄" wide, 24" repeat, 11 yds. per roll. Document in Sanderson Archives. Period colorings: No.WR 7512-1 (alabaster); No.WR 7512-4 (ocean blue).

ॐ BOWERY. English, 1850–1920, block print. 20¹/₄" wide, 21" repeat, 11 yds. per roll. Adaptation. Document in Sanderson Archives. Period coloring: No.WR 7450-2 (bottle, jade, and tartan green on parchment).

ॐ COLERIDGE. English, c. 1870, block print. Designed by Owen Jones. 20¹/₄" wide, 3¹/₄" repeat, 11 yds. per roll. Document in Sanderson Archives. Period coloring: No.WH 7371-1 (copper on bottle).

ॐ OKEFORD. English, 1860–70, block print. Originally printed by Jeffrey & Company. 20¹/₄" wide, 5¹/₄" repeat, 11 yds. per roll. Document in Sanderson Archives. Period colorings: No.WH 7372-1 (grisaille on cream); No.WH 7372-4 (red on garnet).

ॐ SAVILLE. English, 1860–80, block print. Originally printed by Jeffrey & Company. 20¹/₄" wide, 12" repeat, 11 yds. per roll. Document in Sanderson Archives. Period coloring: No.WH 7374-1 (cypress green and rose on white).

SCALAMANDRE

ॐ BUCCLEUCH MANSION. American, 1850–70, block or machine print. 18¹/₂" wide, 6⁷/₁₆" repeat, 8 yds. per s/r. Reproduced for Buccleuch Mansion, New Brunswick, N.J. No.WP81413. Special order.

ॐ THE CEDARS—FRONT HALL AND PARLOR. French or American, 1840–50, block print. 18³/₄" wide, 18¹/₂" repeat, 8 yds. per s/r. Reproduced for Bliss Nash Davis House, Danville, Vt. No.WP81474. Special order.

ॐ EASTMAN. French or American, 1840–50, block or machine print. 23⁵/₈" wide, 20³/₈" repeat, 6 yds. per s/r. Reproduced for George Eastman Birthplace, now at Genesee County Museum, Mumford, N.Y. No.WP81188-001 (green, brown, off-white, and French blue blotch).

❧ FLEUR GOTHIQUE. French, 1840–50, block print. 21" wide, 21" repeat, 7 yds. per s/r. Historic representation. Reproduced from a period design for a wallpaper. Document in Scalamandré Archive. No.WP81463-001 (oyster and silver on ecru).

❧ GENEVIEVE. French, 1840–60, block print. Guibert, fig. 44, p. 6. 27" wide, 24" repeat, 5 yds. per s/r. Historic representation: design slightly reduced. Document at Bibliothèque Forney, Paris. No.WP81401-001 (grays and yellows on ecru and blue).

❧ INGE-STONEHAM HOUSE. English or German, 1860–70, block print with embossing. 18¾" wide, 19" repeat, 8 yds. per s/r. Historic representation. Reproduced for Inge-Stoneham House, Round Top, Tex. No.WP81411. Special order.

❧ INGE-STONEHAM HOUSE GUEST BEDROOM. French, 1860–70, block print. 18½" wide, 16" repeat, 8 yds. per s/r. Historic representation. Reproduced for Inge-Stoneham House, Round Top, Tex. No.WP81412. Special order.

❧ INGE-STONEHAM HOUSE PARLOR. English or German, 1860–70, block print. 18¾" wide, 19" repeat, 8 yds. per s/r. Historic representation. Reproduced for Inge-Stoneham House, Round Top, Tex. No.WP81410. Special order.

❧ JACQUELINE. French, 1860–70, block print. Guibert, fig. 763, p. 117 and pl. 5. 27" wide, 27" repeat, 5 yds. per s/r. Historic representation: scale enlarged. Document at Bibliothèque Forney, Paris. No.WP81394-001 (multi lilac on cream).

❧ KELTON HOUSE RESTORATION. French, 1855–75, machine print. 18½" wide, 19½" repeat, 7 yds. per s/r. Reproduced for Kelton House, Columbus, Ohio. Document at Cooper-Hewitt Museum. No.WP81202-001 (brown, beiges, green, yellow, red, and cocoa). Special order.

❧ LINDENWALD GEOMETRIC. American, 1840–50, machine print. 18" wide, 2" repeat, 8 yds. per s/r. Reproduced for Martin Van Buren National Historic Site, Kinderhook, N.Y. No.WP88031-001 (gold, green, and white on beige). Special order.

❧ LINDENWALD—NORTHWEST BEDROOM. American or French, c. 1840, block print. 18½" wide, 12" repeat, 8 yds. per s/r. Reproduced for Martin Van Buren National Historic Site, Kinderhook, N.Y. No.WP81342-001 (pinks, blues, and grays on polar white). Special order.

❧ LINDENWALD NURSERY. American or French, c. 1850, block print. 27" wide, 10⅝" repeat, 8 yds. per s/r. Reproduced for Martin Van Buren National Historic Site, Kinderhook, N.Y. No.WP81341-001 (mauves, greens, gold, and gray-violet on straw). Special order.

❧ LINDENWALD PARLOR AND DINING ROOM. American or French,

above left
INGE-STONEHAM
HOUSE GUEST
BEDROOM, 1860–70.
Scalamandré.

above right
THE CEDARS—FRONT
HALL AND PARLOR,
1840–50.
Scalamandré.

right
EASTMAN, 1840–50.
Scalamandré.

c. 1840, block print. 18⅝" wide, 9¾" repeat, 8 yds. per s/r. Reproduced for Martin Van Buren National Historic Site, Kinderhook, N.Y. No.WP81339-001 (gray and metallic gold on ecru embossed texture). Special order.

above left
JACQUELINE, 1860–70. Scalamandré.

๑ LINDENWALD—SERVANTS' DINING ROOM. American, c. 1840, block print. 19" wide, 4¾" repeat, 8 yds. per s/r. Reproduced for Martin Van Buren National Historic Site, Kinderhook, N.Y. No.WP81373-001 (white, tangerine, violet, and browns on straw). Special order.

above right
LINDENWALD PARLOR AND DINING ROOM, c. 1840. Scalamandré.

๑ LINDENWALD—SOUTHEAST BEDROOM. American or French, c. 1840, block print. 18⅜" wide, 1¼" repeat, 8 yds. per s/r. Reproduced for Martin Van Buren National Historic Site, Kinderhook, N.Y. No.WP81344-001 (green on chalk white). Special order.

๑ LINDENWALD—SOUTHWEST BEDROOM. American or French, c. 1840, block print. 19" wide, 4¾" repeat, 8 yds. per s/r. Reproduced for Martin Van Buren National Historic Site, Kinderhook, N.Y. No.WP81345-001 (white and pistachio on mushroom). Special order.

๑ LINDENWALD—STRIPE. American, c. 1850, machine print. 18" wide, 8 yds. per s/r. Reproduced for Martin Van Buren National Historic Site, Kinderhook, N.Y. No.WP88030-001 (tans and roses on off-white). Special order.

๑ LORENZO STUDY. American or French, 1860–70, block or machine print. 18½" wide, 25¼" repeat, 8 yds. per s/r. Reproduced for

Lorenzo, Cazenovia, N.Y. No.WP81167-001 (grays, browns, gold, silver, black, and wine). Special order.

❧ LOCUST GROVE FLOWER. English, 1850–60, block print. 18¾" wide, 1⅞" repeat, 8 yds. per s/r. Reproduced for Young-Morse Historic Site, Poughkeepsie, N.Y. No.WP81227-001 (medium gray on polished white). Special order.

❧ MARGOT. French, 1850–60, machine print. Guibert, fig. 51, p. 7. 27" wide, 9¾" repeat, 5 yds. per s/r. Adaptation: floral motifs omitted. Document at Bibliothèque Forney, Paris. No.WP81395-001 (multi cream).

❧ PITTSON HOUSE. American or English, 1840–50, block print. 28" wide, 22" repeat, 5 yds. per s/r. Reproduced for Old Economy Village, Ambridge, Pa. No.WP8788 (white and black on gray). Special order.

❧ POTERLET ARCADE. French, 1840–60, block print. 27" wide, 3" repeat, 5 yds. per s/r. Historic representation. Reproduced from a period design for a wallpaper. Document in Scalamandré Archive. No.WP81459-001 (grays on plum).

❧ RUSSIAN BISHOP'S HOUSE—DINING ROOM. French or English, 1850–60, block print. 21" wide, 21" repeat, 7 yds. per s/r. Reproduced for Russian Bishop's House, Sitka National Historical Park, Sitka, Alaska. No.WP81368. Special order.

❧ RUSSIAN BISHOP'S HOUSE—LAYMAN'S ROOM. English or American, 1850–60, machine print. 21" wide, 8⅜" repeat, 7 yds. per s/r. Reproduced for Russian Bishop's House, Sitka National Historical Park, Sitka, Alaska. No.WP81363-001 (indigo on chalk white). Special order.

❧ RUSSIAN BISHOP'S HOUSE—RECEPTION ROOM. Probably American, 1850–60, block or machine print. 21" wide, 18¾" repeat, 7 yds. per s/r. Reproduced for Russian Bishop's House, Sitka National Historical Park, Sitka, Alaska. No.WP81366-001 (off-white, green, and maroon on warm gray). Special order.

❧ RUSSIAN BISHOP'S HOUSE—STUDY. American, 1850–60, machine print. 21" wide, 10½" repeat, 7 yds. per s/r. Reproduced for Russian Bishop's House, Sitka National Historical Park, Sitka, Alaska. No.WP81371-001 (green and burgundy on coated white). Special order.

❧ STANTON HOUSE—BACK BEDROOM. American, 1850–60, block or machine print. 19" wide, 3⅛" repeat, 8 yds. per s/r. Reproduced for Elizabeth Cady Stanton House, Seneca Falls, N.Y. No.WP81331-001 (beige and golds on polar white). Special order.

❧ STANTON HOUSE—DINING ROOM. American, c. 1846, machine print. 18" wide, 9¾" repeat, 8 yds. per s/r. Reproduced for Elizabeth Cady Stanton House, Seneca Falls, N.Y. No.WP81329-001 (brick, mustard, and green on ivory). Special order.

❧ STANTON HOUSE—DOUBLE PARLOR. American, c. 1846, block or

RUSSIAN BISHOP'S
HOUSE—RECEPTION
ROOM, 1850–60.
Scalamandré.

RUSSIAN BISHOP'S
HOUSE—STUDY,
1850–60. Scalamandré.

STANTON HOUSE—
STAIR HALL, c. 1850.
Scalamandré.

machine print. 18″ wide, 10⅝″ repeat, 8 yds. per s/r. Reproduced for Elizabeth Cady Stanton House, Seneca Falls, N.Y. No.WP81327-001 (Wedgewood and light emerald on polar white). Special order.

ॐ STANTON HOUSE—FRONT BEDROOM. American, c. 1846, block or machine print. 18″ wide, 10¾″ repeat, 8 yds. per s/r. Reproduced for Elizabeth Cady Stanton House, Seneca Falls, N.Y. No.WP81330-001 (gray, kelly green, and brick on polar white). Special order.

ॐ STANTON HOUSE—STAIR HALL. American, c. 1850, block print. 18″ wide, 20″ repeat, 8 yds. per s/r. Reproduced for Elizabeth Cady Stanton House, Seneca Falls, N.Y. No.WP81328-001 (smoke and kelly green on polar white). Special order.

ॐ TOOMBS HOUSE. English or French, 1850–70, block print. 18½″ wide, 9¼″ repeat, 8 yds. per s/r. Reproduced for General Robert Toombs House, Washington, Ga. No.WP81246-001 (grays and metallic gold on haze blue).

ॐ WIDOW CLARKE HOUSE. Probably American, 1840–50, machine print. 19″ wide, 18¾″ repeat, 8 yds. per s/r. Historic representation. Reproduced for Widow Clarke House, Chicago, Ill., a property of Chicago Architecture Foundation. No.WP81231-001 (white and off-white on polished white). Special order.

opposite
ROSES POMPON,
1850–65. Brunschwig
& Fils. Page 101.

ॐ WAYNE HOUSE. American, 1830–50, block print. 28″ wide, 10″ repeat, 5 yds. per s/r. Reproduced for Old Economy Village, Ambridge, Pa. No.WP8821 (brown, blue, and green on tan). Special order.

opposite
HANBURY HALL, 1840–60. Classic Revivals (Silvergate Collection). Page 106.

left
LA DAUPHINE with dado and frieze, 1869. Galacar & Company. Page 109.

ANTEBELLUM BLOCKS, 1845–55. Schumacher. Page 129.

REBECCA, 1840–60.
Lee Jofa. Page 112.

NEO-GREC FLORAL VINE, 1865–75. Schumacher. Page 129.

ISIS, 1865–75. Waterhouse Wallhangings. Page 130.

SMALL ACANTHUS, 1880–1910. Clarence House. Page 147.

IRIS TAPESTRY, 1880–1900. Katzenbach & Warren. Page 156.

ALHAMBRA, 1880–
1900. Katzenbach &
Warren. Page 156.

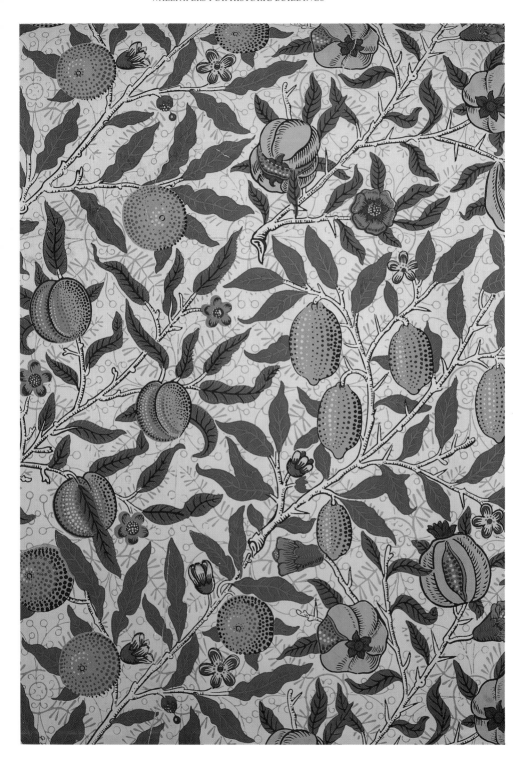

SCHUMACHER

❧ ANTEBELLUM BLOCKS. American, 1845–55, block print. 27" wide, 24¼" repeat, 4½ yds. per s/r. Document in Schumacher Archive. No.512930 (document).

❧ CABBAGE ROSE. French, 1850–70, block print. 20½" wide, 25¼" repeat, 5½ yds. per s/r. Document in Hobe Erwin Collection, Schumacher Archive. No.506191 (antique); No.506194 (spring pink).

❧ FLOWERS AND BERRIES. English, 1840–60, block print. Wells-Cole, no. 18, p. 19. 21" wide, 15" half-drop repeat, 11 yds. per roll. Document at Temple Newsam, Leeds, England. No.TN03 (green).

❧ MONCEAU. French, 1860–70, block print. 54" wide, 36" repeat, 4½ yds. per s/r. Document in Schumacher Archive. No.509313 (coral and seafoam).

❧ MOSS ROSE STRIPE. English or French, 1850–70, block print. 20½" wide, 22¼" repeat, 5½ yds. per s/r. Document in Hobe Erwin Collection, Schumacher Archive. No.506204 (tea rose).

❧ NEO-GREC FLORAL VINE. American, 1865–75, block print. 27" wide, 19" repeat, 4½ yds. per s/r. Document in Schumacher Archive. No.512870 (document).

RICHARD E. THIBAUT

❧ ACORN HALL. English or German, 1860–70, block print. 28" wide, 22" repeat, 4½ yds. per s/r. Adaptation: embossing not reproduced. Historic Homes of America Collection, produced in collaboration with National Preservation Institute. Document at Acorn Hall, Morristown, N.J. No.839-T-7933 (gold on white).

❧ SALEM PAISLEY. American, 1860–80, machine print. 27" wide, 13½" repeat, 4½ yds. per s/r. Historic Homes of America Collection, produced in collaboration with National Preservation Institute. Document at Essex Institute. No.839-T-7925 (multi on white).

❧ TRIMBLE STRIPE. American, 1850–70, machine print. 27" wide, 12⅝" repeat, 4½ yds. per s/r. Historic Homes of America Collection, produced in collaboration with National Preservation Institute. Document at Trimble House, Washington, Ark. No.839-T-7984 (green and brown).

❧ WHIDDEN MARBLE. American, 1865–75, machine print. 27" wide, 12⅝" repeat, 4½ yds. per s/r. Historic Homes of America Collection, produced in collaboration with National Preservation Institute. Document at Whidden House, East Boston, Mass. No.839-T-7909 (taupe and pale green).

THE TWIGS

❧ EMBROIDERED NET. American or French, 1830–60, block print. 27" wide, 25¼" repeat, 5 yds. per s/r. No.A2720/008 (morning glory).

opposite
FRUIT, 1864. Arthur Sanderson & Sons. Page 202.

&❧ GALLOP CLUB. French, 1860–80, machine print. Guibert, fig. 946, p. 139. 21³⁄₄" wide plus 5³⁄₈" border, 21¹⁄₂" repeat, 5 yds. per s/r. No.65400/001 (multi on white).

&❧ LILY OF THE VALLEY. French, 1840–60, block print. 25¹⁄₂" wide, 3¹⁄₂" repeat, 5 yds. per s/r. No.A1010/009 (blue on bone).

&❧ PANIER DES ROSES SIDEWALL. French, 1850–70, block print. 19" wide, 36³⁄₄" half-drop repeat. No.65200/001 (blue ribbon on white).

&❧ ROSES AND RIBBONS. French, 1840–60, block print. 27" wide, 32" half-drop repeat, 5 yds. per s/r. No.98500/001 (pink, cream, and green on clear yellow).

&❧ WOODROSE. French, 1860–70, block print. 27⁷⁄₈" wide, 9³⁄₈" repeat, 5 yds. per s/r. No.67000/003 (coral on off-white).

WATERHOUSE WALLHANGINGS

&❧ BELLE EPOCH. English or German, 1860–70, machine print. 27" wide, 12" repeat, 5 yds. per s/r. Document in Waterhouse Archives. No.183613 (gold on gray). Period coloring: No.183610 (gold on white).

&❧ BISSELL HOUSE. Probably English, 1850–60, machine print. 26¹⁄₂" wide, 5 yds. per s/r. Document at Bissell House, St. Louis, Mo. No.134467 (gold on white).

&❧ CRYSTAL PALACE. English, 1860–70. 27" wide, 26¹⁄₄" repeat, 5 yds. per s/r. Adaptation: design derived from a published design. Document in Waterhouse Archives. No.220635 (multi on white).

&❧ GALLIER HOUSE. French, 1840–50, block print. 18¹⁄₂" wide, 28¹⁄₂" repeat. Document in Waterhouse Archives. Multi on white. Order by name.

&❧ THE GRIFFEN. English or German, 1860–75, block print. 27¹⁄₄" wide, 22¹⁄₂" repeat, 5 yds per s/r. Adaptation: colors altered slightly. Document in Waterhouse Archives. No.221438 (terra cotta). Period coloring: No.221469 (light blue).

&❧ ISIS. English, 1865–75, machine print. 27" wide, 24¹⁄₂" repeat, 5 yds. per s/r. Document in Waterhouse Archives. No.178443 (green and red on blue). Period coloring: No.178700 (blue and red on tan).

&❧ NEW ENGLAND FLORAL. 1850–70, French, probably a block print. 18¹⁄₂" wide, 18³⁄₄" repeat, 7 yds. per s/r. Document in Waterhouse Archives. No.203489 (multi on ivory).

&❧ TRELLIS. American or French, 1860–70, machine print. 21" wide, 11" repeat, 7 yds. per s/r. Document in Waterhouse Archives. No.181335 (pink and green on white).

&❧ VICTORIAN FLORAL. German or English, 1860–70, machine print. 27" wide, 8¹⁄₂" repeat, 5 yds. per s/r. Document in Waterhouse Archives. No.179613 (gold on light gray). Period coloring: No.179610 (gold on white).

above left
MONCEAU, 1860–70.
Schumacher.

above right
WHIDDEN MARBLE,
1865–75. Richard E.
Thibaut.

left
GALLOP CLUB,
1860–80. The Twigs.

GALLIER HOUSE,
1840–50. Waterhouse
Wallhangings.

THE GRIFFEN,
1860–75. Water-
house Wallhangings.

NEW ENGLAND FLORAL,
1850–70. Waterhouse
Wallhangings.

GRIFFON, 1860–80.
Zina Studios.

ZINA STUDIOS

Order by pattern name.

❧ FLOREAL. English or French, 1865–75, block print. 19″ wide, 12″ repeat. Reproduced for Chateau-sur-Mer, Newport, R.I., a property of Preservation Society of Newport County/Newport Mansions. Pink, green, and gold.

❧ GRIFFON. English, 1860–80, block print. Lynn, color pl. 88, p. 351. 23″ wide, 24″ repeat. Reproduced for Chateau-sur-Mer, Newport, R.I., a property of Preservation Society of Newport County/Newport Mansions. Red and gold on brown.

BORDERS

An asterisk (*) indicates a border designed specifically to go with a sidewall listed in the previous section.

BRUNSCHWIG & FILS

❧ CERES BORDER. French, 1850–70, block print. 5″ wide, 18½″ repeat. Period colorings: No.13830.06 (white); No.13832.06 (blue); No.13838.06 (gray). Block print.

❧ CHARTRIDGE BORDER. English, 1844, block print. Originally printed by John Todd Merrick & Company. 6½″ wide, 24″ repeat. Reproduced from a gouache design. Document privately owned. No.14802.06 (cornflower and leaf green).

❧ ELVIRE BORDER NO.1. French, 1840–60, block print. Greysmith, fig. 89, p. 120. 13″ wide, 18¾″ repeat. Adaptation: colors softened. No.10276.06 (coral and blue). Period coloring: No.10279.06 (brown and blue).

❧ ELVIRE BORDER NO.2. French, 1840–60, block print. Greysmith, fig. 89, p. 120. 5⅜″ wide, 18¾″ repeat. No.10286.06 (coral and blue). Period coloring: No.10289.06 (brown and blue).

❧ KENNWORTH BORDER. English, 1856, block print. Originally printed by Heywood, Higgenbottom, Smith & Company. 6″ wide, 18″ repeat. Adaptation: design derived from striped wallpaper. Document privately owned. No.14752.06 (blue).

❧ TAFT BORDER. American, 1850–70, block or machine print. 9¼″ wide, 18½″ repeat. Reproduced for William Howard Taft National Historic Site, Cincinnati. No.366.6C. Custom order.*

❧ TIPPERARY BORDER. French, 1840–60, block print. 4½″ wide, 21¾″ repeat. Adaptation: colors not reproduced exactly. Document in Brunschwig Archives. No.14318.06 (stone green).

❧ VOLUBILIS BORDER. French, 1863–70, block print. 5″ wide, 20″ repeat. Document at Musée des Arts Décoratifs. No.13524.06 (coral and blue on light green).

❧ VOLUBILIS CORNER. French, 1863–70, block print. 14⅝″ wide each side. Document at Musée des Arts Décoratifs. No.13514.06 (coral and blue on light green).

CHARTRIDGE BORDER, 1844. Brunschwig & Fils.

TIPPERARY BORDER, 1840–60. Brunschwig & Fils.

VOLUBILIS BORDER and corner, 1863–70. Brunschwig & Fils.

ᛉ WALTON BORDER. English, 1857, block print. Originally printed by William Cooke. 3" wide, 8" repeat. Adaptation: design derived from striped wallpaper. Document privately owned. Document color not reproduced. Period coloring: No.14761.06 (red).

CLASSIC REVIVALS

Mauny Collection

ᛉ BORDURE ET ANGLE SAINT BRIAC. French, 1840–60, block print. Border: 1" wide; corner: 6½" each side. No.5004 (series). Block print.

ᛉ BORDURE SAINT CAST. French, 1840–60, block print. 1½" wide. No.5003 (series). Block print.

ᛉ DRAPERIE ET ROSES. French, 1840–60, block print. Top: 13¼" wide; bottom: 5¾" wide. No.619J (red and gold). Block print.

ᛉ GROSSE CORDE. French, 1840–60, block print. 2⅛" wide. No.570D (green); No.570G (red); No.570H (blue). Block print.

ᛉ RESTAURATION. French, 1850–70, block print. Top: 7¾" wide; bottom: 2½" wide. No.626F (blue and gray); No.626I (green and gray); No.626K (mauve and gray). Block print.

❧ ROSE MOUSSE. French, 1840–60, block print. 3½" wide. No.546F (pink and white). Block print.

❧ RUBAN FLEURI. French, 1860–75, block print. Border: 3" wide; corner: 7½" each side. No.2617A (blue and rose). Block print.

COWTAN & TOUT

❧ DOG ON WOOD AND IVY STRIPS. English, 1850–80, block print. 8" wide, 25" repeat. No.572 (green and brown).*

❧ FUCHSIA CROWN. English, 1860–70, block print. No.CT-20101 (multi with gold stripe). Block print.*

❧ ROSE AND PANSEY BORDER. English, 1860–80, block print. 5" wide, 21" repeat. No.140 (multi).

❧ SOLANGE BORDER. French, 1835–60, block print. 12½" wide, 14" repeat. No.168-01 (taupe).

❧ SPRING FLOWERS BORDER. English, 1860–70, block print. 5" wide, 21" repeat. No.190 (white); No.191 (black). Block print.

A. L. DIAMENT & COMPANY

❧ ROSE BORDER. French, 1850–60, block print. 10¾" wide, 23¾" repeat. No.150-20 (rose and green on aubergine).

❧ SWAG AND TASSEL. French, 1860–75, block print. 11" wide, 9" repeat. No.158-04 (gold).

GALACAR & COMPANY

❧ LA DAUPHINE DADO. French, 1869, block print. Originally printed by Desfossé et Karth. 16½" wide, 27" repeat, 5 yds. per s/r. Document at Musée des Arts Décoratifs. No.GP-1301 (greens on white).*

❧ LA DAUPHINE FRIEZE. French, 1869, block print. Originally printed by Desfossé et Karth. 16½" wide, 27" repeat, 5 yds. per s/r. Document at Musée des Arts Décoratifs. No.GP-1301 (greens on white).*

CHRISTOPHER HYLAND INCORPORATED

❧ CLASSICAL COLUMN—CAPITAL AND BASE. English or French, 1840–60, block print. 12½" wide. No.AB107/5 (gray, light gray, and dark gray).

❧ CLASSICAL COLUMN—SHAFT. English or French, 1840–60, block print. 8⅞" wide. No.AB108/5 (gray, light gray, and dark gray).

❧ CLASSICAL CORNICE. English or French, 1840-60, block print. 9" wide, 4½" repeat. No.AB110/6B (gray, light gray, and dark gray).

❧ STAFFORD BORDER. English, 1850–70, block print. 10" wide, 10½" repeat. No.WTGASTAB (cream, sienna, light blue, and black).

❧ OWEN JONES BORDER. English, 1855–70, block print. 4⅝" wide, 5" repeat. No.ZZBLJ (period colorings).

KATZENBACH & WARREN

❧ BRAIDED CORD BORDER. French, 1850–60, block print. 3" wide, 9¼" repeat. Document at The Athenaeum of Philadelphia. No.AE1074B (green and gold).

❧ ROCOCO BORDER. French, 1850–60, block print. 7½" wide, 18⅜" repeat. Document at The Athenaeum of Philadelphia. Adaptation: flocking not reproduced. No.AE1112B (multi and tan).

❧ ROSE AND RIBBON BORDER. French, 1850–60, block print. 3¾" wide, 12" repeat. Adaptation: created to accompany "Rose and Ribbon Corner." No.AE1043B (blue and pink). Period coloring: No.AE1042B (yellow and purple).

❧ ROSE AND RIBBON CORNER. French, 1850–60, block print. 20½" wide. Document at The Athenaeum of Philadelphia. No.AE1033B (blue and pink). Period coloring: No.AE1032B (yellow and purple).

❧ SATIN DRAPERY FRIEZE. French, 1840–60, block print. Originally printed by Desfossé et Karth. 10¼" wide (including top and bottom borders), 18" repeat. Document at The Athenaeum of Philadelphia. No.AE1231B (gray and mauve). Period colorings: No.AE1232 (gray and blue); No.AE1233B (gold); No.AE1235B (beige and green).

MT. DIABLO HANDPRINTS

Order by name unless a pattern number is listed.

❧ DIAMOND STRIPE BORDER. French or American, 1860–70, block print. 3" wide, 6½" repeat. Reproduced for Henry Ford Museum & Greenfield Village, Dearborn, Mich. Gold, black, and green on ochre.

❧ SANDRA'S BORDER. American, 1840–60, machine print. 3" wide, 21" repeat. Reproduced for Santa Cruz Mission Adobe, operated by California Department of Parks and Recreation. No.SCB-001 (documentary red and greens).

❧ SANTA CRUZ DADO. American, 1840–60, block or machine print. 21" wide, 19¼" repeat. Reproduced for Santa Cruz Mission Adobe, operated by California Department of Parks and Recreation. No.SCD-001 (documentary orange, blue, and green on clear yellow).

❧ WILLIAM TAFT FRIEZE. American, 1840–70, machine print. 5⅜" wide, 4¾" repeat. Reproduced for William Howard Taft National Historic Site, Cincinnati. Red, gray, gold, and black.

ARTHUR SANDERSON & SONS

❧ BUCKINGHAM ROSE BORDER. English, 1840–70, block print. 5¼" wide, 21" repeat. Document in Sanderson Archives. No.SP 12162 (roses on cream). Block print.

❧ WINDSOR ROSE BORDER. English, 1840–70, block print. 10½" wide, 22" repeat. Document in Sanderson Archives. No.SP 12159 (roses on white). Block print.

ROCOCO BORDER, 1850–60. Katzenbach & Warren.

LINDENWALD—HALL BORDER, c. 1840. Scalamandré.

LINDENWALD— NORTHEAST BEDROOM BORDER, c. 1840. Scalamandré.

LINDENWALD— NORTHEAST PARLOR BORDER, c. 1850. Scalamandré.

LINDENWALD— SOUTHEAST BEDROOM BORDER, c. 1840. Scalamandré.

SCALAMANDRÉ

ᵍᵉ CATALDO MISSION BORDER. French or American, 1850–60, block print with flocking. $4^{7}/_{8}$" wide, $8^{1}/_{4}$" repeat. Historic representation. Reproduced for Old Mission, Cataldo, Idaho. No. WB600-001 (rose, brown, and terra cotta). Special order.

ᵍᵉ LINDENWALD—HALL BORDER. French or English, c. 1840, block print. $2^{3}/_{4}$" wide, $9^{1}/_{4}$" repeat. Reproduced for Martin Van Buren National Historic Site, Kinderhook, N.Y. No.WB81348-001 (olive, greens, and black flock on polar white). Special order.

&❧ LINDENWALD—NORTHEAST BEDROOM BORDER. French, c. 1840, block print. 4½" wide, 10 5/8" repeat. Reproduced for Martin Van Buren National Historic Site, Kinderhook, N.Y. No.WB81346-001 (grays, roses, teals, and brown on polar white). Special order.

&❧ LINDENWALD—NORTHEAST PARLOR BORDER. French or English, c. 1850, block print. 4" wide, 18¾" repeat. Reproduced for Martin Van Buren National Historic Site, Kinderhook, N.Y. No.WB81350-001 (grays, mustard, and turquoise on marble white). Special order.

&❧ LINDENWALD—PARLOR AND DINING ROOM BORDER. French, c. 1840, block print. 2⅜" wide, 4¾" repeat. Reproduced for Martin Van Buren National Historic Site, Kinderhook, N.Y. No.WB81349-001 (maroon and black flock with metallic gold on ecru embossed texture). Special order.

&❧ LINDENWALD—ROSE BORDER. French or English, 1840–60, block print. 4½" wide, 18¾" repeat. Reproduced for Martin Van Buren National Historic Site, Kinderhook, N.Y. No.WB81409-001 (multi lilac on chalk white).

&❧ LINDENWALD—SOUTHEAST BEDROOM BORDER. French, c. 1840, block print. 4½" wide, 9½" repeat. Reproduced for Martin Van Buren National Historic Site, Kinderhook, N.Y. No.WB81351-001 (grays, black, and green on marble white). Special order.

&❧ LOCUST GROVE BORDER. English, 1850–60, block print. 4¾" wide, ⅜" repeat. Reproduced for Young-Morse Historic Site, Poughkeepsie, N.Y No.WB81228-001 (metallic gold, slate gray, and charcoal on pebble gray). Special order.

&❧ RUSSIAN BISHOP'S HOUSE—GUEST ROOM BORDER. French, 1850–60, block print. 2¼" wide, 18" repeat. Reproduced for Russian Bishop's House, Sitka National Historical Park, Sitka, Alaska. No.WB81370-001 (rusts, greens, and browns on black). Special order.

&❧ RUSSIAN BISHOP'S HOUSE—LAYMAN'S ROOM BORDER. French, 1850–60, block print. 3½" wide, 20¼" repeat. Reproduced for Russian Bishop's House, Sitka National Historical Park, Sitka, Alaska. No.WB81364-001 (roses, golds, green, and black on coated white). Special order.

&❧ RUSSIAN BISHOP'S HOUSE—RECEPTION ROOM BORDER. French, 1850–60, block print. 1¾" wide, 10½" repeat. Reproduced for Russian Bishop's House, Sitka National Historical Park, Sitka, Alaska. No.WB81367-001 (roses, greens, and black on warm gray). Special order.

&❧ RUSSIAN BISHOP'S HOUSE—STUDY BORDER. English or French, 1850–60, block print. 1¼" wide, ¾" repeat. Reproduced for Russian Bishop's House, Sitka National Historical Park, Sitka,

Alaska. No.WB81372-001 (roses and greens on coated white). Special order.

SCHUMACHER

&❧ BAROQUE BORDER. French, 1850–70, block print. 3¼" wide, 4¾" repeat. Document in Dornsife Collection, Victorian Society in America. No.5703A (mulberry and spruce).

&❧ BAROQUE CORNER. French, 1850–70, block print. Document in Dornsife Collection, Victorian Society in America. No.5704A (mulberry and spruce).

&❧ BRAID BORDER. French, 1840–70, block print. 3¼" wide, 1½" repeat. Document in Dornsife Collection, Victorian Society in America. No.5706A (document brown and blue).

&❧ ROCOCO CARTOUCHE. American, 1850–60, machine print. 9½" wide, 9½" repeat. Document, a reproduction of c. 1905, in Schumacher Archive. No.512953 (document).

&❧ ROCOCO LEAF BORDER. American, 1850–60, machine print. 3¾" wide, 6¹⁵⁄₁₆" repeat. Document, a reproduction of c. 1905, in Schumacher Archive. No.512963 (document).

&❧ ROCOCO ROSES. American, 1850–60, machine print. 7" wide, 7 ⅜" repeat. Document, a reproduction of c. 1905, in Schumacher Archive. No.512973 (document).

&❧ ROPE BORDER. English or American, 1850–60, block print. 1⁵⁄₁₆" wide, 8" repeat. Document in Dornsife Collection, Victorian Society in America. No.5707A (document cerise and green).

THE TWIGS

&❧ PANIER DES ROSES BORDER. French, 1850–70, block print. 8" wide, 18³⁄₈" repeat. No.65250/001 (blue swag on white).

WATERHOUSE WALLHANGINGS

&❧ ARENENBURG FRIEZE. French, 1860–75, block print. 10½" wide, 9" repeat. Document privately owned. Document coloring: special order. Period colorings: No.225540 (red and gold); No.225476 (green and gold).

&❧ GREEK REVIVAL BORDER. English or French, 1860–75, block print. 3" wide, 18" repeat. Adaptation: flocking not reproduced. Document at New Bedford Glass Museum, New Bedford, Mass. No.226525 (gold on black).

ZINA STUDIOS

Order by pattern name.

&❧ GREEN ANIMALS BORDER. English or French, 1865–80, block print. 8" wide, 9" repeat. Reproduced for Green Animals, Portsmouth, R.I., a property of Preservation Society of Newport County/Newport Mansions. Greens and golds.

ZUBER

SCENIC WALLPAPERS

❧ ELDORADO. French, 1848, block print. Designed by Eugene Ehrmann, Joseph Fuchs, and Hermann Zipelius. *Bulletin,* color pl. 15, no. 4, and p. 159; McClelland, p. 305; Oman and Hamilton, fig. 616, p. 222; Teynac, Nolot, and Vivien, p. 114. Total width: 42'; total height: 12'10"; 21" per panel; 24 panels per set. Block printed in 192 colors from 1,554 wood blocks.

❧ LA GUERRE D'INDEPENDENCE. French, 1852–53, figures painted over Deltil's "Scenic America." *Bulletin,* color pl. 14, no. 3; McClelland, p. 199. Total width: 49'4"; total height: 13'; 18½" per panel; 32 panels per set. Block printed in 223 colors from 1,690 wood blocks.

❧ ISOLA BELLA. French, 1842, block print. Designed by Eugene Ehrmann and Hermann Zipelius. *Bulletin,* color pl. 16; Lynn, fig. 9-26, p. 220. Total width: 27'9"; total height: 12'10"; 18½" per panel; 18 panels per set. Block printed in 85 colors from 742 wood blocks.

❧ LE JARDIN JAPONAIS. French, 1861, block print. Designed by Victor Poterlet. Total width: 17'3½"; total height: 12'10"; 20¾" per panel; 10 panels per set. Block printed in 72 colors from 417 wood blocks.

Zuber also prints a wide variety of wallpapers and borders. The company prefers that inquiries concerning these additional patterns be made directly to its New York showroom.

above
LE JARDIN JAPONAIS (detail), 1861. Zuber.

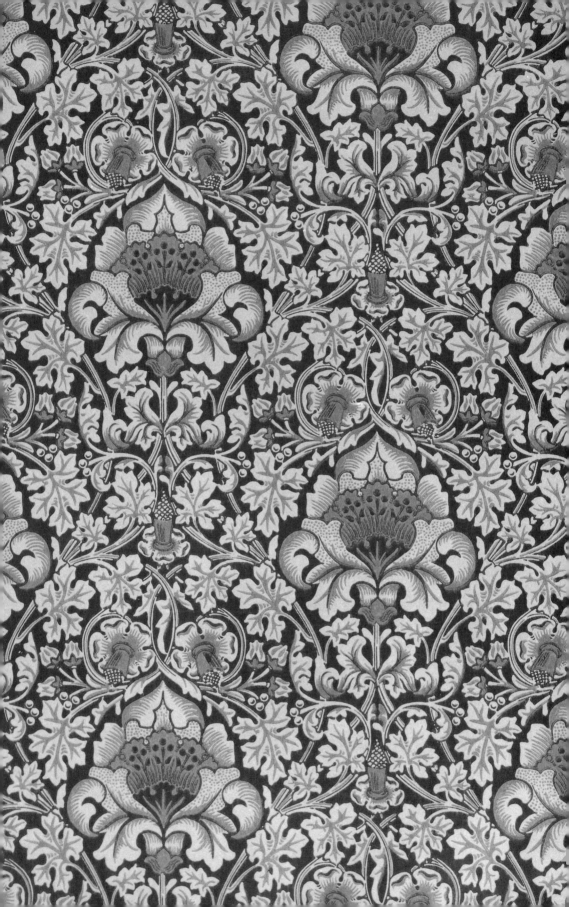

1870 TO 1900:
PATTERN EVERYWHERE

In the United States the late 19th century was unparalled in the manufacture and use of wallpaper. Most residential rooms were papered, including kitchens, closets, attic staircases, and even privies. Ceilings covered with one or more patterns also were fashionable.

Wallpaper was no longer considered only a finish; it became an essential part of a room's overall design. As a result, wallpaper design became a highly regarded branch of the decorative arts. Wallpaper patterns no longer had to imitate other materials such as draped fabric or stone. Indeed, papering a room was likened to bringing art into the home. Books on decorating and pamphlets produced by wallpaper companies promoted the stylized patterns and palettes favored by the English design theorists. As a result, England replaced France and once again became the source for fashionable wallpaper designs.

During this period, many English wallpaper manufacturers hired well-known designers and artists to create a succession of new patterns. One of the most well-known and influential English designers was William Morris, whose patterns of stylized flowers and foliage have remained popular to this day. Some have never gone out of production, and many of those available today are still printed from the original wood blocks. Because wallpapers designed by Morris were expensive, they were not used as extensively in this country as one might expect. His approach to design, however, was widely imitated, and most Americans had to settle for an inexpensive imitation "Morris paper."

Dividing a wall surface into three horizontal units—frieze, fill, and dado—was a popular wall treatment in the 1870s and 1880s. Coordinating borders marked the division between the different but compatible patterns. See, for example, "Chrysanthemum" frieze, fill, dado, and dado border (page 182). Toward the end of the century the dado and dado border were eliminated. However, the wide frieze designed to echo the pattern of the sidewall remained a popular and lucrative offering of the wallpaper manufacturers into the 20th cen-

BROAD MEADOWS, 1880–90. Waterhouse Wallhangings.

143

tury. See, for examples, the patterns "Mary Dailey Crook" (page 186) or "Emperor" (page 189). Ceilings also could be papered with one or more different patterns separated by a judicious use of borders. Often the ceiling paper was designed en suite with the sidewall and wide frieze.

The interest in Japanese design is evident in wallpapers produced during the 1880s. The asymmetrical designs and exotic motifs of patterns in the "Anglo-Japanese" style are direct contrasts to the wallpapers being imported from Japan at the same time; see, for example, "Oriental Garden" (page 168) and "Alhambra" (page 127). Expensive Japanese "leather" papers emulated the stylized English designs and were embossed and highlighted with gilding.

As their name indicates, the Japanese imports were intended to imitate leather. They were only one of several wallcoverings classified as relief decoration and widely used in late 19th-century interiors. Others included Anaglypta and Lincrusta. Both are available today, and many of the patterns are produced from the original rollers. Lincrusta Walton, developed in 1877 by Frederick Walton, the inventor of linoleum, is a composition material whose design is impressed with rollers. Anaglypta is a less substantial copy made from embossed paper. Both receive their decorative coloring after they are applied to the wall.

The elegant effects of many other English and American wallpapers made during the late 19th century were produced by embossing. Because of the expense involved, few firms replicate embossing on reproduction wallpapers. Textured (rather than embossed) wallpapers popular from the 1880s into the 1920s include ingrain and oatmeal papers. Both are considered unsuitable wallcoverings today because of their insubstantial quality and their rough, unwashable surfaces.

By the 1890s designers had stopped emphasizing the use of artistic wallpaper in "tasteful" interiors. Manufacturers catering to the middle-class market returned to producing patterns with floral and scroll motifs, such as "Rococo Rose" (page 188) and "Fortino" (page 189), rendered in a much less stylized manner. Those responsible for decorating interiors for wealthier clients, on the other hand, once again sought wallpaper patterns that imitated more costly textiles. In addition to creating new patterns, many companies reissued the damask and moiré patterns that had been popular a generation earlier. Because of the popularity of damask-patterned wallpapers during this period, most of the reproductions available today are listed in this section rather than in previous sections. Some, however, may be appropriate for earlier restoration projects. If the restoration of an earlier interior requires a wallpaper with a damask pattern, further research should be done on the patterns listed to determine which may be the most appropriate.

The 1980s witnessed an overwhelming interest in Victorian design. As a result a new decorating style called Victorian Revival emerged. Interiors promoted as being decorated in this style are quite diverse. Those that feature floral chintzes, lace curtains, pale colors, and white wicker or stripped furniture—an eclectic combination of English country house and the age of golden oak—would both astonish and confuse our Victorian ancestors. On the other hand, interiors that feature rich combinations of both color and pattern in correct proportion would receive their hearty approval because they are created with a full understanding of Victorian design vocabulary and color theory. The room sets offered by Bradbury & Bradbury are excellent examples of Victorian Revival as it relates to wall decoration. Some of the designs are exact copies of period wallpapers; others copy alternative approaches to Victorian wall decoration, such as stenciling or fresco. Some patterns are derived from published designs that were available to Victorian designers, and others have been developed by contemporary designers to coordinate with them. Like the best revival design in any period, these patterns do not slavishly replicate the past but take the appealing elements from historical designs and combine them in new ways in an attempt to evoke the decorative spirit of an era.

BRADBURY & BRADBURY   WALLPAPERS

&❧ CHILD'S GARDEN. American Victorian Revival, 1980. Designed by S. J. Bauer in the style of a nursery paper by Walter Crane. 27" wide, 27" repeat, 5 yds. per s/r. Code GDW (2 period colorings).

&❧ KNIGHTSBRIDGE DAMASK. American Victorian Revival, 1980. Designed by S. J. Bauer in the style of William Morris. 27" wide, 27" repeat, 5 yds. per s/r. Code KDW.

BRUNSCHWIG & FILS

&❧ FLOWERING TREE. English, 1880–1900, block print. 23½" wide, 39½" repeat, 6 yds. per s/r. Adaptation: scale slightly reduced. Document in Brunschwig Archives. No.11307.06 (indigo and rose).

&❧ FORET FOLIAGE. French, 1890-1900, block print. 21" wide, 24¾" repeat, 11 yds. per s/r. Document privately owned. No.13534.06 (green); No.13538.06 (brown).

&❧ FUCHSIA TRELLIS. French or English, 1870–85, block print. 18½" wide, 23" repeat, 7 yds. per s/r. Document at Cooper-Hewitt Museum. No.12514.06 (pistachio).

&❧ JAPANESQUE. American, 1870–90, machine print. 24½" wide, 15¾" half-drop repeat, 5 yds. per s/r. Document at Cooper-Hewitt Museum. No.12496.6C (gold on light brown). Custom order.

&❧ MAREIKO. French or English, 1870–1900, machine print. 27"

above left
WOODBURY MOIRE,
1890–1915.
Brunschwig & Fils.

above right
FUCHSIA TRELLIS,
1870–85.
Brunschwig & Fils.

wide, 23½" repeat, 5 yds. per s/r. Adaptation: width increased and compatable motif added. Document at Cooper-Hewitt Museum. No.12487.06 (aubergine).

❧ WOODBURY MOIRE. American, 1890–1915, machine print. 28" wide, 13¾" repeat, 5 yds. per s/r. Document at Society for the Preservation of New England Antiquities. Document color, no. 13214.6C (avocado), is a special order. Period colorings: No.13210.06 (sand); No.13213.06 (yellow).

J. R. BURROWS & COMPANY

Order by pattern name and color. All patterns can be custom colored.
❧ ALDAM. English, 1884–95, block print. Designed by Aldam Heaton. 21" wide, 21" repeat, 6 yds. per s/r. Document privately owned. Deep cream. Period coloring: celadon on buff. Also available block printed as a special order.

❧ HEATON. English, 1884–95, block print. Designed by Aldam Heaton. 21" wide, 42" half-drop repeat, 6 yds. per s/r. Document privately owned. Terra cotta on deep cream. Period coloring: celadon on buff. Pattern is made up of two widths of paper, marked A and B; both must be ordered to complete design.

❧ PERSIS. English, 1880–90, block print. 21" wide, 21" repeat, 6 yds. per s/r. Document in Burrows Archive. Sage green. Period colorings:

terra cotta; cream on buff.

&➤ SUMMER STREET DAMASK. English, 1880–95, block print. 21" wide, 36" repeat, 6 yds. per s/r. Document privately owned. Terra cotta. Period colorings: celadon on buff; cream on buff.

CLARENCE HOUSE

&➤ CANONBURY. English, 1890–1910, block print. 21" wide, 21" repeat, 11 yds. per roll. Coles Traditional Collection. No.C260 (gold); No.C264 (blue).

&➤ FLORENTINE DIAPER. English, 1880–1900, block print. 21" wide, 10¹/²" repeat, 11 yds. per roll. Coles Traditional Collection. No.C202 (old rose). Block print.

&➤ MILLIKEN. English, 1880–1900, block print. Designed by Henry H. Mott, originally printed by H. Scott Richmond & Company. Nylander, Redmond, and Sander, front cover and p. 251. 21" wide, 21" repeat, 11 yds. per roll. Coles Traditional Collection. No.C227 (green); No.C229 (white); No.C230 (gold). Block print.

&➤ SAVOY. English, 1870–90, block print. 20¹/²" wide, 5¹/⁴" repeat, 11 yds. per roll. Document in Courtauld Archives, London. No.W9005 (series).

&➤ SMALL ACANTHUS. English, 1880–1910, block print. 21" wide, 24" repeat, 11 yds. per roll. Coles Traditional Collection. Period color-

above left
HEATON, 1884–95.
J. R. Burrows & Company.

above right
PERSIS, 1880–90.
J. R. Burrows & Company.

above left
CANONBURY,
1890–1910.
Clarence House.

above right
MILLIKEN,
1880–1900.
Clarence House.

right
SUMMER STREET
DAMASK, 1880–95.
J. R. Burrows &
Company.

VALLIERE MINOR,
1890–1910. Clarence
House.

ings: No.C217 (parchment); No.C221 (raspberry); No.C220 (green).
Block print.

&⬦ VALLIERE MINOR. English, 1890–1910, block print. 21" wide, 14"
repeat, 11 yds. per roll. Coles Traditional Collection. No.C213
(green); No.C214 (salmon). Block print.

CLASSIC REVIVALS

Authentic Interiors Collection

&⬦ CHARLOTTE. English, 1880–90, machine print. 21" wide, 18" repeat, 11 yds. per roll. Price Collection. No.W-169-4B (ochre and
olive).

&⬦ TRACCY. English, 1880–90, machine print. 21" wide, 20" repeat, 11
yds. per roll. Archival Collection. No.W-205-3A (light green on tan).

Mauny Collection

&⬦ BOUQUET ET GRANDE RAYURE. French, 1890–1930, block print.
21¼" wide, 44" repeat, 11 yds. per roll. Possibly a reproduction of
an 18th-century design. No.140 (pinks and green on blue stripe).
Block print.

&⬦ DAMAS CHOISEUL. French, 1870–90, block print. 18⅛" wide, 26"
repeat, 11 yds. per roll. No.111-I (ochre on ochre). Block print.

&⬦ DAMAS ESPAGNOL. French, 1890–1920, block print. 18½" wide,
21¼" repeat, 11 yds. per roll. No.111-B (white on gray). Block print.

ॐ DAMAS FLAMAND. French, 1890–1920, block print. 18" wide, 20½" repeat, 11 yds. per roll. No.111-C (rust on orange). Block print.

ॐ DAMAS LA CAGE. French, 1890–1920, block print. 18½" wide, 21¾" repeat, 11 yds. per roll. No.111-D (green and gold on white). Block print.

ॐ DAMAS LE NID. French, 1880–1920, block print. 18½" wide, 22¾" repeat, 11 yds. per roll. No.111-E (white on green). Block print.

ॐ DAMAS PALMETTE. French, 1870–80, block print. 18½" wide, 8⅝" repeat, 11 yds. per roll. No.252 (buff on white). Block print.

ॐ DAMAS ROCOCO. French, 1870–1920, block print. 18½" wide, 19⅝" repeat, 11 yds. per roll. No.111-G (white on tan). Block print.

ॐ DAMAS ROYAL. French, 1890–1920, block print. 22" wide, 37⅜" repeat, 11 yds. per roll. No.111-A (rust on off-white). Block print.

ॐ DAMAS UTRECH. French, 1890–1920, block print. 18⅞" wide, 34¼" repeat, 11 yds. per roll. No.111-F (beige on white). Block print.

ॐ PLUMES ET POMMES. French, 1890–1920, block print. 19¼" wide (2 widths required for the complete horizontal repeat), 24¾" repeat, 11 yds. per roll. No.160 (multi on light blue). Block print.

ॐ SEMIS PLUMETS. French, 1890–1920, block print. 18½" wide, 5⅛" repeat, 11 yds. per roll. No.261 (yellow on blue). Block print.

St. James Collection

ॐ FERN FILLER. English, 1892, machine print. Originally printed by Allan, Cockshut and Company. 28" wide, 11" repeat, 11 yds. per roll. No.FF1 (sage); No.FF6 (olive); No.FF11 (rose); No.FF13 (turquoise).

ॐ IRIS FILLER. English, 1885–1900, machine print. 21" wide, 18" repeat, 11 yds. per roll. No.IF6 (olive).

ॐ LARGE CHRYSANTHEMUM FILLER. English, 1890–1900, machine print. 21" wide, 21" repeat, 11 yds. per roll. No.YF14 (old gold).

ॐ PEONY FILLER. English, 1890–1900, machine print. 21" wide, 21" repeat, 11 yds. per roll. No.NF4 (deep red); No.NF7 (pink).

ॐ ROSE BOUQUET FILLER. English, 1890–1900, machine print. 21" wide, 16" repeat, 11 yds. per roll. No.QF7 (pink).

ॐ ROSEBUD FILLER. English, 1892, machine print. Originally printed by Allan, Cockshut and Company. 28" wide, 21" repeat, 11 yds. per roll. No.RF1 (sage); No.RF5 (gray buff); No.RF10 (sienna); No.RF12 (pink olive).

Silvergate Collection

ॐ BROCKHAMPTON SNOWFLAKE. English, c. 1870, block print. 21" wide, 10⅜" repeat, 11 yds. per roll. Document at Brockhampton House, Worcestershire, England. No.AS031. Block print.

ॐ BROCKHAMPTON TRELLIS. English, c. 1870, block print. 21" wide, 3⅞" repeat, 11 yds. per roll. Document at Brockhampton House, Worcestershire, England. No.BS022. Block print.

ॐ BURGES BLOCK. English, c. 1875, block print. Probably designed by William Burges. 21″ wide, 14″ repeat. Document at Knightshayes Court, Devon, England. No.AS141. Block print.

❧ BURGES BUTTERFLY. English, c. 1870. Designed by William Burges. 21″ wide, 5¼″ repeat, 11 yds. per roll. Adaptation: design derived from a sketch for a wallpaper. Document in collection of Royal Institute of British Architects, London. No.CS153. Block print.

❧ EASTLAKE PLAIN HORSE. English, 1872. Designed by Charles Locke Eastlake. 21″ wide, 4¼″ repeat, 11 yds. per roll. Adaptation: design derived from a published design in Eastlake, 1872 ed. No.AS181. Block print.

❧ EASTLAKE SHADOW HORSE. English, 1872. Designed by Charles Locke Eastlake. 21″ wide, 4¼″ repeat, 11 yds. per roll. Adaptation: design derived from a published design in Eastlake, 1872 ed. No.BS192. Block print.

❧ EASTLAKE PLAIN SPRIG. English, 1872. Designed by Charles Locke Eastlake. 21″ wide, 3½″ repeat, 11 yds. per roll. Adaptation: design derived from a published design in Eastlake, 1872 ed. No.AS201. Block print.

❧ EASTLAKE SHADOW SPRIG. English, 1872. Designed by Charles Locke Eastlake. Lynn, fig. 16-9, p. 378. 21″ wide, 3½″ repeat, 11 yds. per roll. Adaptation: design derived from a published design in Eastlake, 1872 ed. No.BS212. Block print.

❧ EASTLAKE PLAIN STAR. English, 1872, block print. Designed by Charles Locke Eastlake. 21″ wide, 3½″ repeat, 11 yds. per roll. Adaptation: design derived from a published design in Eastlake, 1872 ed. No.AS161. Block print.

❧ EASTLAKE SHADOW STAR. English, 1872. Designed by Charles Locke Eastlake. 21″ wide, 3½″ repeat, 11 yds. per roll. Adaptation: design derived from a published design in Eastlake, 1872 ed. No.BS172. Block print.

❧ LAKE DISTRICT ORIGINAL. English, 1880–90, block print. 21″ wide, 18″ repeat, 11 yds. per roll. Document at Townend House, Windermere, England. No.AS091. Block print.

❧ OXBOROUGH TRELLIS. English, 1870–80, block print. 21″ wide, 13¹³/₁₆″ repeat, 11 yds. per roll. Document at Oxburgh Hall, Norfolk, England. No.DS064. Block print.

COLE & SON

Available through Clarence House as custom orders only.

❧ ACANTHUS. English, 1870–90, block print. 21″ wide, 46″ repeat, 11 yds. per roll. Coles Book. No.98874 (red). Block print.

❧ AUDLEY END. English, 1890–1900, block print. 21″ wide, 17″ repeat, 11 yds. per roll. Coles Book. No.98870 (terra cotta). Block print.

❧ BEATRIX DESIGN. English, 1880–90, block print. 21″ wide, 21″ repeat, 11 yds. per roll. Adaptation. Coles Book. No.OEW143 (tan).

above left
OXBOROUGH TRELLIS,
1870–80. Classic
Revivals (Silvergate
Collection).

above right
CADORA, 1870–1910.
Cowtan & Tout.

Period coloring: No.OEW144 (brown). Block print.

&❧ CELTIC. English, 1890, block print. 21″ wide, 8″ repeat, 11 yds. per roll. Coles Book. No.98885 (blue on green). Period coloring: No.98886 (brown on gold). Block print.

&❧ LARGE ADAMS. English, 1890–1900, block print. 21″ wide, 24″ repeat, 11 yds. per roll. Coles Book. No.98816 (white on blue). Block print.

&❧ POPPY. English, 1880–1900, block print. 21″ wide, 17″ repeat, 11 yds. per roll. Coles Book. No.98887 (pink and brown). Block print.

&❧ ROYSTON. English, 1890–1900, block print. 21″ wide, 28″ repeat, 11 yds. per roll. Coles Book. No.PR15013 (green ground). Block print.

COWTAN & TOUT

&❧ AMBERLY. English, 1880–1910, block print. 20½″ wide, 77″ repeat, 11 yds. per roll. No.21065 (blue). Block print.

&❧ BURLINGTON. English, 1880–1900, block print. 21″ wide, 23″ repeat, 11 yds. per roll. No.20576 (hickory). Block print.

&❧ CADORA. English, 1870–1910, block print. 21″ wide, 17″ repeat, 11 yds. per roll. No.20583 (buff); No.20584 (hunter green). Block print.

&❧ GERANIUM. English, 1890–1910, block print. 21″ wide, 16½″ repeat, 11 yds. per roll. No.20580 (reds and greens on white). Block print.

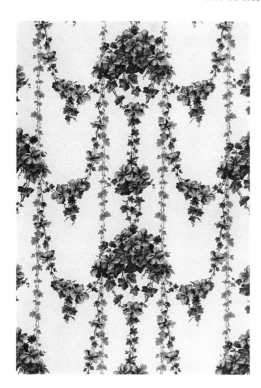

ﱠ HUMMINGBIRD. English, 1890–1900, block print. 21″ wide, 19½″ repeat, 11 yds. per roll. No.20500 (multi on white). Block print.

ﱠ MARLBOROUGH. English, 1880–1900, block print. 20½″ wide, 24″ repeat, 11 yds. per roll. No.7075-08 (gray). Block print.

ﱠ ROSE BOUQUET. English, 1890–1910, block print. 21″ wide, 12″ repeat, 11 yds. per roll. No.20540 (red on white). Block print.

ﱠ SWEET PEA. English, 1890–1910, block print. 21″ wide, 15″ repeat, 11 yds. per roll. No.20570 (multi/stripe). Block print.

ﱠ WESTERN BIRDS. English, 1870–90, block print. 21″ wide, 20″ repeat, 11 yds. per roll. No.27120 (multi on white). Block print.

ﱠ WILD ROSE TRELLIS. English, 1880–1900, block print. 21″ wide, 15½″ repeat, 11 yds. per roll. No.20202 (reds). Block print.

ﱠ WILLOW LEAVES. English, 1880–1900, block print. 24″ wide, 21″ repeat, 5 yds. per s/r. No.25087 (cream and gray); No.25088 (cream and green).

A. L. DIAMENT & COMPANY

ﱠ ESCARPALETTE. French, 1880–90, block print. 19″ wide, 41″ half-drop repeat. No.176-02 (taupe on French blue).

ﱠ CHINAMAN IN SWING. French, 1890–1900, block print. 27″ wide, 30½″ repeat, 5 yds. per s/r. Adapted from an 18th-century design; scale enlarged. No.80264-19 (beige).

above left
GERANIUM,
1890–1910. Cowtan
& Tout.

above right
WESTERN BIRDS,
1870–90. Cowtan &
Tout.

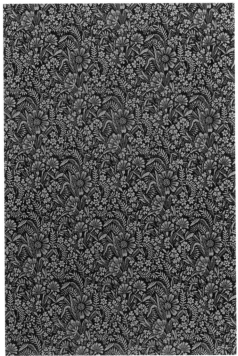

above left

BAMBOO JASMINE,
1870–80. Christopher
Hyland Incorporated.

above right

AESTHETIC GARDEN,
1880–90. Katzenbach
& Warren.

CHRISTOPHER HYLAND INCORPORATED

☙ BAMBOO JASMINE. English, 1870–80, block print. 21" wide, 23³/₄" repeat, 11 yds. per roll. No.WTCBJ2 (beige, green, and light blue).

☙ BODLEY. English, 1870–90, block print. 21" wide, 10¹/₂" repeat, 11 yds. per roll. No.WTCBO7 (greens).

☙ BOKHARA. English, 1880–1900, block print. 21" wide, 24¹/₈" repeat, 11 yds. per roll. No.ZZ93013 (crimson red).

☙ BUCCA CLARENCE. English, 1870–80, block print. 21" wide, 10¹/₄" repeat, 11 yds. per roll. No.WTOCL5 (gray on white).

☙ CORN. English, 1897, block print. Designed by Archibald Knox. 21" wide, 24¹/₈" repeat, 11 yds. per roll. No.AB123/3 (yellow and blue).

☙ GENOESE. English, 1877, block print. Designed by George Gilbert Scott II; printed by Watts & Company. Nylander, Redmond, and Sander, color pl. 44, p. 164, and fig. 60-B, p. 222; Oman and Hamilton, no. 1136, p. 411. 21" wide, 35³/₄" repeat, 11 yds. per roll. No.WTHGN3 (blue-greens). Block print

☙ LACE SUNFLOWER. English, 1880–90, block print. 21" wide, 20¹/₂" repeat, 11 yds. per roll. No.WTOSF5 (white on tan).

☙ LENNEL. English, 1870–90, block print. 20" wide, 12¹/₂" half-drop repeat, 11 yds. per roll. No.ZZBL402 (black on rust).

☙ LITTLE VILLANDRY. English, 1880–90, block print. 21" wide,

154

23$^{1}/_{4}$" repeat, 11 yds. per roll. No.ZZ91004 (mustard beige).

❧ MACKINTOSH STRIPE. English, 1890–1900, block print. 21" wide. 11 yds. per roll. No.AB207.2 (blue ground).

❧ MAGNOLIA. English, 1897, block print. Designed by Archibald Knox. 21" wide, 22$^{1}/_{2}$" repeat, 11 yds. per roll. No.AB125/5.

❧ MALMESBURY. English, 1880–90, block print. 20$^{3}/_{4}$" wide, 63" repeat, 11 yds. per roll. No.WTHML1 (green on creme). Block print.

❧ NIMUE. English, 1880–1900, block print. 22" wide, 19" repeat, 11 yds. per roll. No.WTNIMUE.

❧ OAKLEAF. English, 1870–90, block print. 21" wide, 15" repeat, 11 yds. per roll. No.WTCOA8 (blue).

❧ OLD ENGLISH. English, 1880–90, block print. 21" wide, 59$^{1}/_{2}$" repeat, 11 yds. per roll. No.WTSTOE3 (gray on white).

❧ PEAR. English, 1880–90, block print. 21" wide, 35" repeat (two widths required for the complete horizontal repeat), 11 yds. per roll. No.WTHPR.

❧ RAVENNA. English, 1880–90, block print. 21" wide, 27" repeat, 11 yds. per roll. No.WTHRV5 (blue and white).

❧ ROCK MAPLE HOUSE DAMASK. English, 1880–90, block print. 21" wide, 21" repeat, 11 yds. per roll. No.AB179/2A (creme, beige, and white).

❧ ROSE. English, 1880–90, block print. 21" wide, 28" repeat, 11 yds. per roll. No.WTHRS3 (tan and red). Block print.

❧ ROSE AND CORONET. English, 1875–90, block print. 21" wide, 17$^{3}/_{4}$" repeat, 11 yds. per roll. No.WTHRC2 (rose and blue).

❧ ROSY BUDS. English, 1897, block print. Designed by Archibald Knox. 21" wide, 25" repeat, 11 yds. per roll. No.AB117/4AB (aquamarine).

❧ TEA ROSE. English, 1897, block print. Designed by Archibald Knox. 21" wide, 22$^{1}/_{2}$" repeat, 11 yds. per roll. No.AB124/3 (blue and green).

❧ TRELLIS. English, 1875–85, block print. 21" wide, 7" repeat, 11 yds. per roll. No.WTSTTE.

❧ VENETIAN. English, 1880–90, block print. 21" wide, 47$^{1}/_{2}$" drop repeat, 11 yds. per roll. No.WTHVT1 (green).

❧ VERSAILLES. English, 1880–1900, block print. 21" wide, 41$^{1}/_{2}$" repeat, 11 yds. per roll. No.ZZ0106. Period colorings.

❧ VIOLA. English, 1870–80, block print. 20$^{1}/_{2}$" wide, 15" repeat, 11 yds. per roll. No.41002 (multi on blue-gray); No.41005 (multi on beige).

KATZENBACH & WARREN

❧ AESTHETIC GARDEN. American, 1880–90, machine print. 27" wide, 12$^{5}/_{8}$" repeat, 4$^{1}/_{2}$ yds. per s/r. Document at The Athenaeum of Philadelphia. No.AE1163 (terra cotta and gold). Period coloring: No.AE1161 (olive and gold).

ॐ ALHAMBRA. American, 1880–1900, machine print. 27" wide, 25¼" repeat, 4½ yds. per s/r. Document at The Athenaeum of Philadelphia. No.AE1141 (tan and maroon).

ॐ BIRDS & BOUGHS. French, 1875–80, block print. 27" wide, 25¼" repeat, 4½ yds. per s/r. Document at The Athenaeum of Philadelphia. No.AE1104 (blue ground). Period coloring: No.AE1101 (green and tan).

ॐ BYZANTIUM. American, 1880–1900, machine print. 27" wide, 5⅜" repeat, 4½ yds. per s/r. Document at The Athenaeum of Philadelphia. No.AE1151 (olive and maroon).

ॐ GRAND DAMASK. French, 1880–90, block print. 20½" wide, 24¼" repeat, 6 yds. per s/r. Adaptation: design slightly enlarged; flocking not reproduced. Document at The Athenaeum of Philadelphia. No.AE1063 (red). Period colorings: No.AE1062 (gold); No.AE1065 (green).

ॐ IRIS TAPESTRY. French, 1880–1900, block print. 20½" wide, 25¼" drop repeat, 6 yds. per s/r. Adaptation: embossing not reproduced. Document at The Athenaeum of Philadelphia. No.AE1123 (multi).

ॐ NOSEGAYS. French, 1870–90. 27" wide, 25¼" repeat, 4½ yds. per s/r. Adaptation. No.AE1053 (blue and pink).

LEE JOFA

ॐ COLETTE. French, 1880–90, block print. 27" wide, 36" repeat, 5 yds. per s/r. Reproduced from a period design for a wallpaper. No.P912003 (dove).

ॐ MARGARET CLAIRE. French, 1875–90. 27" wide, 27⅝" repeat, 5 yds. per s/r. Created as a companion to a document border. No.912105 (silver).

ॐ RIBBON AND TRAIL TRELLIS. American or English, 1880–1900, machine print. 27" wide, 15⅝" repeat, 5 yds. per s/r. No.P779003 (cream).

MT. DIABLO HANDPRINTS

Order by name unless pattern number is listed.

ॐ ANGLO-JAPANESE COLLAGE WALL. American, 1880–90, machine print. 18¾" wide, 19¾" repeat. Reproduced for Fallon Hotel, Columbia, Calif., operated by California Department of Parks and Recreation. Greens, blues, maroon, and gold.

ॐ BIBLIO DAMASK. American, 1890–1910, machine print. 18" wide, 17¾" repeat. Reproduced for Byers-Evans House, Denver, Colo., a property operated by Colorado Historical Society. No.BDW-001 (document browns and greens on chestnut).

ॐ BILLINGS ACANTHUS. American, 1890–1900, machine print. 18" wide, 16" repeat. Reproduced for Billings Farm & Museum, Wood-

above left
GRAND DAMASK,
1880–90. Katzenbach
& Warren.

above right
Original document
for "Colette," a
wallpaper of 1880–90
reproduced by
Lee Jofa.

left
BILLINGS ACANTHUS,
1880–90. Mt. Diablo
Handprints.

above left
GRIFFITHS FLORAL,
1880–90. Mt. Diablo
Handprints.

above right
KATHERINE'S BED-
ROOM, 1890–1910.
Mt. Diablo Hand-
prints.

right
NOUVEAU ROSE,
1890–1910.
Mt. Diablo Hand-
prints.

stock, Vt. No.BAW-001 (document custard on camel).

❧ BILLINGS BEDROOM WALL. American, 1890–1900, machine print. 17³/₄" wide, 15¹/₂" repeat. Reproduced for Billings Farm & Museum, Woodstock, Vt. Gold, copper, mica, and light greens.

❧ CAMPBELL HOUSE DAMASK. American, 1870–90, block or machine print. 24" wide, 12" repeat. Reproduced for Campbell House Foundation, St. Louis, Mo. Chocolate on pale blue.

❧ FALLON'S FOLLEY. American, 1880–1900, machine print. 18" wide, 15³/₄" repeat. Reproduced for Fallon Hotel, Columbia, Calif., operated by California Department of Parks and Recreation. Brown, burgundy, and yellow on tan.

❧ GREENFIELD ANGLO-JAPANESE. American, 1880–90, machine print. 18¹/₂" wide, 16³/₈" repeat. Reproduced for Henry Ford Museum & Greenfield Village, Dearborn, Mich. Olives and gray.

❧ GRIFFITHS FLORAL. American, 1880–1900, machine print. 20" wide, 18" repeat. Reproduced for Alan Griffiths House, San Francisco, Calif. No.GFW-001 (document lilac, sage, dove gray, and gold).

❧ KATHERINE'S BEDROOM. American, 1890–1910, machine print. 21" wide, 12" repeat. Reproduced for Byers-Evans House, Denver, Colo., a property of Colorado Historical Society. No.KBW-001 (document rose and green on pale cream).

❧ McFADDEN-WARD FLORAL. American, 1890–1900, machine print. 18" wide, 24" repeat. Reproduced for McFadden-Ward House, Beaumont, Tex. No.MFW-001 (document buttercream on custard).

❧ NAVARRE. American, 1880–1900, machine print. 18" wide, 19" repeat. Reproduced for Navarre Hotel, Columbia, Calif. Butternut and gold on eggshell.

❧ NOUVEAU ROSE. American, 1890–1910, machine print. 18" wide, 12¹/₂" repeat. Reproduced for Byers-Evans House, Denver, Colo., a property of Colorado Historical Society. No.NRW-001 (document pink and green on mica).

❧ OGLESBY DAMASK. English or American, 1870–80, block or machine print. 22¹/₂" wide, 8³/₄" repeat. Reproduced for Governor Oglesby Mansion, Decatur, Ill. Chinese red, maroon, and gold on umber.

❧ PLAZA HOTEL WALLPAPER AND BORDER. American, 1880–1900, machine print. 18" wide plus 6" border, 12" repeat. Reproduced for Plaza Hotel Saloon, San Juan Bautista, Calif. Burnt orange and cream.

❧ POPPY. American, 1890–1910, machine print. 18¹/₈" wide, 16" repeat. Reproduced for Byers-Evans House, Denver, Colo., a property of Colorado Historical Society. Reds and greens.

❧ RENAISSANCE DAMASK. American, 1890–1900. 27" wide, 25⁵/₈" repeat. Adaptation: scaled-down version of "Whittier Damask" (see page 160). Tusk on robin's egg.

❧ ROUND TILE. American, 1880–90, machine print. 17⁵/₈" wide, 6¹/₄" repeat. Reproduced for Byers-Evans House, Denver, Colo., a property of Colorado Historical Society. Blue and umber on cream.

ᛒ SQUARE TILE. American, 1880–90, machine print. 18³/₈" wide, 6¹/₄" repeat. Reproduced for Byers-Evans House, Denver, Colo., a property of Colorado Historical Society. Blues and gray on camel.

ᛒ TEXARKANA FLORAL STRIE. American, 1890–1900, machine print. 21" wide, 18" repeat. Reproduced for Texarkana Museums and Historical Society, Texarkana, Tex. No.TFS-001 (document red, greens, and tans).

ᛒ TOTEM WALL. American, 1880–1900, machine print. 19¹/₂" wide, 12¹/₂" repeat. Reproduced for Henry Ford Museum & Greenfield Village, Dearborn, Mich. Red, olive, and robin's egg on tan.

ᛒ WHITTIER DAMASK. American, 1890–1900. 22¹/₂" wide, 31" repeat. Adapted from a wall stencil. Reproduced for Whittier Museum, San Francisco, a property of California Historical Society. Pumpkin on chestnut.

ᛒ WILD WEST. American, 1875–90, machine print. 21" wide, 18" repeat. Reproduced for Buffalo Bill Historical Center, Cody, Wyo. Browns.

ARTHUR SANDERSON & SONS

ᛒ BEAUMONT. English, 1890–1910, machine print. Originally printed by Jeffrey & Company. 20¹/₄" wide, 15¹/₂" repeat, 11 yds. per roll. Document in Sanderson Archives. Period coloring: No.WH 7378-4 (chalk on khaki).

ᛒ BUCKINGHAM. English, 1880–1900, machine print. Originally printed by Jeffrey & Company. 20¹/₄" wide, 10¹/₂" repeat, 11 yds. per roll. Document in Sanderson Archives. Period colorings: No.WR 7517-3 (sage); No.WR 7517-4 (terra cotta).

ᛒ GLOUCESTER. English, 1890–1920, block print. Originally printed by Chas. Knowles & Company. 20¹/₄" wide, 14" repeat, 11 yds. per roll. Document in Sanderson Archives. Period coloring: No.WR 7513-2 (cameo blue and coral).

ᛒ GROSVENOR. English, 1890–1910, block print. 20¹/₄" wide, 23³/₄" repeat, 11 yds. per roll. Document in Sanderson Archives. Period colorings: No.WR 7376-1 (sage on green); No.7376-5 (Medici crimson on red); No.7376-6 (satinwood on cream).

ᛒ IN MY GARDEN. English, 1870–1920, block print. Originally printed by William Woollams & Company. 20¹/₄" wide, 24" repeat, 11 yds. per roll. Adaptation. Document in Sanderson Archives. Period coloring: No.WR 7451-1 (pinks and moss green on white).

ᛒ LANSDOWNE. English, 1870–1920, block print. Originally printed by William Woollams & Company. 20¹/₄" wide, 21" repeat, 11 yds. per roll. Adaptation. Document in Sanderson Archives. Period coloring: No.WR 7346-3 (gray, azure, and blues on yellow).

ᛒ SOMERVILLE. English, 1870–1920, block print. Originally printed

above left
TEXARKANA FLORAL
STRIE, 1890–1900.
Mt. Diablo Hand-
prints.

above right
IN MY GARDEN,
1870–1920. Arthur
Sanderson & Sons.

left
WILD WEST,
1875–90. Mt. Diablo
Handprints.

by William Woollams & Company. 20¼" wide, 21" repeat, 11 yds. per roll. Adaptation. Document in Sanderson Archives. Period coloring: No.WR 7349-1 (pink, lavender, and green on white).

❧ THE TRAIL. English, 1880–90, block print. 21" wide, 14¾" repeat, 11 yds. per roll. Document in Sanderson Archives. Period colorings: No.WH 7373-1 (slate green on oyster); No.WH 7373-2 (flaxen on cream).

❧ WESTMORELAND. English, 1880–1900, block print. 20¼" wide, 21" repeat, 11 yds. per roll. Document in Sanderson Archives. Period coloring: No.WR 7518-3 (pearl).

❧ YORK. English, 1880–1900, block print. 20¼" wide, 14" repeat, 11 yds. per roll. Document in Sanderson Archives. Period coloring: No.WR 7520-3 (green baize).

SCALAMANDRE

❧ ACORN HALL DINING ROOM. American, 1890–1900, machine print with embossing. 28" wide, 18¾" repeat, 5 yds. per roll. Historic representation. Reproduced for Acorn Hall, Morristown, N.J. No.WP81068-001 (metallic gold, mustard, cream, burgundy, and black). Special order.

❧ ACORN HALL LIBRARY. English or American, 1880–90, machine print. 24" wide, 12" repeat. Historic representation. Reproduced for Acorn Hall, Morristown, N.J. No.WP81067-001 (metallic golds on burgundy). Special order.

❧ BILTMORE. American, 1880–90, machine print. Nylander, Redmond, and Sander, cover and fig. 72-a, p. 251. 21⅛" wide, 21⅛" repeat, 7 yds. per s/r. Reproduced for Biltmore, Asheville, N.C. No. WP81171. Special order.

❧ CHATEAU-SUR-MER. French, 1870–80, block print with embossing. 28½" wide, 17½" repeat, 5 yds. per s/r. Historic representation: embossing not reproduced. Reproduced for Chateau-sur-Mer, Newport, R.I., a property of Preservation Society of Newport County/ Newport Mansions. Additional sample at Cooper-Hewitt Museum. Document color, no. WP81490-999, is a special order.

❧ CAPTAIN EDWARD PENNIMAN HOUSE—CAPTAIN'S BEDROOM. American, c. 1870, machine print. 18" wide, 18" repeat, 8 yds. per s/r. Reproduced for Capt. Edward Penniman House, Eastham, Mass., a property operated by National Park Service. No.WP81385-001 (taupes, greens, and golds on warm gray). Special order.

❧ FAIRFIELD PLANTATION PAPER. English or American, 1870–80, machine print. 27" wide, 18" repeat, 5 yds. per s/r. Historic representation. Reproduced for Historic Charleston Reproductions, Charleston, S. C. No.WP81273-001 (grays and beige on pebble gray).

❧ GLENDALE—GUEST BEDROOM. American, 1890–1900, machine print with embossing. 20" wide, 12" repeat, 7 yds. per s/r. Historic

representation. Reproduced for Glendale Historical Society, Glendale, Calif. No.WP81292-001 (metallic on restoration base). Special order.

☙ GLENDALE—PARLOR/DINING ROOM. American, 1890–1900, machine print. 18¹/₈" wide, 18³/₈" repeat, 8 yds. per s/r. Reproduced for Glendale Historical Society, Glendale, Calif. No.WP81290-001 (silver and deep rose on old rose). Special order.

☙ GOODWIN PARLOR FLORAL. American or English, 1880–90, block print. 18⁵/₈" wide, 21" repeat, 8 yds. per s/r. Historic representation. Reproduced from a photograph for Wadsworth Athenaeum, Hartford, Conn. No.WP81469. Special order.

☙ GRANT KOHRS RANCH. American, 1890–1900, machine print. 18¹/₂" wide, 19⁷/₈" repeat, 8 yds. per s/r. Historic representation. Reproduced for Grant Kohrs Ranch National Historic Site, Deer Lodge, Mont. No.WP81309-001 (ivory, gray-green, metallic gold, and peach blotch). Special order.

☙ HIRSCHFELD HOUSE—DOWNSTAIRS MAIN HALL. American, 1890–1910, machine print. 18" wide, 19" repeat, 8 yds. per s/r. Reproduced for Hirschfeld House, Austin, Tex. No.WP81 192-1 (maroon and brown on beige). Special order.

☙ THE MOLLY BROWN HOUSE. American, 1890–1900, machine print. 18⁵/₈" wide, 18⁵/₈" repeat, 8 yds. per s/r. Historic representation. Re-

above left
THE TRAIL, 1880–90.
Arthur Sanderson &
Sons.

above right
GLENDALE—PARLOR/
DINING ROOM, 1890–
1900. Scalamandré.

above left
GOODWIN PARLOR
FLORAL, 1880–90.
Scalamandré.

above right
PHOENIX WALLS,
1890–1910. Scala-
mandré.

right
SAGAMORE HILL
LIBRARY FIELD PAPER,
1890–1900. Scala-
mandré.

produced for Molly Brown House, Denver Colo. No.WP81229-001 (blue, black, rust, and red on citron). Special order.

&» MONTEZUMA FLORAL. American, 1890–1900, machine print. 36" wide, 18³/₄" repeat, 4 yds. per s/r. Historic representation. Repro-duced for Villa Montezuma, San Diego, Calif. No.WP 81132-001 (creams, tan, dusty rose, plum, seafoam, and antique metallic gold blotch). Special order.

&» PARSONAGE. American, 1880–90, machine print. 18³/₄" wide, 6 ¹/₄" repeat, 8 yds. per s/r. Reproduced for the Parsonage, Peru, Vt. No.WP81414. Special order.

&» PHOENIX TILE. American, 1890–1910, machine print. 27" wide, 6" repeat, 5 yds. per s/r. Reproduced for Rosson House, Phoenix, Ariz. No.WP81152 (blue and white). Special order.

&» PHOENIX WALLS. American, 1890–1910, machine print. 20¹/₂" wide, 22¹/₈" repeat, 7 yds. per s/r. Historic representation. Repro-duced for Rosson House, Phoenix, Ariz. No.WP81150-001 (greens, aqua, turquoise, chamois, wine, and black on horse-carriage brown). Special order.

&» ROSSON DINING ROOM. American, 1890–1910, machine print. 36" wide, 15¹/₂" repeat, 4 yds. per s/r. Historic representation. Repro-duced for Rosson House, Phoenix, Ariz. No.WP81151-001 (gray, chamois, metallic gold, and taupe). Special order.

&» ROSSON NURSERY. American, 1890–1900, machine print. 25" wide, 15¹/₂" repeat, 6 yds. per s/r. Historic representation. Reproduced for Rosson House, Phoenix, Ariz. No.WP81185 (pink and blue on beige). Special order.

&» ROSSON TILE. American, 1890–1910, machine print. 25" wide, 6¹/₈" repeat, 6 yds. per s/r. Historic representation. Reproduced for Rosson House, Phoenix, Ariz. No.WP81155-001 (blues, greige, and white on ivory).

&» ROSSON WALLS. American, 1890–1910, machine print. 48" wide, 7³/₄" repeat, 3 yds. per s/r. Reproduced for Rosson House, Phoenix, Ariz. No.WP81163-001 (pinks, peach, celery, rose, silver, and dusty rose).

&» SAGAMORE HILL LIBRARY FIELD PAPER. American, 1890–1900, ma-chine embossed. 27" wide, 18¹/₄" repeat, 8 yds. per s/r. Historic rep-resentation. Reproduced for Sagamore Hill, Oyster Bay, N.Y. No.WP81259-001 (browns, grays, olive, metallic gold, and copper blotch). Special order.

&» THOMAS WOLFE MEMORIAL DINING ROOM. American, 1890–1910, machine print. 24¹/₂" wide, 15⁷/₈" repeat, 6 yds. per s/r. Reproduced for Thomas Wolfe Memorial, Asheville, N.C. No.WP81197-001 (light green, off-white, beige, silver, plum, and deep maroon). Spe-cial order.

&» THOMAS WOLFE MEMORIAL HALL WALLS. American, 1890–1910,

above left
WETMORE LEAVES,
1875–90.
Scalamandré.

above right
Original document
for "Ogden's Floral,"
a wallpaper of 1890–
1900 reproduced by
Schumacher.

machine print. 27¹/₂" wide, 15³/₄" repeat, 6 yds. per s/r. Reproduced for Thomas Wolfe Memorial, Asheville, N.C. No.WP81198-001 (gold, olive, and silver).

❧ WETMORE LEAVES. English, 1875–80, block print. Lynn, color pl. 86, p. 349. 21³/₄" wide, 21" repeat, 7 yds. per s/r. Historic representation. Reproduced for Chateau-sur-Mer, Newport, R.I., a property operated by Preservation Society of Newport County/Newport Mansions. No.WP81495. Special order.

SCHUMACHER

❧ CHINTZ. English, 1870–90, block print. Sugden and Edmundson, p. 105; Wells-Cole, no. 15, p. 18. 30" wide, 33" repeat, 11 yds. per s/r. Document at Temple Newsam, Leeds, England. No.TN01 (multi on tan).

❧ CONSTANTINE. French, 1870–90, block or machine print. 27" wide, 13" repeat, 4¹/₂ yds. per s/r. Adaptation: pattern enlarged. Document in Hobe Erwin Collection, Schumacher Archive. No.508405 (delft).

❧ CONTINENTAL DAMASK. English or French, 1880–1900, block or machine print. 20¹/₂" wide, 18³/₄" repeat, 5¹/₂ yds. per s/r. Document in Hobe Erwin Collection, Schumacher Archive. No.506210 (birch).

❧ ESTATE VINE. American, 1890–1900, machine print. 27" wide, 25¹/₂" half-drop repeat, 4¹/₂ yds. per s/r. Document in Hobe Erwin Collection, Schumacher Archive. No.508520 (document teal).

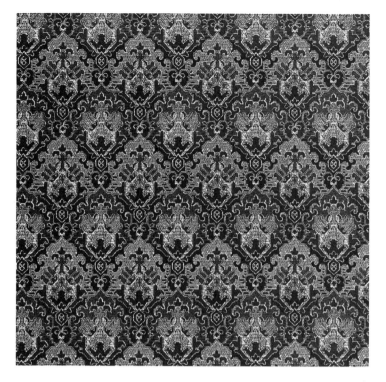

left
NEW HARMONY,
1893–1910.
Richard E. Thibaut.

୬ OGDEN'S FLORAL. American, 1890–1900, machine print. 27" wide, 25¼" repeat, 4½ yds. per s/r. Document in Schumacher Archive. No.512850 (document tan).

୬ STORKS AND THRUSHES. English, 1875–90, block print. Sugden and Edmundson, pl. 65, p. 104; Wells-Cole, no. 14, pp. 16–17. 30" wide, 36" repeat, 11 yds. per roll. Document at Temple Newsam, Leeds, England. No.TN07 (blue on ivory).

RICHARD E. THIBAUT

୬ ALLEN ROSE. American, 1880–1900, machine print. 28" wide, 22" repeat, 4½ yds. per s/r. Adaptation: number of colors reduced from 16 to 10; width of pattern increased. Historic Homes of America Collection, produced in collaboration with National Preservation Institute. Document at Candace Allen House, Providence, R.I. No.839-T6523 (multi on white).

୬ LEESBURG. American, 1890–1920, machine print. 27" wide, 12⅝" repeat, 4½ yds. per s/r. Historic Homes of America Collection, produced in collaboration with National Preservation Institute. Document at Carrier House, Leesburg, Va. No.839-T-7968 (yellow and blue).

୬ NEW HARMONY. American, 1893–1910, machine print. 28" wide, 7⅜" repeat, 4½ yds. per s/r. Historic Homes of America Collection, produced in collaboration with National Preservation Institute. Doc-

ORIENTAL GARDEN,
1880–90. Richard E.
Thibaut.

ument at Schnee-Eliot House, New Harmony, Ind. No.839-T-7972
(red and ochre). Period coloring: No.839-T-7974 (blue and rust).

➷ ORIENTAL GARDEN. American, 1880–90, machine print. 27" wide,
19" repeat, 4¹/₂ yds. per s/r. Historic Homes of America Collection,
produced in collaboration with National Preservation Institute. Document at Prater's Jewelry Store, Humbolt, Neb. No.839-T-7929 (tan
and olive).

➷ THE HERMITAGE. American, 1890–1915, machine print. 27" wide,
13¹/₂" repeat, 4¹/₂ yds. per s/r. Historic Homes of America Collection, produced in collaboration with National Preservation Institute.
Document at Hermitage, Ho-Ho-Kus, N.Y. No.839-T-7992 (tan, gold,
and burnt orange).

➷ THE WILLOWS. American, 1890–1910, machine print. 27" wide,
19" repeat, 4¹/₂ yds. per s/r. Historic Homes of America Collection,
produced in collaboration with National Preservation Institute. Document at the Willows, Morristown, N.J. No.839-T-7964 (copper). Period colorings: No.839-T-7965 (burgundy); No.839-T-7966 (silver);
No.839-T-7967 (rose).

VICTORIAN COLLECTIBLES LIMITED

All documents are in the Brillion Collection. Samples from the same
collection are at the Cooper-Hewitt Museum. Selected samples are
also at the Victoria and Albert Museum.

❧ VICTORIAN STRIPE. American, 1890–1910, machine print. 27" wide, 2" repeat, 5 yds. per s/r. No.45-001 (green, ivory, and silver on putty).

WATERHOUSE WALLHANGINGS

❧ BROAD MEADOWS. English or American, 1880–90, machine print. 21" wide, 14" repeat, 7 yds. per s/r. Document in Waterhouse Archives. No.212548 (light and dark green on cream).

❧ BRODSWORTH. English or American, 1880–1910, machine print. 27" wide, 30" repeat, 5 yds. per s/r. Document in Waterhouse Archives. No.187540 (red on red).

❧ CHINESE POPPY. English, 1870–80, machine print. 18½" wide, 18½" repeat, 7 yds. per s/r. Document in Waterhouse Archives. Document color, red on beige, is a special order.

❧ FLOWERS AND FRUIT. American, 1880–1920, machine print. 18" wide, 15¾" repeat, 7 yds. per s/r. Document in Waterhouse Archives. No.205540 (red on red). Period colorings: No.205431 (white on pale green); No.205252 (white on yellow); No.205467 (beige on white).

❧ MOSES-KENT HOUSE. English, 1870–1900, block print. 27" wide, 20" repeat, 5 yds. per s/r. Adaptation: original printed on burlap. Document privately owned. Document color, green, is a special order.

❧ NORWICH. American, 1880–1920, block print. 27" wide, 23" repeat, 5 yds. per s/r. Reproduced for Longfellow National Historic Site, Cambridge, Mass. No.201449 (mustard on yellow).

❧ PILLEMENT. French, 1890–1910, block print. 28" wide, 44" repeat, 5 yds. per s/r. Reproduces an 18th-century design. Document in Waterhouse Archives. No.100635 (multi on white).

❧ QUINCY LACE. English or American, 1890–1900, machine print. 20½" wide, 18" repeat, 7 yds. per s/r. Document in Waterhouse Archives. No.180163 (yellow). Period colorings (series).

❧ WAYSIDE FLORAL. American, 1870–90, machine print. 25" wide, 15¾" repeat, 5 yds. per s/r. Document at the Wayside, Concord, Mass., a property operated by Minute Man National Historical Park. No.142635 (white on beige).

ZINA STUDIOS

Order by pattern name.

❧ KINGSCOTE LEAVES. American, 1890–1910, machine print. 18" wide, 19⅛" repeat. Reproduced for Kingscote, Newport, R.I., a property of Preservation Society of Newport County/Newport Mansions. Blues.

❧ ROSE TRELLIS. English, 1890–1910, block print. 18⅝" wide, 21½" drop repeat. Reproduced for Kingscote, Newport, R.I., a property of Preservation Society of Newport County/Newport Mansions. Pinks, green, and gray on beige.

right
NORWICH,
1880–1920. Water-
house Wallhangings.

bottom left
WAYSIDE FLORAL,
1870–90. Water-
house Wallhangings.

bottom right
KINGSCOTE LEAVES,
1890–1910. Zina
Studios.

Coordinating wallpaper patterns include two or more designs that were intended to be used together. The sidewall is called the fill and the top border is called the frieze. Patterns are grouped in the following combinations under each manufacturer: roomsets; fills, friezes, dados, and borders; fills, friezes, and ceiling papers; and fills and friezes.

BRADBURY & BRADBURY

Bradbury & Bradbury roomsets include coordinated fills, friezes, dados, borders, and ceiling patterns. Elements may be purchased separately.

Aesthetic Movement Roomset

CHERRY BLOSSOM. English, 1878, block print. Designed by Lewis F. Day. 27" wide, 13^1/$_2$" repeat, 5 yds. per s/r. Code CBW (4 period colorings).

EMELITA'S FRIEZE. American, 1880–90, machine print. 15^1/$_2$" wide plus 3" borders, 21^1/$_2$" repeat. Code EMF (4 period colorings).

ICE BLOSSOM CEILING. American, 1870–90, machine print. 27" wide, 27" repeat, 5 yds. per s/r. Code ICC (4 period colorings).

ORIENTAL BROCADE PANEL. American, 1870–90. 28^1/$_2$" wide, 27" high. Adapted from a stencil design. Code OBP (2 period colorings).

COORDINATING WALLPAPER PATTERNS

EMELITA'S FRIEZE, 1880–90, from Aesthetic Movement Roomset. Bradbury & Bradbury.

Detail from Anglo-Japanese Roomset ceiling, 1870–80. Bradbury & Bradbury.

ICE BLOSSOM CEILING, 1870–90, from Aesthetic Movement Roomset. Bradbury & Bradbury.

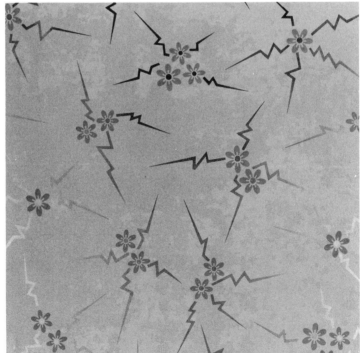

❧ PENELOPE BORDER. American Victorian Revival, 1980. Designed by Burt Kallander. 6″ wide, 9″ repeat. Code PEB (4 period colorings).

❧ PENELOPE CORNER BLOCK. American, 1870–90. 20″ by 24″. Adapted from a stencil design. Code PET (4 period colorings).

❧ WESTWIND ENRICHMENT. American, 1870–90, machine print. 27″ wide, 6¾″ repeat. Code WWE (8 period colorings).

Anglo-Japanese Roomset

❧ CLAIRE'S WILLOW. English, 1870–80. 27″ wide, 13½″ repeat, 5 yds. per s/r. Adaptation of a Morris background. Code CWW (13 period colorings).

❧ EASTLAKE COMBINATION ORNAMENT. American, 1870–80. 6″ wide, 9″ repeat. Adapted from an anonymous published design. Code ECB (5 period colorings).

❧ EASTLAKE DADO. English, 1870–80, machine print. Designed by Christopher Dresser. 26″ wide, 3″ repeat. Adapted from a published design. Reproduced for Camron-Stanford House, Oakland, Calif. Code ELD (5 period colorings).

❧ EASTLAKE FRIEZE. English, 1870–80, machine print. Based on a design by Christopher Dresser. Greysmith, fig. 105, p. 146; Lynn, color pl. 92, p. 435. 18″ plus borders, 12″ repeat. Adaptation. Reproduced for Camron-Stanford House, Oakland, Calif. Document at Cooper-Hewitt Museum. Code ELF (5 period colorings).

❧ IVY BLOCK ENRICHMENT. American Victorian Revival, 1980. Designed by S. J. Bauer. 27″ wide, 3″ repeat. Code IBE (5 period colorings).

❧ JAPANESE LATTICE. English, 1878, block print. 27″ wide, 2½″ repeat, 5 yds. per s/r. Code JLW (4 period colorings).

❧ SUNBURST CEILING. American, 1880–1900, machine print. 27″ wide, 9″ repeat, 5 yds. per s/r. Code SBC (5 period colorings).

❧ SUNFLOWER CORNER BLOCK. American Victorian Revival, 1980. Designed by S. J. Bauer. 21″ wide, 21″ high. Code SFT (5 period colorings).

❧ SUNFLOWER PANEL. American Victorian Revival, 1980. Designed by S. J. Bauer. 18″ wide, 36″ high. Code SFP (2 period colorings).

❧ SUNFLOWER ROSETTE. American Victorian Revival, 1980. Designed by S. J. Bauer. 18″ diamater. Code SFR (3 period colorings).

❧ VALENCIA PANEL. American Victorian Revival, 1980. Designed by S. J. Bauer. Panel size: 27″ wide, 12″ high. Code VLP (4 period colorings).

In the Dresser Tradition I

❧ ALGERNON. American Victorian Revival, 1980. Designed by Burt Kallander. 27″ wide, 13½″ repeat, 5 yds per s/r. Code AGW (4 period colorings).

❧ BACHELOR'S BUTTON. English, 1862. Designed by Christopher

Dresser. 27″ wide, 7¹/₂″ repeat, 5 yds. per s/r. Adapted from a published design. Code BBW (4 period colorings).

❧ DRESSER CEILING. English, 1875. Designed by Christopher Dresser. Adapted from a published design. 27″ wide, 8″ repeat, 5 yds. per s/r. Code DSC (4 period colorings).

❧ FALLON BORDER. American, 1880–90, machine print. 10¹/₂″ wide, 27″ repeat. Code FAB (4 period colorings).

❧ FALLON CORNER BLOCK. American, 1880–90, machine print. 18¹/₄″ wide, 18¹/₄″ high. Code FAT (4 period colorings).

❧ PINSTRIPE BORDER. English, 1870–80. Designed by Christopher Dresser. 1″ or 3″ wide, depending on how it is cut. Code PNB (5 period colorings).

❧ PINSTRIPE CORNER TURN. English, 1870–80. Designed by Christopher Dresser. 5¹/₂″ wide, 5¹/₂″ high. Adapted from a published design. Code PNT (4 period colorings).

❧ QUENTIN BORDER. English, 1870–80. Designed by Christopher Dresser. 6³/₄″ wide, 3¹/₂″ repeat. Adapted from a published design. Code QUB (4 period colorings).

❧ RANDOM STAR CEILING. English, 1870–80. Designed by Christopher Dresser. 27″ wide, 27″ repeat, 5 yds. per s/r. Adapted from a published design. Code RSC (light blue or midnight blue).

❧ STAR TRELLIS ENRICHMENT. English, 1870–80. Designed by Owen Jones. 27″ wide, 2¹/₄″ repeat. Adapted from a published design. Code STE (9 period colorings).

❧ WATKINS GLEN FRIEZE. English or American, 1875–90, machine print. Based on a design by Christopher Dresser. 18″ wide, 18¹/₄″ repeat. Code WGF (4 period colorings).

In the Dresser Tradition II

❧ LILY. American, 1875–80. *In Pursuit of Beauty*, fig. 3.2, p. 70. 27″ wide, 10³/₄″ repeat, 5 yds. per s/r. Adaptation of a sketch for a wall treatment by P. B. Wight. Document at Burnham Architectural Library, Chicago. Code LYW (4 period colorings).

❧ PINSTRIPE BORDER (see above).

❧ PINSTRIPE CORNER TURN (see above).

❧ PLAZA CEILING. American, 1880–1900, machine print. 27″ wide, 9″ repeat. 5 yds. per s/r. Reproduced for Plaza Hotel Saloon, San Juan Bautista, Calif. Code PLC (4 period colorings).

❧ RANDOM STAR CEILING (see above).

❧ ROLAND. English, 1875. Designed by Christopher Dresser. 27″ wide, 10³/₄″ repeat, 5 yds. per s/r. Adapted from a published design. Code RLW (4 period colorings).

❧ VICTORY FRIEZE. English, 1875–90. Designed by Christopher Dresser. 18″ wide, 26″ repeat. Adapted from a published design. Code VIF (4 period colorings).

❧ WESTWIND ENRICHMENT (see page 173).

Fenway Roomset

❧ FIDDLEHEAD DADO. American Victorian Revival, 1980. Designed by Carmen Reid. 27" wide, 9" repeat. Code FHD (4 period colorings).

❧ GOSSAMER CEILING. American Victorian Revival, 1980. Designed by S. J. Bauer. 27" wide, 27" repeat, 5 yds. per s/r. Code GSC (5 period colorings).

❧ IRIS FRIEZE. English, 1876, block print. Designed by Walter Crane. 18" wide plus one 6" and one 3" border, 9" repeat. Adaptation. Code IRF (4 period colorings).

❧ MOTH BORDER. American Victorian Revival, 1980. Designed by S. J. Bauer. 4" wide, 6³/₄" repeat. Code MOB (3 period colorings).

❧ NEPTUNE. American Victorian Revival, c. 1980. 27" wide, 13¹/₂" repeat, 5 yds. per s/r. Code NPW (4 period colorings).

❧ RAINDROP ENRICHMENT. American Victorian Revival, 1980. Designed by S. J. Bauer. 27" wide, 1¹/₂" repeat. Code RDE (4 period colorings).

❧ SERPENTINE. Adapted from traditional Japanese wood block. 27" wide, 6³/₄" repeat, 5 yds. per s/r. Code SPW (4 period colorings).

❧ SPIRAL CORNER BLOCK. American Victorian Revival, 1980. Designed by S. J. Bauer. Each block 6" by 6". Code SPT (3 period colorings).

above left

LILY, 1875–80, from Dresser Tradition II Roomset. Bradbury & Bradbury.

above right

VICTORY FRIEZE, 1875–90, from Dresser Tradition II Roomset. Bradbury & Bradbury.

In the Morris Tradition

• ACANTHUS BORDER. English, 1875–90. 9" wide, 13½" repeat. Adapted from stencil designs by Morris & Company. Code ACB (5 period colorings).

• ASTER CORNER BLOCK. American Victorian Revival, 1980. Designed by S. J. Bauer. Each block 3" by 3". Code AST (4 period colorings).

• BIRD AND ANEMONE (see page 202 under Wallpapers by William Morris and Morris & Company).

• CHEQUERBOARD. American Victorian Revival, 1980. Designed by S. J. Bauer. 27" wide, 3" repeat, 5 yds. per s/r. Code CQW (4 period colorings).

• CHEVRON BORDER. English or American, 1875–90, block print. 1" wide, 3" repeat. Code CVB (2 period colorings).

• CLAIRE'S WILLOW (see page 173).

• CLEMENTINA. English, 1883, block print. Adapted from William Morris's "Christchurch." 27" wide, 13½" repeat, 5 yds. per s/r. Code CLW (4 period colorings).

• KELMSCOTT FRIEZE. English, 1875–90. 18" wide, 27" repeat. Adapted from stencil designs by Morris & Company. Code KSF (5 period colorings).

• KENSINGTON CEILING. American Victorian Revival, 1980. Designed by S. J. Bauer. 27" wide, 13½" repeat, 5 yds. per s/r. Code KNC (5 period colorings).

• LEAF BORDER. English, 1875–90. 3" wide, 6¾" repeat. Adapted from stencil designs by Morris & Company. Code LEB (3 period colorings).

• MARIGOLD (see page 204 under Wallpapers by William Morris and Morris & Company).

• POMEGRANATE PANELS. American Victorian Revival, 1980. Designed by S. J. Bauer. 27" wide, 27" repeat. Code PGP (5 period colorings).

• RASPBERRY BRAMBLE. American Victorian Revival, 1980. Designed by Bruce Bradbury. 27" wide, 17" repeat, 5 yds. per s/r. Code RBW (4 period colorings).

• ROSE CORNER BLOCK. American Victorian Revival, 1980. Designed by S. J. Bauer. Each block 9" by 9". Code RST (3 period colorings).

• WALDEN. English, 1875–90. Adapted from a design by William Morris. 27" wide, 13½" repeat, 5 yds. per s/r. Code WAW (5 period colorings).

• WILLOW (see page 205 under Wallpapers by William Morris and Morris & Company).

Neo-Grec Roomset

• ANTHEMION WALL FILL. English, 1880–90. Designed by George and Maurice Ashdown Audsley. 27" wide, 9" repeat, 5 yds. per s/r. Adapted from a published design. Code AFW (5 period colorings).

BAYBERRY FRET BORDER. English, 1880–90. Designed by Owen Jones. 5¹/₂" wide, 8" repeat. Adapted from a published design. Pattern Code BFB (5 period colorings).

CHAIN BORDER. American Victorian Revival, 1980. Designed by S. J. Bauer. 1" wide, 2¹/₄" repeat. Code CHB (4 period colorings).

LAUREL BORDER. English, 1880–90. Designed by Owen Jones. 3" wide, 2¹/₄" repeat. Adapted from a published design. Code LRB (4 period colorings).

NEO-GREC CORNER BLOCK. English, 1880–90. Designed by George and Maurice Ashdown Audsley. 8" wide, 8" high. Adapted from a published design. Code NGC (5 period colorings).

NEO-GREC CORNER FAN. English, 1880–90. Designed by George and Maurice Ashdown Audsley. 24" wide, 24" high. Adapted from a published design. Code NGT (5 period colorings).

NEO-GREC MAIDENS. English, 1880–90. Designed by Walter Crane. Each block 18" by 18". Adapted from a published design. Code NGM (5 period colorings).

NEO-GREC DADO. English, 1880–90. Designed by George and Maurice Ashdown Audsley, 27" wide, 13¹/₂" repeat. Adapted from a published design. Code NGD (5 period colorings).

NEO-GREC FRET BORDER. English, 1880–90. Designed by George and Maurice Ashdown Audsley. 9" wide, 4" repeat. Adapted from a published design. Code NGB (5 period colorings).

NEO-GREC FRIEZE. English, 1880–90. Designed by George and Maurice Ashdown Audsley. 14" wide plus 4" border, 13¹/₂" repeat. Adapted from a published design. Code NGF (5 period colorings).

Detail from Neo-Grec Roomset ceiling, 1880–90. Bradbury & Bradbury.

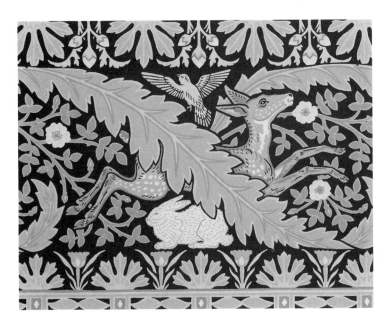

DEER AND RABBIT
FRIEZE, 1887, from
Woodland Roomset.
Bradbury & Bradbury.

๑ STAR TRELLIS ENRICHMENT (see page 174).

๑ SWYRE CROSS CEILING. English, 1880–90. Designed by Bruce Talbert. 27" wide, 2" repeat. 5 yds. per s/r. Adapted from a published design. Code SWC (5 period colorings).

๑ WAVE BORDER. English, 1870–80. Designed by Owen Jones. 3" wide, 3½" repeat. Adapted from a published design. Code WVB (4 period colorings).

Woodland Roomset

๑ ASTER BORDER. English or American, 1880–90, block print. 3" wide, 9" repeat. Code ASB (4 period colorings).

๑ ASTER CORNER BLOCK (see page 176).

๑ BLOSSOM AND BLOCK. American Victorian Revival, 1980. Designed by S. J. Bauer. 27" wide, 6¾" repeat, 5 yds. per s/r. Code BKW (4 period colorings).

๑ CRAB APPLE. American Victorian Revival, 1980. Designed by S. J. Bauer. 27" wide, 13½" repeat, 5 yds. per s/r. Code SRW (4 period colorings).

๑ DAISY CORNER BLOCK. American Victorian Revival, 1980. Each block 6" by 6". Code DST (3 period colorings).

๑ DEER AND RABBIT FRIEZE. English, 1887. Designed by Walter Crane; originally printed by Jeffrey & Company. 18" plus 6" border, 19" repeat. Minor changes in design. Document at Victoria and Albert Museum. Code DRF (4 period colorings).

๑ MORRIS CEILING (see page 201 under Wallpapers by William Morris and Morris & Company).

๑ ROSE BORDER. English, 1880–90. Designed by George and Maurice Ashdown Audsley. 6" wide, 13" repeat. Adapted from a stencil design. Code ROB (4 period colorings).

❧ SWEET BRIAR (see page 246 under Wallpapers by William Morris and Morris & Company).

❧ WOODLAND BORDER. 1880–1900, block print. 6" wide, 6½" repeat. Code WOB (4 period colorings).

Additional Patterns

The following group includes a fill, a frieze, and a ceiling pattern.

❧ SEASHELL WALL. American, 1880–1900, machine print. 27" wide, 27" one third–drop repeat, 5 yds. per s/r. Code SHW. Special order.

❧ SEASHELL FRIEZE. American, 1880–1900, machine print. 18" wide plus 7½" border, 19" repeat. Code SHF. Special order.

❧ STARFISH CEILING. American, 1880–1900, machine print. 27" wide, 27" repeat, 5 yds. per s/r. Code SFC. Special order.

CLASSIC REVIVALS

Authentic Interiors Collection

The following group includes a fill, a frieze, a dado, and a border.

❧ ARCADIA FILL. English, 1880–90, machine print. 21" wide, 18" repeat, 11 yds. per s/r. Archival Collection. No.W-191-5A (yellow and brown).

❧ ROSAL FRIEZE. English, 1880–90, machine print. 5" wide, 16½" repeat. Archival Collection. No.F-194-6A (yellow and brown).

❧ MANWEL BORDER. English, 1880–90, machine print. 5" wide, 12" repeat. Archival Collection. No.B-192-6A (yellow and brown).

❧ JASMIN DADO. English, 1880–90, machine print. 24" wide, 20½" repeat. Archival Collection. No.D-193-6A (yellow and brown).

The following group includes a fill, a frieze, and a dado.

❧ KLARA FILL. English, 1870–80, machine print. Murphy, no. 12, p. 16. 20¾" wide, 22¾" repeat, 11 yds. per roll. Price Collection. No.W-180-1A (deep olive).

❧ BAGHA FRIEZE. English, 1870–80, machine print. Murphy, no. 12, p. 16. 6¾" wide, 20¾" repeat. Price Collection. No.F-179-5A (deep olive).

❧ BENARES DADO. English, 1870–80, machine print. 26" wide, 21" repeat, 11 yds. per roll. Price Collection. No.D-178-5A (deep olive).

The following group includes a fill and a frieze.

❧ OWEN FILL. English, 1880–90, machine print. Murphy, no. 18, p. 22. 21" wide, 15" repeat, 11 yds. per roll. Price Collection. No.W-166-1A (tan).

❧ ISIS FRIEZE. English, 1880–90, machine print. Murphy, no. 18, p. 22. 7" wide, 15" repeat. Price Collection. No.F-167-2A (tan).

St. James Collection

The following group includes a fill, a frieze, a dado, and a border.

❧ CHRYSANTHEMUM DADO. English, 1892, machine print. Originally

KLARA FILL, BAGHA
FRIEZE, and BENARES
DADO, 1870–80.
Classic Revivals
(Authentic Interiors
Collection).

printed by Allan, Cockshut and Company. 21" wide, 16½" repeat, 11 yds. per roll. No.CD5 (gray buff); No.CD6 (olive); No.CD9 (citron); No.CD10 (sienna); No.CD12 (pink olive); No.CD16 (drab olive); No.CD18 (slate); No.CD23 (acid green); No.CD26 (khaki); No.CD27 (vivid green).

❧ CHRYSANTHEMUM DADO BORDER. English, 1892, machine print. Originally printed by Allan, Cockshut and Company. 5¼" wide, 10 ½" repeat. No.CB5 (gray buff); No.CB6 (olive); No.CB9 (citron); No.CB10 (sienna); No.CB12 (pink olive); No.CB16 (drab olive); No.CB18 (slate); No.CB23 (acid green); No.CB26 (khaki); No.CB27 (vivid green).

❧ CHRYSANTHEMUM FILLER. English, 1892, machine print. Originally printed by Allan, Cockshut and Company. 28" wide, 21" repeat, 11 yds. per roll. No.CF6 (olive); No.CF12 (pink olive); No.CF18 (slate); No.CF27 (vivid green); No.CF28 (ginger).

❧ CHRYSANTHEMUM FRIEZE. English, 1892, machine print. Originally printed by Allan, Cockshut and Company. 10¾" wide, 12" repeat. No.CZ1 (sage); No.CZ5 (gray buff); No.CZ6 (olive); No.CZ8 (teal); No.CZ10 (sienna); No.CZ11 (rose); No.CZ12 (pink olive); No.CZ16 (drab olive); No.CZ18 (slate); No.CZ23 (acid green); No.CZ26 (khaki).

The following group includes fills and friezes.

❧ BURWOOD FILLER. English, 1892, machine print. Originally printed by Allan, Cockshut and Company. 21" wide, 16" repeat, 11 yds. per roll. No.BF1 (sage); No.BF11 (rose); No.BF13 (turquoise); No.BF14 (old gold); No.BF19 (burnt sienna).

❧ BURWOOD FRIEZE. English, 1892, machine print. Originally printed by Allan, Cockshut and Company. 10" wide, 21" repeat. No.BZ1 (sage); No.BZ11 (rose); No.BZ13 (turquoise); No.BZ14 (old gold); No.BZ19 (burnt sienna).

❧ POMEGRANATE FILLER. English, 1892, machine print. Originally printed by Allan, Cockshut and Company. 28" wide, 18" repeat, 11 yds. per roll. No.GF1 (sage); No.GF7 (pink); No.GF27 (vivid green); No.GF28 (ginger).

❧ POMEGRANATE FRIEZE. English, 1892, machine print. Originally printed by Allan, Cockshut and Company. 10" wide. No.GZ1 (sage); No.GZ7 (pink); No.GZ9 (citron).

❧ POPPY FILLER. English, 1892, machine print. Originally printed by Allan, Cockshut and Company. 28" wide, 18" repeat, 11 yds. per roll. No.PF2 (olive rust); No.PF3 (pink blue); No.PF4 (deep red); No.PF14 (old gold); No.PF18 (slate).

❧ POPPY FRIEZE. English, 1892, machine print. Originally printed by Allan, Cockshut and Company. 16½" wide. No.PZ2 (olive rust); No.PZ3 (pink blue); No.PZ4 (deep red); No.PZ5 (gray buff); No.PZ28 (ginger).

CHRYSANTHEMUM
FRIEZE, with filler,
dado border and
dado, 1892. Classic
Revivals (St. James
Collection).

POPPY FRIEZE, 1892.
Classic Revivals
(St. James Collection).

POMEGRANATE FRIEZE,
1892. Classic Revivals
(St. James Collection).

MT. DIABLO HANDPRINTS

Order by name unless a pattern number is listed. The following group includes a fill, a frieze, a dado, and two borders.

➳ MARSH CREEK WALL. English, 1870–80, block or machine print. 21" wide, 18" repeat. Reproduced for Raheen, Kew, Victoria, Australia. No.MCW-001 (document blues, greens, and gold).

➳ MARSH CREEK KINGFISHER DADO/ FRIEZE. English, 1870–80, block or machine print. 28" wide, 24" repeat. Reproduced for Raheen, Kew, Victoria, Australia. No.MCK-001 (document blues, greens, pink, and gold).

➳ MARSH CREEK FISH DADO. English, 1870–80, block or machine print. 10³/₄" wide, 22³/₄" repeat. Reproduced for Raheen, Kew, Victoria, Australia. No.MCF-001 (document greens, khaki, and gold).

➳ MARSH CREEK FLORAL BORDER. English, 1870–80, block or machine print. 5¹/₄" wide, 10³/₄" repeat. Reproduced for Raheen, Kew, Victoria, Australia. No.MCD-001 (document greens, yellow, and red).

➳ MARSH CREEK LILY PAD BORDER. English, 1870–80, block or machine print. 3³/₄" wide, 21" repeat. Reproduced for Raheen, Kew, Victoria, Australia. No.MCL-001 (document greens, blues, and ochre). The following group includes fills and friezes.

➳ BARNUM WALL. American, c. 1893, machine print. 18" wide, 7⁷/₈" repeat. Reproduced for Barnum Museum, Bridgeport, Conn. Reds, green, and tans.

➳ BARNUM FRIEZE. American, c. 1893, machine print. 18" wide, 12" repeat. Reproduced for Barnum Museum, Bridgeport, Conn. Reds, green, and tans.

❧ BILLINGS PARLOR WALL. American, 1890–1900, machine print. 18" wide, 12½" repeat. Reproduced for Billings Farm & Museum, Woodstock, Vt. Rose, burgundy, and gold on tan.

❧ BILLINGS PARLOR FRIEZE. American, 1890–1900, machine print. 9½" wide, 12½" repeat. Reproduced for Billings Farm & Museum, Woodstock, Vt. Rose, burgundy, and gold on tan.

❧ ETRUSCAN MOSAIC. American, 1880–1900, machine print. 18" wide, 18¾" repeat. Reproduced for Fallon Hotel, Columbia, Calif., a property operated by California Department of Parks and Recreation. Copper, metallic blue, umber, and gray-green on deep ochre.

❧ ETRUSCAN MOSAIC FRIEZE. American, 1880–1900, machine print. 21¼" wide, 18¾" repeat. Reproduced for Fallon Hotel, Columbia, Calif., a property operated by California Department of Parks and Recreation. Copper, metallic blue, umber, and gray-green on deep ochre.

❧ FALLON FLORAL WALL. American, 1880–1900, machine print. 18½" wide, 15½" repeat. Reproduced for Fallon Hotel, Columbia, Calif., a property operated by California Department of Parks and Recreation. Gold and mica on cream.

❧ FALLON FLORAL FRIEZE. American, 1880–1900, machine print. 18½" wide, 15¾" repeat. Reproduced for Fallon Hotel, Columbia, Calif., a property operated by California Department of Parks and Recreation. Gold and mica on cream.

❧ KLINE CREEK FARM WALL. American, c. 1889, machine print. 18⅞" wide, 12½" repeat. Reproduced for Kline Creek Farmhouse, Dupage, Ill. Mica, gold, and lavender on cream.

❧ KLINE CREEK FARM BORDER. American, c. 1889, machine print. 9¾" wide, 12½" repeat. Reproduced for Kline Creek Farmhouse, Dupage, Ill. Mica, gold, and lavender on cream.

VICTORIAN COLLECTIBLES LIMITED

All documents are in the Brillion Collection. Samples from the same collection are at the Cooper-Hewitt Museum, and selected samples are at the Victoria and Albert Museum. The following groups include a fill, a frieze, and a ceiling paper. Some of the ceiling patterns are interchangeable.

❧ DAYLE. American, 1890–1910, machine print. Originally printed by Standard Wall Paper Company. 27" wide, 18¾" repeat, 5 yds. per s/r. No.21-001 (burgundy, gold, and bisque on butternut).

❧ DAYLE BORDER. American, 1890–1910, machine print. 9" wide, 15¾" repeat. No.21-061 (burgundy, gold, and bisque on butternut).

❧ DAYLE CEILING. American, 1890–1910, machine print. 24" wide,

MARSH CREEK WALL,
with borders, frieze,
and dado, 1870–80.
Mt. Diablo Hand-
prints.

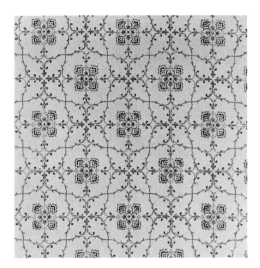

above left

DAYLE CEILING,
1890–1910. Victorian
Collectibles Limited.

above right

MARY DAILEY CROOK
and border,
1890–1910. Victorian
Collectibles Limited.

12¹/₂" repeat, 5 yds. per s/r. No.21-031 (blue and gold on amber crackle).

᪐ HERALDIC. American, 1890–1910, machine print. Originally printed by Standard Wall Paper Company. 18" wide, 15¹/₂" repeat, 5 yds. per s/r. No.40-001 (burgundy, rose, green, and golds on brown). Period coloring: No.40-003 (black, brown, terra cotta, gold, and copper on beige weave).

᪐ HERALDIC BORDER. American, 1890–1910, machine print. 18" wide, 18" repeat. No.40-051 (burgundy, rose, green, and golds on brown). Period coloring: No.40-053 (black, brown, terra cotta, gold, and copper on beige weave).

᪐ HERALDIC BORDER (narrow). American, 1890–1910, machine print. 9" wide, 8" repeat. Half-scale adaptation of preceding pattern. No.40-061 (burgundy, rose, green, and golds on brown). Period coloring: No.40-063 (black, brown, terra cotta, gold, and copper on beige weave).

᪐ HERALDIC CEILING. American, 1890–1910, machine print. 24" wide, 18" repeat, 5 yds. per s/r. No.40-031 (golds and brown on burgundy). Period colorings: No.40-032 (golds and brown on ivory); No.40-033 (green and golds on off-white).

᪐ MARY DAILEY CROOK. American, 1890–1910, machine print. 24" wide, 15¹/₂" repeat, 5 yds. per s/r. No.25-001 (mauve, green, ivory, and navy on Victorian blue). Period colorings: No.25-002 (rose, gold, and cream on pink); No.25-003 (toasts, greens, and gold on beige).

ᔥ MARY DAILEY CROOK BORDER. American, 1890–1910, machine print. Originally printed by S. A. Maxwell & Company. 18" wide, 18³/₄" repeat. No.25-055 (mauve, green, ivory, and navy on Victorian blue). Period colorings: No.25-052 (rose, gold, and cream on pink); No.25-053 (toasts, greens, and gold on beige).

ᔥ MARY DAILEY CROOK CEILING. American, 1890–1910, machine print. Originally printed by Standard Wall Paper Company. 18¹/₂" wide plus two 2¹/₂" borders, 18³/₄" repeat, 5 yds. per s/r. No.25-031 (mauve, green, gold, and blue on ivory). Period colorings: No.25-032 (rose, gold, and cream on ivory); No.25-033 (toasts, green, and gold on off-white).

ᔥ MILLARD. American, 1890–1910, machine print. 24" wide, 10" repeat, 5 yds. per s/r. No.24-001 (burgundy, white, and gold on gray). Period coloring: No.24-003 (brown and greens on green crackle).

ᔥ MILLARD BORDER. American, 1890–1910, machine print. 18" wide, 18¹/₂" repeat. No.24-051 (burgundy, white, and gold on gray). Period coloring: No.24-053 (brown and greens on green crackle).

ᔥ MILLARD BORDER (narrow). American, 1890–1910, machine print. 9" wide, 18¹/₂" repeat. Half-scale adaptation of preceding pattern. No.24-061 (burgundy, white, and gold on gray). Period coloring: No.24-063 (brown and greens on green crackle).

ᔥ MILLARD CEILING. American, 1890–1910, machine print. Originally printed by S. A. Maxwell & Company. 24" wide, 12¹/₂" repeat, 5 yds. per s/r. No.24-031 (burgundy, gray, and gold on white).

ᔥ ROCOCO ROSE. American, 1890–1910, machine print. Originally printed by S. A. Maxwell & Company. 24" wide plus 2¹/₂" border, 12¹/₂" repeat, 5 yds. per s/r. No.31-001 (cream, green, and gold on beige).

ᔥ ROCOCO ROSE BORDER. American, 1890–1910, machine print. Originally printed by S. A. Maxwell & Company. 18" wide, 16" repeat. No.31-051 (cream, green, and gold on beige).

ᔥ ROCOCO ROSE BORDER (narrow). American, 1890–1910, machine print. 9" wide, 8" repeat. Half-scale adaptation of preceding pattern. No.31-061 (cream, green, and gold on beige).

ᔥ ROCOCO ROSE CEILING. American, 1890–1910, machine print. Originally printed by S. A. Maxwell & Company. 24" wide plus 3" border, 12" repeat, 5 yds. per s/r. No.31-031 (gold, cream, and green on ivory).

ᔥ VICTORIAN TEA ROSE. American, 1890–1910, machine print. 24" wide, 15³/₄" repeat, 5 yds. per s/r. No.42-001 (rose, burgundy, tan, and silver on pink). Period colorings: No.42-002 (rose, burgundy, tan, and silver on beige); No.42-003 (rose, burgundy, tan, and silver on Victorian gold).

above left
MILLARD and border, 1890–1910. Victorian Collectibles Limited.

above right
ROCOCO ROSE and border. 1890–1910. Victorian Collectibles Limited.

ॐ VICTORIAN TEA ROSE BORDER. American, 1890–1910, machine print. 18″ wide, 19″ repeat. No.42-051 (rose, burgundy, tan, silver, and pink on beige). Period coloring: No.42-003 (rose, burgundy, tan, silver, and pink on Victorian gold).

ॐ VICTORIAN TEA ROSE BORDER (narrow). American, 1890–1910, machine print. 18″ wide, 19″ repeat. Half-scale adaptation of preceding pattern. No.42-061 (rose, burgundy, tan, silver, and pink on beige). Period coloring: No.42-063 (rose, burgundy, tan, silver, and pink on Victorian gold).

ॐ VICTORIAN TEA ROSE CEILING. American, 1890–1910, machine print. 25″ wide, 12″ repeat, 5 yds. per s/r. No.42-035 (gold, pink, silver, and green on beige). Period coloring: No.42-032 (gold, pink, silver, and green on white).

The following group includes fills and friezes.

ॐ EMPEROR. American, 1890–1910, machine print. 24″ wide, 18½″ repeat, 5 yds. per s/r. No.19-001 (dark green and gold on pumpkin). Period coloring: No.19-004 (greens on green crackle).

ॐ EMPEROR BORDER. American, 1890–1910, machine print. 18″ wide, 16″ repeat. No.19-051 (dark green and gold on pumpkin). Period coloring: No.19-054 (greens on green crackle).

ॐ EMPEROR BORDER (narrow). American, 1890–1910, machine print. 9″ wide, 16″ repeat. Half-scale adaptation of preceding pattern.

No.19-061 (dark green and gold on pumpkin). Period coloring: No.19-064 (greens on green crackle).

᪣ FORTINO. American, 1890–1910, machine print. 27" wide, 18³/₄" repeat, 5 yds. per s/r. No.20-001 (green, gold, and cream on sage).

᪣ FORTINO BORDER. American, 1890–1910, machine print. Originally printed by Janeway & Company. 18" wide, 15³/₄" repeat. No.20-051 (green, gold, and cream on sage).

᪣ REGAL MEDALLION. American, 1890–1915, machine print. 24" wide, 26¹/₂" repeat, 5 yds. per s/r. No.15-001 (burgundy on beige). Period coloring: No.15-006 (burgundy and green on beige).

᪣ REGAL MEDALLION BORDER. American, 1890–1915, machine print. 18" wide, 19" repeat. No.15-051 (burgundy on beige). Period coloring: No.15-056 (burgundy and green on beige).

above left
EMPEROR and border, 1890–1910. Victorian Collectibles Limited.

above right
FORTINO and border, 1890–1910. Victorian Collectibles Limited.

ZINA STUDIOS

Order by pattern name. The following group includes a fill, a freize, and a border.

᪣ PASSION FLOWER. English, 1875–85, machine print. Lynn, color pl. 89, p. 352, and dust jacket. 21¹/₂" wide, 19⁷/₈" repeat, 5 yds. per s/r. Reproduced for Camron-Stanford House, Oakland, Calif. Document at Cooper-Hewitt Museum. Turquoise and orange on cream.

᪣ PASSION FLOWER BORDER. English, 1875–85, machine print. 3³/₄" wide, 5" repeat. Document at Cooper-Hewitt Museum. Turquoise on cream.

❧ PASSION FLOWER FRIEZE. English, 1875–85, machine print. Lynn, color pl. 89, p. 352, and dust jacket. 21" wide, 5" repeat. Reproduced for Camron-Stanford House, Oakland, Calif. Document at Cooper-Hewitt Museum. Turquoise and orange on cream.

BORDERS, DADOS, AND PANELS

BRADBURY & BRADBURY

❧ PEACOCK FRIEZE. English, 1889, block print. Designed by Walter Crane; originally printed by Jeffrey & Company. 21³/₄" wide, 21³/₄" repeat. Design derived from a printed advertisement. Document at Victoria and Albert Museum. Code PKF. Special order.

❧ PERSIA BORDERS. French, 1870–80. 10" wide, 18" repeat. Design derived from a published design by Racinet. Code PSB. Special order.

❧ VERMILLION STAR FRIEZE. American, 1890-1900. 18" wide, 9¹/₂" repeat. Reproduced from a photograph for Clay County Historical Society, Vermillion, S.D. Code VSF. Special order.

J. R. BURROWS & COMPANY

Order by pattern name and color.

❧ CHAUNCY FRIEZE. American, 1885–95, machine print. 18" wide, 22¹/₄" repeat. Document privately owned. Brown on brown. Can be printed on oatmeal paper as special order.

❧ PERSIS FRIEZE. American Victorian Revival. 9¹/₂" wide, 20" repeat. Designed to complement "Persis" sidewall (page 146). Period colorings: sage green; terra cotta; celadon on buff.

CLASSIC REVIVALS

Authentic Interiors Collection

❧ BETTINGTON FRIEZE. English, 1880–90, machine print. Murphy, no. 23 (5th frieze from top), p. 28. 5¹/₄" wide, 15" repeat. Archival Collection. No.F-197-10A (multi).

❧ SWALLOW FRIEZE. English, 1880–90, block or machine print. 10¹/₂" wide, 20¹/₂" repeat. Archival Collection. No.F-170-11A (blue).

❧ TESSA FRIEZE. English, 1870–80, machine print. 8¹/₂" wide, 16" repeat. Price Collection. No.F-202-2A.

St. James Collection

❧ DAISY FRIEZE. English, 1890–1900, machine print. 12" wide. No.DZ28 (ginger).

❧ GALLICA FRIEZE. English, 1892, machine print. Originally printed by Allan, Cockshut and Company. 7" wide. No.AZ2 (rust olive); No.AZ3 (pink blue); No.AZ4 (deep red); No.AZ18 (slate); No.AZ27 (vivid green).

❧ GOTHIC BORDER. Australian, 1890–1900. 7¹/₂" wide. Reproduced from a stencil design. No.GB22 (terra cotta).

PASSION FLOWER,
1875–85.
Zina Studios.

CHAUNCEY FRIEZE,
1885–95.
J. R. Burrows &
Company.

SWALLOW FRIEZE,
1880–90. Classic
Revivals (Authentic
Interiors Collection).

DAISY FRIEZE, 1880–90. Classic Revivals (St. James Collection).

GALLICA FRIEZE, 1892. Classic Revivals (St. James Collection).

WHISTLER DADO BORDER, 1892. Classic Revivals (St. James Collection).

RIBBONS AND BOWS BORDER, 1890–1920. Cowtan & Tout.

❧ HAWTHORN DADO. English, 1892, machine print. Originally printed by Allan, Cockshut and Company. 21″ wide, 5½″ repeat, 11 yds. per roll. No.HD15 (china blue); No.HD16 (drab olive); No.HD17 (salmon); No.HD22 (terra cotta).

❧ HAWTHORN DADO BORDER. English, 1892, machine print. Originally printed by Allan, Cockshut and Company. 4½″ wide, 5½″ repeat. No.HB15 (china blue); No.HB16 (drab olive); No.HB17 (salmon); No.HB22 (terra cotta).

❧ JAPANESE DADO. English, 1890–1900, machine print. 28″ wide, 18″ repeat, 11 yds. per roll. No.SD6 (olive); No.SD28 (ginger).

❧ JAPANESE DADO BORDER. English, 1892, machine print. Originally printed by Allan, Cockshut and Company. 4⅞″ wide. No.SB6 (olive); No.SB28 (ginger).

❧ JUNIPER HALL DADO. English, 1885–1900, machine print. 26″ wide, 19″ repeat, 11 yds. per roll. No.JD2 (olive rust); No.JD13 (turquoise).

❧ JUNIPER HALL DADO BORDER. English, 1885–1900, machine print.

4¼" wide, 2⅜" repeat. No.JB2 (olive rust); No.JB13 (turquoise).

🙠 LOUISA BORDER. English, 1892, machine print. Originally printed by Allan, Cockshut and Company. 5" wide, 12" repeat. No.LB13 (turquoise); No.LB15 (china blue); No.LB19 (burnt sienna); No.LB20 (eau de Nil); No.LB21 (antique blue); No.LB22 (terra cotta).

🙠 MATHER BORDER. English, 1885–1900, machine print. 4½" wide, No.MB6 (olive).

🙠 MENINGOORT DADO. English, 1885–1900, machine print. 21" wide, 11 yds. per roll. No.MD14 (old gold).

🙠 PRIMROSE FRIEZE. English, 1885–1900, machine print. 7" wide. No.EZ3 (pink blue); No.EZ10 (sienna); No.EZ17 (salmon).

🙠 QUEENSCLIFF. English, 1890–1900, machine print. 10" wide. No.QZ1 (sage).

🙠 WHISTLER DADO. English, 1892, machine print. Originally printed by Allan, Cockshut and Company. 28" wide, 18" repeat, 11 yds. per roll. No.WD1 (sage); No.WD2 (olive rust); No.WD8 (teal).

🙠 WHISTLER DADO BORDER. English, 1892, machine print. Originally printed by Allan, Cockshut and Company. 4⅞" wide. No.WB1 (sage); No.WB2 (olive rust); No.WB8 (teal).

COWTAN & TOUT

🙠 HAWTHORNE BORDER. English, 1890–1910, block print. 4" wide, 21" repeat. No.133 (multi). Block print.

🙠 MYRTLE BORDER. English, 1890–1910, block print. 5" wide, 7¼" repeat. No.181 (pink). Block print.

🙠 RIBBONS AND BOWS BORDER. English, 1890–1920, block print. 5" wide, 24" repeat. No.128 (green); No.128-1 (rose). Block print.

🙠 RIBBONS AND BOWS BORDER. English, 1890–1920, block print. 5" wide, 21" repeat. No.132 (pink); No.132-1 (blue). Block print.

🙠 SWEET PEA BORDER. English, 1890–1920, block print. 5" wide, 21" repeat. No.134 (multi). Block print.

CHRISTOPHER HYLAND INCORPORATED

🙠 ETIENNE. French, 1870–1900, block print. 18½" wide, 10" repeat. No.AB170/5 (gold, brown, and green).

🙠 LOGRIS. English, 1880–90, block print. 7" wide, 6" repeat. Sold only in 11-yard rolls. No.WTLB101 (rust, creme, mint, and forest).

🙠 OLEANDER TRELLIS. English, 1870–90, block print. 18¾" wide, 18" repeat. No.AB161/20 (multi on document original colors).

🙠 POIMA. English or French, 1890–1910, block print. 21" wide, 23½" repeat. No.AB101/10A (multi).

LEE JOFA

🙠 COLETTE BORDER. French, 1880–90, block print. 13⅜" wide, 36" repeat. Design derived from a period design for a wallpaper. No.P912023 (dove).

მ⊶ MARGARET CLAIRE BORDER. French, 1875–90, block print. 13$^1/_2$" wide, 27" repeat. Adaptation: flocking not reproduced. No.P912124 (silver).

მ⊶ PETIT MARGARET BORDER. French, 1875–90, block print. 5" wide, 27" repeat. Adaptation: scale reduced. No.P912154 (silver).

MT. DIABLO HANDPRINTS

მ⊶ FALLON FRIEZE. American, 1880–1900, machine print. 19" wide, 20$^7/_8$" repeat. Reproduced for Fallon Hotel, Columbia, Calif., operated by California Department of Parks and Recreation. Golds and silver on gray.

მ⊶ FLORAL GARLAND FRIEZE. American, 1880–90, machine print. 17" wide, 16" repeat. Reproduced for Woodland Opera House, Woodland, Calif. Pinks, greens, taupe, and cream.

მ⊶ FLORAL SCENIC BORDER. American, 1880–90, machine print. 6$^1/_4$" wide, 16$^1/_4$" repeat. Reproduced for Henry Ford Museum & Greenfield Village, Dearborn, Mich. Burgundy, blue, and greens.

მ⊶ GOLD LEAF FLORAL BORDER. American, 1880–90, machine print. 7$^1/_2$" wide, 21$^3/_4$" repeat. Reproduced for Fallon Hotel, Columbia, Calif., operated by California Department of Parks and Recreation.

მ⊶ GROS POINT FRIEZE. American, 1880–1900, machine print. 9$^1/_2$" wide, 21" repeat. Reproduced for Fallon Hotel, Columbia, Calif., operated by California Department of Parks and Recreation. Blues, green, drab, and maroon.

მ⊶ OGLESBY "ARABIC" FRIEZE. English or American, 1870–80, block or machine print. 21" wide, 20" repeat. Reproduced for Governor Oglesby Mansion, Decatur, Ill. Chinese red, maroon, and gold on umber.

მ⊶ WOODLAND OPERA FRIEZE. American, 1890–1900, machine print. 19" wide, 19" repeat. Reproduced for Woodland Opera House, Woodland, Calif. Roses and gold.

SCALAMANDRE

მ⊶ BYERS-EVANS PARLOR FRIEZE. American, 1890–1915, machine print. 18" wide, 21$^7/_8$" repeat. Reproduced for Byers-Evans House, Denver, Colo. No.WB81465. Special order.

მ⊶ GRANT KOHRS RANCH—DINING ROOM BORDER. American, 1890–1900, machine print. 18" wide, 24" repeat. Historic representation. Reproduced for Grant Kohrs Ranch National Historic Site, Deer Lodge, Mont. No.WB81264-001 (oatmeal and metallic silver on smoke).

მ⊶ GRANT KOHRS RANCH FRIEZE. American, 1890–1900, machine print. 18" wide, 24" repeat. Historic representation. Reproduced for Grant Kohrs Ranch National Historic Site, Deer Lodge, Mont. No.WB81263-001 (cinnamon, slate, topaz, and metallic gold). Special order.

GRANT KOHRS RANCH
FRIEZE, 1890–1900.
Scalamandré.

SAGAMORE HILL
LIBRARY FRIEZE, 1890–
1900. Scalamandré.

&❧ MONTEZUMA DADO. English or American, 1890–1900, machine print. 36" wide, 20⁵⁄₈" repeat. Historic representation. Reproduced for Villa Montezuma, San Diego, Calif. No.WB81131-001 (multi). Special order.

&❧ MONTEZUMA FLORAL BORDER. American, 1890–1900, machine print. 7¹⁄₄" wide, 15¹¹⁄₁₆" repeat. Historic representation. Reproduced for Villa Montezuma, San Diego, Calif. No.WB81130 (multi on bronze). Special order.

&❧ PHOENIX FRIEZE. American, 1890–1910, machine print. 18" wide, 22¹⁄₈" repeat. Historic representation. Reproduced for Rosson House, Phoenix, Ariz. No.WB81161 (multi on brown). Special order.

&❧ ROSE SWAG BORDER. American, 1890–1900, machine print. 18" wide, 14" repeat. Adaptation. Central City Collection. No.WB81142-001 (green and pink on yellow). Special order.

&❧ ROSSON HOUSE FRIEZE. American, c. 1900, machine print. 17" wide, 9³⁄₈" repeat. Reproduced for Rosson House, Phoenix, Ariz. No.WB81147-001 (pinks, peach, celery, rose, silver, and dusty rose blotch).

&❧ SAGAMORE HILL LIBRARY FRIEZE. American, 1890–1900, machine print. 9¹⁄₂" wide, 18³⁄₁₆" repeat. Historic representation. Design reconstructed from photographs. Reproduced for Sagamore Hill, Oyster Bay, N.Y. No.WB81258-001 (browns, gray, olive, metallic gold, and copper blotch). Special order.

&❧ SAVANNAH HOUSE BORDER. American, 1890–1900, machine print. 18¹⁄₈" wide, 19" repeat. Savannah Collection. Document at Werms House, Savannah, Ga. No.WB81087 (brown and rust on beige). Special order.

MAY TREE FRIEZE, 1896. Victorian Collectibles Limited.

GRIFFON BORDER, 1875. Zina Studios.

SCHUMACHER

୬ CHRYSANTHEMUM BORDER. English or American, 1890–1900, machine print. 9" wide, 10" repeat. Document at Whitworth Art Gallery, Manchester, England. Period coloring: No.5702B (mulberry and spruce).

୬ DAUPHIN BORDER. American, 1890–1910, machine print. 22" wide, 23" repeat. Document in Schumacher Archive. No.512680 (aqua).

VICTORIAN COLLECTIBLES LIMITED

୬ BENSON BORDER. American, 1890–1910, machine print. 9" wide, 16" repeat. No.26-061 (gold and brown on brown).

୬ LIBERTY FLOWER BORDER. American, 1890–1910, machine print. 6" wide, 29³/₄" repeat. No.35-061 (cream, burgundy, and gold on buff).

୬ MAY TREE FRIEZE. English, 1896, block print. Designed by Walter Crane for Jeffrey & Company. Oman and Hamilton, color pl. p. 321; Teynac, Nolot, and Vivien, color pl. p. 159. 21¹/₂" wide, 36" repeat. No.36-051 (greens, blues, black, terra cotta, and cream on putty).

ঌ OPERA SCROLL BORDER. American, 1890–1910, machine print. Originally printed by S. A. Maxwell & Company. 18" wide, 15¹/₂" repeat. No.33-051 (greens, gold, and white on beige).

WATERHOUSE WALLHANGINGS

ঌ SAMANTHA. American, 1890–1920, machine print. 13¹/₂" wide, 9¹/₂" repeat. Document in Waterhouse Archive. Period coloring: No.228328 (brown and blue).

ZINA STUDIOS

Order by pattern name.

ঌ GRIFFON BORDER. English, 1875, block print. Designed by William Burges. Lynn, color pls. 87–88, pp. 250–51. 11³/₄" wide, 21" repeat. Reproduced for Chateau-sur-Mer, Newport, R.I., a property of Preservation Society of Newport County/Newport Mansions. Document at Cooper-Hewitt Museum. Blue and white.

ঌ THE WILLOWS. American, 1890–1910, machine print. 19⁷/₈" wide, 18⁵/₈" repeat. Reproduced for the Willows, operated by Morris County (N.J.) Park Commission. Red and terra cotta.

CEILING PAPERS, CEILING BORDERS, AND CORNERS

For additional ceiling papers, see listings under coordinated patterns (pages 171–88).

BRADBURY & BRADBURY

ঌ MOSSWOOD BORDERS. American, 1870–80. Two 7" and two 4" borders per sheet, 7" repeat. Design derived from a sketch for a ceiling treatment by P. B. Wight. Document at Burnham Architectural Library, Chicago. Code MWB (3 period colorings).

ঌ MOSSWOOD ROSETTE. American, 1870–80. Panel 24" by 24". Design derived from a sketch for a ceiling treatment by P. B. Wight. Document at Burnham Architectural Library, Chicago. Code MWR (3 period colorings).

J. R. BURROWS & COMPANY

Order by pattern name and color. All patterns can be custom colored.

ঌ PERSIS CEILING. American Victorian Revival. 21" wide, 21" repeat, 6 yds. per s/r. Design based on motifs in "Persis" wallpaper (page 146). Period coloring: gold on buff.

ঌ ALDAM CEILING. American Victorian Revival. Block printed with custom stencils in neoclassical manner of Aldam Heaton. Deep cream with blue.

CLASSIC REVIVALS

Authentic Interiors Collection

∂♦ BURGIS. English, 1880–90, machine print. 21" wide, 21" repeat, 11 yds. per roll. Archival Collection. No.C-201-1A (silver on beige).

St. James Collection

∂♦ MOSAIC CEILING. English, 1890–1900, machine print. 21" wide, 11 yds. per roll. No.MC9 (citron).

∂♦ SWALLOW CEILING. English, 1890–1900, machine print. 18" wide, 18⅞" repeat, 11 yds. per roll. No.SC12 (pink olive).

∂♦ VICTORIAN CEILING. English, 1892, machine print. Originally printed by Allan, Cockshut and Company. 21" wide, 10½" repeat, 11 yds. per roll. No.VC1 (sage); No.VC5 (gray buff); No.VC10 (sienna); No.VC14 (old gold); No.VC17 (salmon); No.VC29 (mauve); No.VC30 (lustre).

MT. DIABLO HANDPRINTS

Order by name unless pattern number is listed.

∂♦ BILLINGS CEILING. American, 1880–1900, machine print. 18¼" wide, 12¼" repeat. Reproduced for Billings Farm & Museum, Woodstock, Vt. Copper, gold, peach, and ochre on buff.

∂♦ CHAMPAGNE CEILING. American, 1880–1900, machine print. 18" wide, 15¾" repeat. Reproduced for Fallon Hotel, Columbia, Calif., operated by California Department of Parks and Recreation. Gold, silver, and copper on cream.

∂♦ CRACKED ICE CEILING. American, 1880–90, machine print. 27" wide, 6¾" repeat. Reproduced for Alameda Historical Society, Alameda, Calif. Dark umber and gold on ochre.

∂♦ FALLON CEILING. American, 1880–1900, machine print. 19½" wide, 19" repeat. Reproduced for Fallon Hotel, Columbia, Calif., operated by California Department of Parks and Recreation. Green, gold, mica, and yellow on pink.

∂♦ RAVEL CEILING. American, 1890–1910, machine print. 18" wide, 18½" repeat. Reproduced for Byers-Evans House, Denver, Colo., a property of Colorado Historical Society. No.RVC-001 (document yellow and umber on kraft).

∂♦ SUNBURST CEILING. American, 1880–1900, machine print. 19" wide, 13" repeat. Reproduced for Fallon Hotel, Columbia, Calif., a property of California Department of Parks and Recreation. Gold, mica, pine, and blue on cream.

SCALAMANDRE

∂♦ MONTEZUMA CEILING. American, 1890–1900, machine print. 35½" wide, 15¹³⁄₁₆" repeat, 4 yds. per s/r. Document at Villa Montezuma, San Diego, Calif. No.WP81127-1 (green and metallic on terra cotta). Special order.

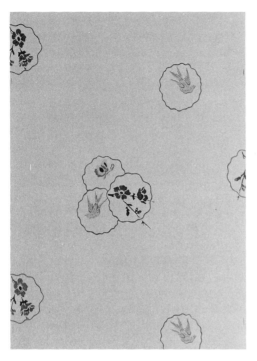 

꙳ THOMAS WOLFE MEMORIAL HALL CEILING. American, 1880–1900, machine print. 27" wide, 5⅝" repeat, 5 yds. per s/r. Reproduced for Thomas Wolfe Memorial, Asheville, N.C. No.WP81199-001 (taupe and off-white). Special order.

꙳ WERMS HOUSE DIAMOND. American, 1870–80, machine print. 48" wide, 6" repeat, 3 yds. per s/r. Adaptation. Savannah Collection. Document at Werms House, Savannah, Ga. No.WP81112 (green and ecru on beige). Special order.

VICTORIAN COLLECTIBLES LIMITED

꙳ LIBERTY BIRD CORNER. American, 1890–1910, machine print. 18" each side. Order with "Liberty Bird 18" Ceiling Set." No.1886B1 (golds, burgundy, cream, and blue on buff).

꙳ ROCOCO BOWS. American, 1890–1920, machine print. 25" wide, 12" repeat, 5 yds. per s/r. No.43-031 (brown on ivory).

SCALAMANDRE

꙳ TEKKO FIRST CLASS. Austria (now produced in Switzerland), 1890–1900, machine embossed. 31½" wide, 3½" repeat, 5 yds. per s/r. No.TB7-124 (champagne).

꙳ TEKKO FIRST CLASS. Austria (now produced in Switzerland), 1890–1900, machine embossed. 31½" wide, 6½" repeat, 5 yds. per s/r. No.TB8-127 (sand).

above left
SWALLOW CEILING, 1890–1900. Classic Revivals (St. James Collection).

above right
LIBERTY BIRD CORNER, 1890–1910. Victorian Collectibles Limited.

EMBOSSED PAPERS

❧ TEKKO FIRST CLASS. Austria (now produced in Switzerland), 1890–1900, machine embossed. 31½" wide, 24" repeat, 5 yds. per s/r. No.TC2-173 (jade).

❧ TEKKO FIRST CLASS. Austria (now produced in Switzerland), 1890–1900, machine embossed. 31½" wide, 4½" repeat, 5 yds. per s/r. No.TC3-174 (gold).

❧ TEKKO FIRST CLASS. Austria (now produced in Switzerland), 1890–1900, machine embossed. 31½" wide, 5 yds. per s/r. No.TD1-174 (gold).

❧ TEKKO FIRST CLASS. Austria (now produced in Switzerland), 1890–1900, machine embossed. 31½" wide, 22" half-drop repeat, 5 yds. per s/r. No.TD2-175 (cognac).

❧ TEKKO FIRST CLASS. Austria (now produced in Switzerland), 1890–1900, machine embossed. 31½" wide, 10½" repeat, 5 yds. per s/r. No.TD3-152 (lavender-blue).

❧ TEKKO FIRST CLASS. Austria (now produced in Switzerland), 1890–1900, machine embossed. 31½" wide, 8¾" repeat, 5 yds. per s/r. No.TD7-154 (corn).

❧ TEKKO FIRST CLASS. Austria (now produced in Switzerland), 1890–1900, machine embossed. 31½" wide, 28" half-drop repeat, 5 yds. per s/r. No.TE1-123 (cream).

❧ TEKKO FIRST CLASS. Austria (now produced in Switzerland), 1890–1900, machine embossed. 31½" wide, 17" half-drop repeat, 5 yds. per s/r. No.TE6-124 (champagne).

❧ TEKKO FIRST CLASS. Austria (now produced in Switzerland), 1890–1900, machine embossed. 31½" wide, 25½" half-drop repeat, 5 yds. per s/r. No.TF7-174 (gold).

RELIEF DECORATIONS— LINCRUSTA AND LINCRUSTA BORDERS

CROWN DECORATIVE PRODUCTS

Crown Decorative Products are available through Bentley Brothers, Classic Ceilings, and Mile Hi Crown. Product comes unfinished and must be painted.

❧ ANNE FRIEZE. English, 1890–1910, impressed composition. 10½" wide, 21" repeat. No.RD 1947.

❧ BYZANTINE. English, 1895–1910, impressed composition. 20½" wide, 2¹/₁₀" repeat, 11 yds. per roll. No.RD 1954.

❧ EMPIRE FRIEZE. English, 1890–1910, impressed composition. 10⅞" wide, 21" repeat. No.RD 1957.

❧ ITALIAN RENAISSANCE. English, 1895–1910, impressed composition. 20½" wide, 40" repeat, 11 yds. per roll. No.RD 1952.

WALLPAPERS BY WILLIAM MORRIS AND MORRIS & COMPANY

BRADBURY & BRADBURY

Bradbury & Bradbury's reproductions of William Morris patterns are reduced in scale by 13 percent. They are screen printed in period colorings.

❧ BIRD AND ANEMONE. English, 1882, block print. Clark, no. 16, p. 72; Oman and Hamilton, no. 1065, p. 377. 27" wide, 22" repeat, 5 yds. per s/r. Document at Victoria and Albert Museum. Code BAW (8 period colorings).

❧ MARIGOLD. English, 1875, block print. Clark, no. 16, p. 27; Lynn, no. 16-5, p. 371. 27" wide, 9" repeat, 5 yds. per s/r. Document at Victoria and Albert Museum. Code MAW (8 period colorings).

❧ MORRIS CEILING. English, 1888, block print. Oman and Hamilton, no. 1065, p. 375. 27" wide, 13½" repeat, 5 yds. per s/r. Design based on Morris's "Borage Ceiling" (page 202). Document at Victoria and Albert Museum. Code MOC (4 period colorings).

ARTHUR SANDERSON & SONS

Unless otherwise noted, the patterns listed in this section were designed by William Morris. Morris & Company's wallpapers were originally printed by Jeffrey & Company. The original wood blocks are now owned by Arthur Sanderson & Sons, and the following patterns are printed from them. Other Morris patterns printed from the original blocks are available as special orders with a minimum of six rolls of 11 yards each.

❧ ACORN. English, 1879, block print. Clark, no. 26, p. 34; Oman and Hamilton, no. 1065, p. 373. 21" wide, 19" repeat, 11 yds. per s/r.

above left
ITALIAN RENAISSANCE, 1895–1910. Crown Decorative Products.

top right
EMPIRE FRIEZE , 1890–1910. Crown Decorative Products.

above right
ANNE FRIEZE , 1890–1910. Crown Decorative Products.

Page from the *William Morris Log Book*, 1864–c. 1896, illustrating DAISY and FRUIT, both from 1864 and now printed by Arthur Sanderson & Sons.

Document in Sanderson Archives. No.114 (green). Block print.

ॐ BIRD AND ANEMONE. English, 1882, block print. Clark, no. 16, p. 72; Oman and Hamilton, no. 1065, p. 377. 21" wide, 20½" repeat, 11 yds. per roll. Document in Sanderson Archives. No.143 (red); No.144 (yellow). Block print.

ॐ BORAGE CEILING. English, 1888, block print. Oman and Hamilton, no. 1065, p. 375. 21" wide, 20" repeat, 11 yds. per roll. Document in Sanderson Archives. No.142190 (yellow on cream); No.479 (white). Block print.

ॐ CHRYSANTHEMUM. English, 1877, block print. Clark, no. 22, p. 31; Greysmith, fig. 100, p. 137; Oman and Hamilton, no. 1065, p. 373. 21" wide, 21" repeat, 11 yds. per roll. Document in Sanderson Archives. No.118 (green). Block print.

ॐ DAISY. English, designed in 1862, first printed in 1864, block print. Clark, no. 1, p. 19; Lynn, color pl. 81, p. 345; Sugden and Edmundson, color pl. 110; Teynac, Nolot, and Vivian, color pl. p. 150. 21" wide, 14" repeat, 11 yds. per roll. Document in Sanderson Archives. No.1 (dark green); No.75 (light green). Block print.

ॐ FRUIT (also POMEGRANATE). English, designed in 1862, first printed in 1864, block print. Clark, no. 2, p. 20; Oman and Hamilton, no. 1067, p. 381; Sugden and Edmundson, color pl. 11. 21" wide, 21" repeat, 11 yds. per roll. Document in Sanderson Archives. No.4 (dark green); No.5 (cream). Block print.

ॐ GOLDEN LILY. English, 1899, block print. Designed by John Henry Dearle. Oman and Hamilton, no. 1076, p. 385. 21" wide, 17½" repeat, 11 yds. per roll. Document in Sanderson Archives. No.346 (multicolor). Block print.

GRANVILLE. English, 1895, block print. Designed by John Henry Dearle. Oman and Hamilton, no. 1066, p. 378. 21" wide, 19³/₄" repeat, 11 yds. per roll. Document in Sanderson Archives. No.325 (blue and green). Block print.

HONEYSUCKLE. English, 1883, block print. Designed by May Morris. Oman and Hamilton, no. 1065, p. 373. 21" wide, 21" repeat, 11 yds. per roll. Document in Sanderson Archives. No.147 (green); No.263 (light). Block print.

INDIAN. English, 1868–70, block print. Clark, no. 5, p. 21; Oman and Hamilton, no. 1066, p. 380. 21" wide, 26¹/₂" repeat, 11 yds. per roll. Document in Sanderson Archives. No.14 (light blue); No.32 (green; No.470 (red). Block print.

IRIS. English, 1888, block print. Designed by John Henry Dearle. Oman and Hamilton, no. 1066, p. 377. 21" wide, 16¹/₂" repeat, 11 yds. per roll. Document in Sanderson Archives. No.224 (green). Block print.

LARKSPUR. English, 1874, block print. Clark, no. 11, p. 23; Oman and Hamilton, no. 1065, p. 372. 21" wide, 14" repeat, 11 yds. per roll. Document in Sanderson Archives. No.30 (yellow); No.64 (green); No.160 (salmon). Block print.

LOOP TRAIL. English, 1877, block print. Designed by Kate Faulkner. Oman and Hamilton, no. 1066, p. 380. 21" wide, 11 yds.

below left
GOLDEN LILY, 1899.
Arthur Sanderson
& Sons.

below right
GRANVILLE, 1895.
Arthur Sanderson
& Sons.

LARKSPUR, 1874.
Arthur Sanderson &
Sons.

per roll. Document in Sanderson Archives. No.94 (blue); No.95 (yellow); No.169 (red). Block print.

ᔰ MALLOW. English, 1879, block print. Designed by Kate Faulkner. Oman and Hamilton, no. 1066, p. 380. 21″ wide, 12″ repeat, 11 yds. per roll. Document in Sanderson Archives. No.107 (yellow); No.140 (red); No.145 (green); No.159 (salmon). Block print.

ᔰ MARIGOLD. English, 1875, block print. Clark, no. 16, p. 27; Lynn,

204

fig. 16-5, p. 371. 21" wide, 10½" repeat, 11 yds. per roll. Document in Sanderson Archives. No.39 (dark); No.532 (olive). Block print.

❧ POPPY. English, 1881, block print. Clark, no. 27, p. 35; Oman and Hamilton, no. 1065, p. 373. 21" wide, 16¼" repeat, 11 yds. per roll. Document in Sanderson Archives. No.440 (red); No.531 (brown). Block print.

❧ SUNFLOWER. English, 1879, block print. Clark, no. 25, p. 33; Oman and Hamilton, no. 1065, p. 373. 21" wide, 18" repeat, 11 yds. per roll. Document in Sanderson Archives. No.274 (green); No.530 (white). Block print.

❧ TRELLIS. English, designed in 1862, first produced in 1864, block print. Clark, no. 3, p. 21; Oman and Hamilton, color pl., p. 363; Sugden and Edmondson, color pl. 109. 21" wide, 21" repeat, 11 yds. per roll. Document in Sanderson Archives. No.7 (green); No.157 (cream). Block print.

❧ VINE. English, 1874, block print. Clark, no. 14, p. 26; Nylander, Redmond, and Sander, fig. 68.1, p. 241; Oman and Hamilton, no. 1065, p. 372. 21" wide, 21" repeat, 11 yds. per roll. Document in Sanderson Archives. No.45 (black). Block print.

❧ WILLOW. English, 1874, block print. Clark, no. 17, p. 27; Oman and Hamilton, no. 1065, p. 372. 21" wide, 17½" repeat, 11 yds. per roll. Document in Sanderson Archives. No.66 (sage); No.67 (green). Block print.

❧ WILLOW BOUGH. English, 1887, block print. Clark, no. 35, p. 41; Oman and Hamilton, no. 1065, p. 374; Sugden and Edmondson, color pl. 114. 21" wide, 18" repeat, 11 yds. per roll. Document in Sanderson Archives. No.210 (green); No.229 (blue). Block print.

The following Morris designs have been transferred to rollers and are printed by machine.

❧ ACORN. English, 1879, block print. Clark, no. 26, p. 34; Oman and Hamilton, no. 1065, p. 373. 21" wide, 18" repeat, 11 yds. per roll. Document in Sanderson Archives. Period coloring: No.WM 7422-2 (nutmeg on tan).

❧ CHRISTCHURCH. English, 1882, block print. Clark, no. 30, p. 37; Greysmith, fig. 101, p. 141; Oman and Hamilton, no. 1066, p. 380. 21" wide, 10½" repeat, 11 yds. per roll. Document in Sanderson Archives. Period coloring: No.WM 7423-3 (blue on white).

❧ CHRYSANTHEMUM. English, 1877, block print. Clark, no. 22, p. 31; Greysmith, fig. 100, p. 137; Oman and Hamilton, no. 1065, p. 373. 21" wide, 21" repeat, 11 yds. per s/r. Document in Sanderson Archives. Period coloring: No.WM 7612 (series).

❧ FOLIAGE. English, 1899, block print. Designed by John Henry Dearle. Oman and Hamilton, no. 1076, p. 387. 21" wide, 24" repeat, 11 yds. per roll. Document in Sanderson Archives. Period colorings:

No.WM 7424-1 (moss green and khaki on green); No.WM 7424-3 (charcoal and taupe on black).

❧ HONEYSUCKLE. English, 1883, block print. Designed by May Morris. Oman and Hamilton, no. 1065, p. 373. 21" wide, 21" repeat, 11 yds. per roll. Document in Sanderson Archives. Period coloring: No.WM 7611 (series).

❧ SPRAY. English, c. 1871, block print. Produced by Morris & Company. Clark, no. 8, p. 22; Oman and Hamilton, no. 1067, p. 382. 21" wide, 19³⁄₄" repeat, 11 yds. per roll. Document in Sanderson Archives. Period coloring: No.WH 7367-4 (cafe-au-lait on oyster).

❧ VINE. English, 1873, block print. Clark, no. 14, p. 26; Nylander, Redmond, and Sander, fig. 68.1, p. 241; Oman and Hamilton, no. 1065, p. 372. 21" wide, 21" repeat, 11 yds. per roll. Document in Sanderson Archives. Period coloring: No.WM 7613-3 (maroon and green on midnight ground).

❧ WILLOW BOUGH. English, 1887, block print. Clark, no. 35, p. 41; Oman and Hamilton, no. 1065, p. 374; Sugden and Edmondson, color pl. 114. 21" wide, 18" repeat, 11 yds. per roll. Document in Sanderson Archives. No.WM 7614-1 (greens and tan on parchment ground).

SCALAMANDRE

The patterns listed here are screen-printed reproductions of designs by William Morris and Morris & Company.

❧ BORAGE. English, 1888, block print. Oman and Hamilton, no. 1065, p. 375. 20⁷⁄₈" wide, 20⁷⁄₈" repeat, 7 yds. per s/r. Reproduced for North American Branch of William Morris Society. No.WP81240 (pearlized white). Special order.

❧ MORRIS CEILING. English, 1883, block print. Original pattern name was "The Wreath." Oman and Hamilton, no. 1065, p. 374. 21" wide, 21" repeat, 7 yds. per s/r. Reproduced for North American Branch of William Morris Society. No.WP81236-001 (greens, rose, yellow, and beige on snow white).

❧ MORRIS IRIS. English, 1888, block print. Original pattern name was "Iris," designed by John Henry Dearle. Oman and Hamilton, no. 1066, p. 377. 21" wide, 17¹⁄₂" repeat, 7 yds. per s/r. Reproduced for North American Branch of William Morris Society. No.WP81239-001 (greens, multi, and blue blotch). Special order.

❧ MYRTLE. English, 1899, block print. Clark, no. 49, p. 52. 22" wide, 33³⁄₄" repeat, 7 yds. per s/r. Reproduced for North American Branch of William Morris Society. No.WP81237-001 (multi greens, blues, pinks, and yellows).

❧ PIMPERNEL. English, 1876, block print. Clark, no. 19, p. 29; Greysmith, color pl. 22, p. 134; Lynn, color pl. 83, p. 346; Oman and Hamilton, no. 1065, p. 372. 21¹⁄₂" wide, 16¹³⁄₁₆" repeat, 7 yds. per s/r. Reproduced for North American Branch of William Morris Society.

PIMPERNEL, 1876.
Scalamandré.

No.WP81226-001 (multi greens, aqua, gold, and forest-green blotch).

➣ WALLFLOWER. English, 1890, block print. Clark, no. 39, p. 45; Oman and Hamilton, no. 1065, p. 375. 21″ wide, 14½″ repeat, 7 yds. per s/r. Reproduced for North American Branch of William Morris Society. No.WP81233-001 (terra cotta, brick, and salmon on ivory).

SOCIETY FOR THE PRESERVATION OF NEW ENGLAND ANTIQUITIES

➣ JEWETT HOUSE LITHOGRAPH. American, 1880–1920, roller print. Originally printed by Frederick Beck & Company, New York. Nylander, Redmond, and Sander, fig. 65.1. p. 233. 20½″ wide, 15½″ repeat, 7 yds. per roll. Reproduced for Sarah Orne Jewett House, South Berwick, Maine. Document at Society for Preservation of New England Antiquities. Blue and tan.

CUSTOM PATTERNS FROM MUSEUMS

1900 TO 1930:
CHANGING TASTES IN
A NEW CENTURY

The opinions about wallpaper formed during the 1890s had an effect on its use in the 20th-century interior. "The wallpaper is killing me; one of us must go"—Oscar Wilde's reputed last words in 1900 echoed the disdain for wallpapers held by many taste makers. In *The Decoration of Houses*, published in 1897, Edith Wharton and Ogden Codman pronounced wallpaper "inferior as a wall-decoration" and stated emphatically, "These hangings have, in fact, little to recommend them."

Wallpaper manufacturers, however, disagreed. The 1899 brochure of a Worcester, Massachusetts, company claimed that "the decorative possibilities of the new WALL PAPERS are almost boundless." Manufacturers began to produce wallpaper sample books, often twice a year, so that their latest offerings could be distributed nationwide to an eager public. Brochures and pamphlets promoted repapering rooms as an integral part of spring cleaning. Mail-order houses followed the lead of the larger manufacturers. The wallpaper sample books produced by Sears, Roebuck & Company and others present an enormous array of patterns that were available to enhance middle-class homes. They also reveal how inexpensive it was to paper a room. In 1905 one could purchase wallpaper for a room 11 feet by 11 feet, including borders and the ceiling paper, for only 26 cents.

Many wallpaper styles developed in the 1890s remained fashionable into the first decades of the 20th century (consult the previous chapter for appropriate listings). This is especially true of the sidewalls and their wide companion friezes. Many friezes became even wider during this period; their designs filled the entire 18-or 21-inch width of the printing stock. The concept of the wooded forest depicted in Walter Crane's "May Tree Frieze" (page 196) was widely copied. Such friezes were used in combination with painted walls or walls covered with plain papers or wide striped wallpapers.

Floral borders, often incorporating ribbons, enjoyed a renaissance in the years preceding World War I. Note the similarities among

Strawberry Hill Room at Beauport,Gloucester, Massachusetts. The paper installed here is the document on which Brunschwig & Fils's "Beauport Promenade" is based. (Society for the Preservation of New England Antiquities)

"Rosedale" (page 239), "Rose and Ribbon Frieze" (page 237), and "Aurelia" (page 236). Narrower borders were used to form panels on walls papered with plain-colored papers, often of the ingrain or oatmeal type, or wallpapers with small repeating patterns.

Although some block printing was still done in America, most block-printed wallpapers used during this time were imported from England or France. "Beauport Promenade" (page 227) exemplifies the exotic appearance of many of these imports. Other imported patterns were more traditional. Many reproduced 18th-century fabric designs. Others like "Adam" (page 217) and "Dorset" (page 228) were based on late 18th-century neoclassical styles; the inspiration for the design, however, was 18th-century architectural decoration, not 18th-century wallpaper design.

Some elaborate floral designs of the 1850s that had not lost their appeal were still available. William Morris's wallpapers were still considered appropriate and were often used in 20th-century interiors. Most new designs offered by Morris & Company were designed by John Henry Dearle, who became the firm's artistic director after Morris's death in 1896.

The designs advertised as "novelty" papers perhaps hold the most appeal for late 20th-century taste. The term encompasses a wide variety of pattern types and styles: Arts and Crafts—for example, "Accomack" and "Accomack Border" (page 222); tapestry papers—for example, "Gobelin's Forest" (page 232); and Native American motifs—for example, "New Harmony" (page 167). The most appealing of this group to contemporary consumers are the Art Nouveau patterns, listed here and in the previous chapter, which may be more popular today than in their own time. A small interest in Art Nouveau patterns existed; however, Art Nouveau never evolved into a major wallpaper style. In his book *Home Furnishing* (1913) George Leland Hunter dismissed the style saying, "Its sinuous stems and parabolic curves have long since uncoiled themselves into nothingness."

As noted in the introduction, the interest in early wallpapers began to develop in the early 20th century. Scenic wallpapers enjoyed a new round of popularity, and the Zuber factory reissued many of its earlier patterns. In the early 19th century, when they were first imported, they were used only in best parlors, but now these colorful panoramas were considered appropriate for dining rooms and front halls.

In 1924 Nancy McClelland published *Historic Wall-Papers*. In contrast to previous articles, which discussed the "romance" of early wallpapers, this book provided the most accurate information about historic wallpapers available before 1930 and was the standard work on the subject for the next 56 years. McClelland's work as a decorator as well as her writings influenced what was considered appropriate for historic and traditional interiors. She collected wallpaper samples and later had many designs reproduced for sale. She also distributed the block-printed wallpapers made in France by André Mauny, which included many reproductions of 18th-century designs made by his predecessor Robert Caillard.

Modernists took another view. Because the purpose of wallpaper was decorative, not functional, they dismissed it as superfluous. Beginning in the 1930s plain-colored walls and textures became the prevalent treatment for stylish interiors. Having few good examples to emulate, the general public became almost afraid to apply bold patterns to walls. Today this attitude has changed, and colorful patterns are once again returning to the walls of domestic interiors.

BRADBURY & BRADBURY   WALLPAPERS

&❧ BOWER. English, c. 1910, block print. 27" wide, 13½" repeat, 5 yds. per s/r. Code BOW (2 period colorings).

&❧ BRIAR ROSE. English, 1901, block print. Designed by C. F. A. Voysey. Oman and Hamilton, no. 1242, p. 443. 27" wide, 9" repeat, 5 yds per s/r. Adaptation. Document at Victoria and Albert Museum. Code BRW (2 period colorings).

&❧ HONEYSUCKLE. English, 1900–20, block print. 27" wide, 15½" repeat, 5 yds. per s/r. Code HSW (2 period colorings).

&❧ ORCHARD. English, c. 1900, block print. Adaptation of "The Fairyland" by C. F. A. Voysey. Oman and Hamilton, no. 1260, p. 445. 27" wide, 13½" repeat, 5 yds. per s/r. Code ORW (2 period colorings).

&❧ ROSAMUND. English, 1900–20, block print. Designed by Walter Crane. 27" wide, 18" half-drop repeat, 5 yds. per s/r. Code RMW (2 period colorings).

&❧ THISTLE. English, 1900–20, block print. 17" wide, 21" repeat, 5 yds. per s/r. Code THW (2 period colorings).

BRUNSCHWIG & FILS

&❧ APPLEDORE. French, 1920–30, block print. 20" wide, 21" half-drop repeat, 6 yds. per s/r. Document in Brunschwig Archives. No.13828.06 (cream ground).

&❧ ART NOUVEAU TULIP. American, 1900–20, machine print. 24¼" wide, 15¾" repeat. Reproduced for Odessa Historical Society, Odessa, Tex. No.343.6C. Custom order.

&❧ BEAUPORT PROMENADE. English, 1907, block print. 18¼" wide, 34" repeat, 7 yds. per s/r. Adaptation: design slightly enlarged. Document at Beauport, Gloucester, Mass., a property of Society for the Preservation of New England Antiquities. No.13369.06 (black).

&❧ CANDIDE. French, 1900–20, block print. 21" wide, 40¼" repeat. Document in McClelland Collection, Brunschwig Archives. No. 11500.6C. Custom order.

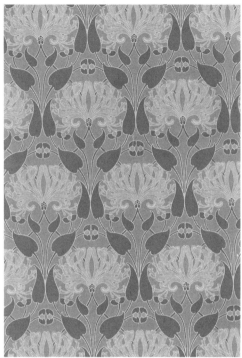

above left
ORCHARD, c. 1900.
Bradbury & Bradbury.

above right
HONEYSUCKLE,
1900–20. Bradbury
& Bradbury.

right
ROSAMUND,
1900–20. Bradbury
& Bradbury.

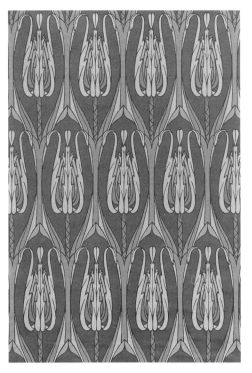 

ॐ TOBACCO LEAF STRIPE. American, 1900–20, machine print. 27" wide, 19" repeat. Reproduced for Odessa Historical Society, Odessa, Tex. No.340.6C. Custom order.

ॐ TULIP STRIPE AND BORDER. American, 1900–10, machine print. 22¾" wide plus 4" border. Reproduced for Odessa Historical Society, Odessa, Tex. No.7885.6C. Custom order.

above left
THISTLE, 1900–20.
Bradbury & Bradbury.

above right
APPLEDORE, 1920–30.
Brunschwig & Fils.

CLARENCE HOUSE

ॐ BELVEDERE. English, 1900–20, block print. 21" wide, 16" repeat, 11 yds. per s/r. Coles Traditional Collection. No.C253 (rose); No.C254 (cream); No.C255 (blue).

ॐ DORSET. English, 1900–15, block print. 21" wide, 18" repeat, 11 yds. per s/r. Coles Traditional Collection. Period colorings: No.C223 (yellow); No.C224 (green); No.C226 (gold).

ॐ SWANS. American or English, 1920–30, machine print. 27" wide, 9" repeat, 5 yds. per s/r. No.9180/1 (brown); No.9180/3 (green); No.9180/4 (silver).

CLASSIC REVIVALS

Authentic Interiors Collection
ॐ AUSTIN. English, 1920–30, machine print. 20½" wide, 20½" repeat. Archival Collection. No.T-209-3A (tan).

above left
BELVEDERE, 1900–20.
Clarence House.

above right
MODERNE CHINOIS,
1920–30. Classic
Revivals (Mauny
Collection).

Mauny Collection

ঌ BOUQUET CHINOIS. French, 1910–30, block print. 17¼" wide, 19" repeat, 11 yds. per roll. No.201 (blues on gray). Block print.

ঌ CAMPANULES. French, 1900–30, block print. 19¾" wide, 10¾" repeat, 11 yds. per roll. Possibly reproduces an earlier design. No.294. Block print.

ঌ CACTUS. French, 1900–30, block print. 21¼" wide, 29" repeat, 11 yds. per roll. No.172 (red, gold, and yellow on blue). Block print.

ঌ FLEURETTE. French, 1900–30, block print. 18½" wide, 15¾" repeat, 11 yds. per roll. No.237 (gray on cream). Block print.

ঌ GRAND PILLEMENT. French, 1900–20, block print. 21⅝" wide, 21⅝" repeat, 11 yds. per roll. Possibly reproduces an earlier design. No.204 (multi on white). Block print.

ঌ GUIRLAND FLEURIE. French, 1900–30, block print. 21¼" wide, 20" repeat, 11 yds. per roll. No.130 (green and orange). Block print.

ঌ INDIEN. French, 1920–30, block print. 18½" wide, 13" repeat, 11 yds. per roll. No.120 (brown and green on white). Block print.

ঌ JARDIN DE MOSSOEL. French, 1915–30, block print. 18½" wide, 37½" repeat, 11 yds. per roll. No.1500 (multi on black). Block print.

ঌ LE MARMOURER. French, 1920–30, block print. 21⅝" wide, 19¼" repeat, 11 yds. per roll. No.209 (multi on cream). Block print.

ঌ MODERNE CHINOIS. French, 1920–30, block print. 19¼" wide,

36$\frac{1}{2}$" repeat, 11 yds. per roll. No.157 (brown and green on tan). Block print.

❧ MONTGOLFIER. French, 1920–30, block print. 24$\frac{3}{4}$" wide, 19$\frac{3}{4}$" repeat, 11 yds. per roll. Possibly reproduces an earlier design. No.280 (red on white). Block print.

❧ MOSAIQUE. French, 1920–30, block print. 23$\frac{5}{8}$" wide, 23$\frac{5}{8}$" repeat, 11 yds. per roll. No.282 (gold and blue). Block print.

❧ PAGODE. French, 1920–30, block print. 27$\frac{1}{2}$" wide, 11 yds. per roll. No.185 (multi on blue). Block print.

❧ PALMETTE VIRGINIE. French, 1920–30, block print. 18$\frac{1}{2}$" wide, 24$\frac{3}{8}$" repeat, 11 yds. per roll. No.240 (gray on buff). Block print.

❧ PETIT MARTIN DE MONSIEUR MEAN. French, 1920–30, block print. 20$\frac{7}{8}$" wide, 20$\frac{7}{8}$" repeat, 11 yds. per roll. No.196 (multi on blue). Block print.

❧ PRIMEVERES. French, 1920–30, block print. 21$\frac{1}{4}$" wide, 40$\frac{1}{4}$" repeat, 11 yds. per roll. No.158 (rust and yellow on cream). Block print.

❧ PROMENADE CHINOISE. French, 1920–30, block print. 26$\frac{3}{8}$" wide, 29$\frac{1}{4}$" repeat, 11 yds. per roll. Possibly reproduces an earlier design. No.216 (multi on cream). Block print.

❧ P. DU ROY. French, 1920–30, block print. 21$\frac{1}{4}$" wide, 7$\frac{1}{8}$" repeat, 11 yds. per roll. No.281 (gold on white). Block print.

❧ ROSACE TOURANTE. French, 1920–30, block print. 20$\frac{1}{2}$" wide, 19$\frac{5}{8}$" repeat, 11 yds. per roll. No.102 (mauve on light blue). Block print.

❧ RUBANS ET FLEURS. French, 1920–30, block print. 21$\frac{5}{8}$" wide, 20$\frac{7}{8}$" repeat, 11 yds. per roll. Possibly reproduces an earlier design. No.298 (multi on cream). Block print.

❧ RUBAN ET PETIT RAYURE. French, 1900–30, block print. 20$\frac{7}{8}$" wide, 20$\frac{7}{8}$" repeat, 11 yds. per roll. No.144 (multi on yellow). Block print.

❧ RUBANS ET RAISINS. French, 1900–30, block print. 24" wide, 32$\frac{1}{4}$" repeat, 11 yds. per roll. No.131 (multi on light yellow). Block print.

❧ SEMIS COQUILLE. French, 1900–30, block print. 18$\frac{1}{2}$" wide, 5$\frac{1}{8}$" repeat, 11 yds. per roll. No.258 (buff on cream). Block print.

❧ SEMIS PLUMES. French, 1900–20, block print. 18$\frac{1}{2}$" wide, 5$\frac{1}{4}$" repeat, 11 yds. per roll. No.254 (gold on off-white). Block print.

❧ TREILLAGE. French, 1920–30, block print. 18$\frac{1}{2}$" wide, 7$\frac{1}{8}$" repeat, 11 yds. per roll. No.148 (gray on light gray). Block print.

❧ VOLUBILIS. French, 1920–30, block print. 22" wide, 10$\frac{3}{4}$" repeat, 11 yds. per roll. No.284 (lavender and black on tan). Block print.

Silvergate Collection

❧ SWEETPEA. English, 1900–20, block print. 21" wide, 21" repeat, 11 yds. per roll. Document at Achnacloich House, Argylshire, England. No.FS046. Block print.

❧ TOWNEND. English, 1900–10, block print. 21″ wide, 18″ repeat, 11 yds. per roll. Document at Townend House, Windermere District, England. No.ES285. Block print.

COWTAN & TOUT

❧ ADAM. English, 1900–10, block print. 21″ wide plus 5″ border, 22″ repeat, 5 yds. per s/r. No.13690 (platinum and white).

❧ LILAC TIME. American or English, 1910–30, machine print. 27″ wide, 20″ repeat, 5 yds. per s/r. No.20159-13 (periwinkle and white).

❧ MISSENDEN MINOR. English, 1900–20, block print. 21″ wide, 10″ repeat, 11 yds. per s/r. No.20544 (beige). Block print.

❧ WINDSOR ROSE. English or American, 1900–20, machine print. 27″ wide, 36″ repeat, 5 yds. per s/r. Adaptation. No.82000 (multi on off-white). Period coloring: No.821000-07 (antique).

CHRISTOPHER HYLAND INCORPORATED

❧ AMOUR ET AGEON. French, 1920–30, block print. 23½″ wide, 25″ repeat, 11 yds. per s/r. No.MN5839 (violet). Block print.

❧ ART DECO ABSTRACT. English or French, 1925–30, block print. 21″ wide, 22½″ repeat, 11 yds. per s/r. No.AB157/1 (lavender on gray).

❧ ART DECO FANS. French, 1925–30, block print. 21″ wide, 11 yds. per s/r. No.AB159/1 (peach).

❧ NINEVEH. English, 1900–30, block or machine print. 18″ wide, 11 yds. per s/r. No.ABNIN (rustic red and old gold).

❧ OPIN. English or French, 1900–30, block print. 21″ wide, 11 yds. per s/r. No.ABOPIN (black and gold).

❧ PARIS, 1930. French, 1930, block print. 20¼″ wide, 22″ repeat, 11 yds. per s/r. No.AB157/1B (peach and beige).

❧ PERROQUETS. French, 1920–30, block print. 19½″ wide, 24″ repeat, 11 yds. per s/r. No.MN5801 (green). Block print.

❧ PASTORALE. French, 1920–30, block print. 21½″ wide, 24″ repeat, 11 yds. per s/r. No.MN2008 (pale blue). Block print.

MT. DIABLO HANDPRINTS

Order by name unless a pattern number is listed.

❧ DRUMMOND MEDALLION STRIPE. American, c. 1910, machine print. 18″ wide, 15″ repeat. Reproduced for Drummond Home, Hominy, Okla. Maroon and gold on cream.

❧ DRUMMOND SEISMIC STRIPE. American, c. 1910, machine print. 18¾″ wide, 15⅜″ repeat. Reproduced for Drummond Home, Hominy, Okla. Umber, gold, and custard on eggshell.

❧ HUMMINGBIRD LATTICE. French, 1900–10, block print. 18¾″ wide, 23¾″ repeat. Reproduced for Kearney Mansion, Fresno, Calif. No.HBW-001 (document greens, creams, and roses on buff).

above left
ADAM, 1900–10.
Cowtan and Tout.

above right
ART DECO ABSTRACT,
1925–30. Christopher
Hyland Incorporated.

left
ART DECO FANS,
1920–30. Christopher
Hyland Incorporated.

above left
PASSION FLOWER,
1900–10. Mt. Diablo
Handprints.

above right
HUMMINGBIRD
LATTICE, 1900–10.
Mt. Diablo Hand-
prints.

right
ROSE LATTICE,
1900–10. Mt. Diablo
Handprints.

◈ PASSION FLOWER. French, 1900–10, block print. 21½" wide, 21" repeat. Reproduced for Kearney Mansion, Fresno, Calif. No.PFW-001 (document greens and mauve on light green).

◈ ROSE LATTICE. French, 1900–10, block print. 20½" wide, 19" repeat. Reproduced for Kearney Mansion, Fresno, Calif. No.RLW-001 (document white, pinks, and greens).

ARTHUR SANDERSON & SONS

◈ LINCOLN. English, 1900–20, machine print. 20¼" wide, 3" repeat, 11 yds. per roll. Adaptation: embossing not reproduced. Document in Sanderson Archives. Period coloring: No.WR 7516-4 (linen).

◈ ROSE AND PEONY. English, 1917, machine print. 20¼" wide, 21" repeat, 11 yds. per roll. Document in Sanderson Archives. Period colorings: No.WR 359-8 (rose and tan); No.WR 359-19 (pink and blue).

◈ ROWAN. English, 1901, block print. Designed by C. F. A. Voysey. 20¼" wide, 18" repeat, 11 yds. per roll. Document in Sanderson Archives. Period colorings: No.WH 7370-3 (fawn on oyster); No.WH 7370-4 (olivewood on black).

◈ THE MANDERIN. English, 1920–30, machine print. 20¼" wide, 20½" repeat, 11 yds. per roll. Document in Sanderson Archives. Period coloring: No.WH 7368-1 (Ming blue on white).

left
ROSE AND PEONY, 1917. Arthur Sanderson & Sons.

above
ROWAN, 1901. Arthur Sanderson & Sons.

ᛏᛏ QUADRILLE. English, 1900–15, block print. 20¼" wide, 4½" repeat, 11 yds. per roll. Document in Sanderson Archives. Period coloring: No.WH 7366-5 (malachite on khaki).

ᛏᛏ WARWICK. English, 1890–1900, block print. 20¼" wide, 24" repeat, 11 yds. per roll. Document in Sanderson Archives. Period colorings: No.WR 7514-2 (pale yellow); No.WR 7514-3 (gray).

SCALAMANDRE

ᛏᛏ BARTON HOUSE. American, 1900–20, machine print. 47½" wide, 18¾" repeat, 3 yds. per s/r. Historic representation. Reproduced for Barton House, Lubbock, Tex. No.WP81104 (brown). Special order.

ᛏᛏ BARTON HOUSE RESTORATION. American, 1900–10, machine print. 36⅜" wide, 22" repeat, 4 yds. per s/r. Reproduced for Barton House, Lubbock, Tex. No.WP 81116-001 (beige and gold tones). Special order.

ᛏᛏ BARTON HOUSE RESTORATION. American, 1900–10, machine print. 27" wide, 26" repeat. Reproduced for Barton House, Lubbock, Tex. No.WP 81126 (red and green on metallic ground). Special order.

ᛏᛏ BARTON HOUSE RESTORATION BEDROOM. American, 1900–10, machine print. 27" wide, 15½" repeat, 5 yds. per s/r. Reproduced for Barton House, Lubbock, Tex. No.WP81110 (pink and green on white). Special order.

ᛏᛏ BARTON HOUSE RESTORATION HALL WALLS. American, 1900–10, machine print. 46¾" wide, 18¾" repeat, 3 yds. per s/r. Reproduced for Barton House. No.WP81105 (beige and brown). Special order.

ᛏᛏ BARTON LILY. American, 1900–10, machine print. 45" wide, 22" repeat, 3 yds. per s/r. Reproduced for Barton House, Lubbock, Tex. No.WP81115 (pink and green on brown). Special order.

ᛏᛏ FRANKLIN D. ROOSEVELT'S HOME—BIRTH ROOM–MORNING ROOM. American, c. 1916, machine print. Originally printed by Thomas Strahan Company. 23" wide, 6¹/₁₆" repeat, 6 yds. per s/r. Historic representation. Reproduced for Home of Franklin D. Roosevelt National Historic Site, Hyde Park, N.Y. No.WP81315-001 (ginger, tan, and white on straw). Special order.

ᛏᛏ FRANKLIN D. ROOSEVELT'S HOME—BEDROOM. American, c. 1916, machine print. 18½" wide, 9½" repeat, 8 yds. per s/r. Reproduced for Home of Franklin D. Roosevelt National Historic Site, Hyde Park, N.Y. No.WP81319-001 (ecru on sand). Special order.

ᛏᛏ FRANKLIN D. ROOSEVELT'S HOME—BOYHOOD ROOM. American, c. 1916, machine print. 21" wide, 20¾" repeat, 7 yds. per s/r. Reproduced for Home of Franklin D. Roosevelt National Historic Site, Hyde Park, N.Y. No.WP81316-001 (pale multi and white on antique white). Special order.

ᛏᛏ FRANKLIN D. ROOSEVELT'S HOME—CHINTZ ROOM. American, c. 1916, machine print. 20½" wide, 21" repeat, 7 yds. per s/r. Repro-

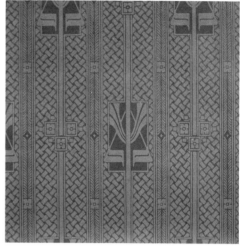

duced for Home of Franklin D. Roosevelt National Historic Site, Hyde Park, N.Y. No.WP81318-001 (multi and metallic gold on ivory). Special order.

ଚ୬ FRANKLIN D. ROOSEVELT'S HOME—PINK ROOM. American or English, c. 1916, block print. 21" wide, 17³/₈" repeat, 7 yds. per s/r. Reproduced for Home of Franklin D. Roosevelt National Historic Site, Hyde Park, N.Y. No.WP81317-001 (rose, pinks, gray, and greens on antique white). Special order.

ଚ୬ GLENRIDGE HALL. American, 1929, machine print. 18" wide, 8" repeat, 8 yds. per s/r. Reproduced for Glenridge Hall, Atlanta, Ga. No.WP81391-1 (rust on cream). Special order.

ଚ୬ GREEN LEAVES BOUQUET. English, 1900–30, machine print. 27" wide, 27" repeat, 5 yds. per s/r. Adaptation: moiré background added. No.WP81393-001 (multi on Persian rose).

ଚ୬ PEARCE-McALLISTER COTTAGE. American, 1920–30, machine print. 28³/₈" wide, 5 yds. per s/r. No.WP81384-001 (caramel and sand on special cream). Special order.

ଚ୬ SAVANNAH TULIP. American, 1900–15, machine print. 27³/₈" wide, 18¹/₂" repeat, 5 yds. per s/r. Reproduced for Historic Savannah Foundation, Savannah, Ga. Document at John Barlow House, Savannah, Ga. No.WP81092 (brown on bisque). Special order.

ଚ୬ SCHREINER ROSE. American, 1900–10, machine print. 19" wide,

above left
FRANKLIN D. ROOSEVELT'S HOME— CHINTZ ROOM, c. 1916. Scalamandré.

above right
BARTON HOUSE, 1900– 20. Scalamandré.

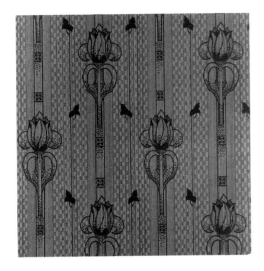

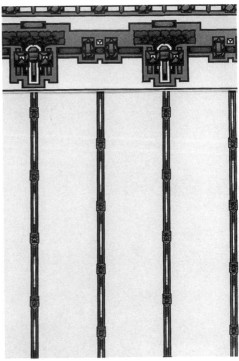

19″ repeat, 8 yds. per s/r. Reproduced for Schreiner Mansion, Kerrville, Tex. No.WP81235-001 (ivory, yellows, old rose, greens, and olive blotch). Special order.

ᔰ SCHREINER STRIPE. American, 1900–10, machine print. 18″ wide, 15³⁄₈″ repeat, 8 yds. per s/r. Reproduced for Schreiner Mansion, Kerrville, Tex. No.WP81244-001 (ivory, yellow, taupe, gold metallic, and beige blotch). Special order.

ᔰ SORRELL-WEED HOUSE. Probably American, 1900–10, machine print. 48″ wide, 22¹⁄₂″ repeat, 3 yds. per s/r. Reproduced for Historic Savannah Foundation, Savannah, Ga. Document at Sorrell-Weed House, Savannah, Ga. No.WP81119-001 (celadon and white). Special order.

ᔰ STANROD MANSION FOYER. American, 1900–10, machine print. 36″ wide, 18³⁄₄″ repeat, 4 yds. per s/r. Reproduced for Stanrod Mansion, Pocatello, Idaho. No.WP81079. Special order.

ᔰ TELLER'S THISTLE. American, 1900–10, machine print. 48″ wide, 20″ repeat, 3 yds. per s/r. Reproduced for Lake House, Central City, Colo. No.WP81145-1 (birch color ground). Special order.

SCHUMACHER

ᔰ GOBELIN'S FOREST. American, 1900–10, machine print. 27″ wide, 25¹⁄₄″ repeat, 4¹⁄₂ yds. per s/r. Document in Schumacher Archive.

Adaptation: pattern enlarged 25 percent. No.512830 (forest green).

✥ GREEN LEAVES LACE STRIPE. American, 1900–15, machine print. 27" wide, 25¼" half-drop repeat, 4½ yds. per s/r. Reproduced for Historic Natchez Foundation. No.504742 (green house).

✥ GREEN LEAVES OAK. American, 1900–15, machine print. 27" wide, 25¼" repeat, 4½ yds. per s/r. Reproduced for Historic Natchez Foundation. No.504670 (forest).

✥ RICHMOND PRIMAVERA. American, 1900–10, machine print. 27" wide, 25¼" repeat, 4½ yds. per s/r. Adaptation. Reproduced for Historic Natchez Foundation. No.504763 (cranberry and green).

✥ SPLATTER TEXTURE. American, 1900–20, machine print. 20½" wide, 12½" repeat, 5½ yds. per s/r. Document in Hobe Erwin Collection, Schumacher Archive. No.506165 (coco).

RICHARD E. THIBAUT

✥ ACCOMACK. American, 1904–20, machine print. 27" wide, 6¼" repeat, 4½ yds. per s/r. Historic Homes of America Collection, produced in collaboration with National Preservation Institute. Document at Harmanson House, Onancock, Va. No.839-T-7976 (rust and ochre on ivory).

✥ ANDOVER. American, 1920–30, machine print. 20½" wide, 19" repeat, 5½ yds. per s/r. No.839-T-7660 (pale orange).

✥ ELIZABETH. American, 1920–30, machine print. 20½" wide, 19" repeat, 5½ yds. per s/r. Historic Homes of America Collection, produced in collaboration with National Preservation Institute. Document at Clarence Wilson House, Gastonia, N.C. No.839-T-7955 (multi on gray).

✥ LORENZO. American, 1910–30, machine print. 20½" wide, 25¼" repeat, 4½ yds. per s/r. Historic Homes of America Collection, produced in collaboration with National Preservation Institute. Document at Lorenzo, Cazenovia, N.Y. No.839-T-7941 (multi on gray).

✥ NEWTON. American, 1900–20, machine print. 27" wide, 12⅝" repeat, 5 yds. per s/r. No.839-T-274 (beige).

VICTORIAN COLLECTIBLES LIMITED

All documents are in the Brillion Collection. Samples from the same collection are at the Cooper-Hewitt Museum, and selected samples are also at the Victoria and Albert Museum.

✥ HERRINGBONE. American, 1900–20, machine print. 27" wide, 36" repeat, 5 yds. per s/r. No.49-001 (brown on brown). Period coloring: No.49-004 (white mica on filagree cream).

✥ ORCHARD HALL. American, 1900–20, machine print. Originally printed by S. A. Maxwell & Company. 24" wide, 19" repeat, 5 yds.

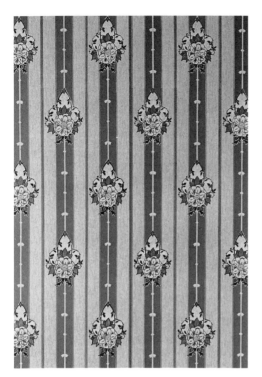 

above left

ORCHARD HALL, 1900–20. Victorian Collectibles Limited.

above right

WELLINGTON HOUSE, 1900–10. Waterhouse Wallhangings

per s/r. No.18-001 (sage and gold on gold string). Period coloring: No.18-003 (brown, gold, and green on straw string).

ও PETITE FLEURS. American, 1900–20, machine print. 28" wide, 29¹/₂" repeat, 5 yds. per s/r. No.40-001 (brown and gold on brown).

WATERHOUSE WALLHANGINGS

ও GEORGETOWN FLORAL. American, 1900–20, machine print. 20¹/₂" wide, 19" repeat, 7 yds. per s/r. Document in Waterhouse Archives. No.192519 (gray-green ground).

ও JARDIN CHINOIS. Probably American, 1915–25, machine print. 22" wide, 21" repeat, 7 yds. per s/r. Document color unknown. Period colorings: No.172519 (gray on white); No.172810 (beige on Chinese red).

ও WELLINGTON HOUSE. American, 1900–10, machine print. 21" wide, 18³/₄" repeat, 5 yds. per s/r. Document in Waterhouse Archives. No.198513 (gold and white on gold). Period coloring: No.198635 (white and gold on ivory).

ZINA STUDIOS

Order by pattern name.

ও OLD GREENWICH. American, 1900–30, machine print. 24" wide, 4" repeat. Green and yellow on gray.

224

CHATEAU-SUR-MER,
1870–80. Scalamandré.
Page 162.

LION AND DOVE
FRIEZE, 1900. Brad-
bury & Bradbury.
Page 235.

BEAUPORT PROMENADE,
1907. Brunschwig &
Fils. Page 211.

DORSET, 1900–15.
Clarence House.
Page 213.

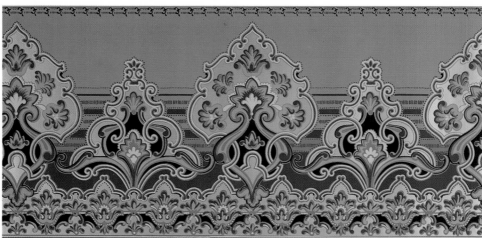

top
TULIP FRIEZE, 1903.
Arthur Sanderson &
Sons. Page 246.

above
STUPA BORDER,
c. 1905. Schumacher.
Page 238.

right
APPLEDORE, 1920–30.
Brunschwig & Fils.
Page 211.

opposite
FRANKLIN ROOSEVELT'S
HOME—PINK ROOM,
c. 1916. Scalamandré.
Page 221.

The following groups include a fill and a frieze.

Classic Revivals

St. James Collection

ॐ BELLEVUE HOMESTEAD FILLER. English, 1900–10, machine print. 21″ wide, 11 yds. per roll. Reproduced by National Trust of Queensland for Bellevue Homestead, Coominya, Queensland, Australia. No.VF4 (deep red); No.VF7 (pink); No.VF21 (antique blue).

ॐ BELLEVUE HOMESTEAD FRIEZE. English, 1900–10, machine print. 16″ wide. Reproduced by National Trust of Queensland for Bellevue Homestead, Coominya, Queensland, Australia. No.VZ4 (deep red); No.VZ7 (pink); No.VZ21 (antique blue).

Mt. Diablo Handprints

Order by name unless pattern number is listed.

ॐ DRUMMOND STRIPE. American, c. 1910, machine print. $18^7/_8$″ wide. Reproduced for Drummond Home, Hominy, Okla. Raspberry and mauve.

ॐ DRUMMOND PANEL. American, c. 1910, machine print. $24^3/_4$″ wide, 22″ repeat. Reproduced for Drummond Home, Hominy, Okla. Raspberry, mauve, and cream.

Victorian Collectibles Limited

All documents are in the Brillion Collection. Samples from the same collection are at the Cooper-Hewitt Museum, and selected samples are also at the Victoria and Albert Museum.

ॐ BRILLION TULIP. American, 1900–20, machine print. Originally printed by Standard Wall Paper Company. 24″ wide, $16^1/_4$″ repeat, 5 yds. per s/r. Adaptation: document color not reproduced exactly. No.22-001 (green, gold, and brown on gold crespi). Period colorings: No.22-002 (browns and pearl on beige weave); No.22-005 (greens, terra cotta, and gold on beige).

ॐ BRILLION TULIP BORDER. American, 1900–20, machine print. Originally printed by Standard Wall Paper Company. 18″ wide, 19″ repeat. Adaptation: document color not reproduced exactly. No.22-051 (green, gold, and brown on gold crespi). Period colorings: No.22-052 (browns and pearl on beige weave). No.22-055 (greens, terra cotta, and gold on beige).

ॐ IVY. American, 1910–20, machine print. 29″ wide, $12^1/_2$″ repeat, 5 yds. per s/r. Adaptation. No.39-001 (gold on cream).

ॐ IVY BORDER. American, 1910–20, machine print. $10^1/_2$″ wide, 19″ repeat. Adaptation. No.39-051 (gold on cream).

ॐ LACEY ROSE. American, 1900–20, machine print. Originally printed by Gledhill Wall Paper Company. 18″ wide plus three 2″ borders, 19″ repeat, 5 yds. per s/r. No.38-001 (tan, pinks, golds, and

COORDINATING
WALLPAPER
PATTERNS

opposite
GOBELIN'S FOREST,
1900–10. Schumacher.
Page 222.

greens on cream). Period coloring: No.38-002 (pinks, golds, and greens on cream).

below left
BELLEVUE HOMESTEAD
FRIEZE, 1900–10.
Classic Revivals
(St. James Collection).

bottom left
BELLEVUE HOMESTEAD
FILLER, 1900–10.
Classic Revivals
(St. James Collection).

below right
LACEY ROSE and border, 1900–20. Victorian Collectibles
Limited.

☙ LACEY ROSE BORDER. American, 1900–20, machine print. Originally printed by Gledhill Wall Paper Company. 18″ wide, 19″ repeat. No.38-051 (tan, pinks, golds, and greens on cream). Period coloring: No.38-052 (pinks, golds, and greens on cream).

☙ LACEY ROSE BORDER (narrow). American, 1900–20, machine print. 9″ wide, 9½″ repeat. Half-scale adaptation of preceding pattern. No.38-061 (tan, pinks, golds, and greens on cream). Period coloring: No.38-062 (pinks, golds, and greens on cream).

☙ NOUVEAU FLEUR. American, 1910–30, machine print. 23″ wide, 9½″ repeat, 5 yds. per s/r. No.37-001 (mint plaid on ivory). Period coloring: No.37-002 (beige plaid on beige weave).

☙ NOUVEAU FLEUR BORDER. American, 1910–30, machine print. 9″ wide, 19″ repeat. No.37-061 (pale pinks, blues, and green on ivory). Period coloring: No.37-062 (greens, brown, gold, and dark mauve on beige weave).

☙ URN. American, 1900–20, machine print. 27″ wide, 18¾″ repeat, 5 yds. per s/r. No.27-001 (gold, and brown on brown).

☙ URN BORDER. American, 1900–20, machine print. 18″ wide, 16″ repeat. No.27-051 (gold and brown on brown).

BRADBURY & BRADBURY

BORDERS

৯৯ LION AND DOVE FRIEZE. English, 1900, block print. Designed by Walter Crane; originally printed by Jeffrey & Company. 26¹/₂" wide, 46" repeat. Document at Victoria and Albert Museum. Code LDF. Special order.

BRUNSCHWIG & FILS

৯৯ AURELIA BORDER. American, 1900–20, machine print. 13" wide, 18³/₄" repeat. Adaptation: bottom motif added. Document in Brunschwig Archives. No.14037.06 (bisque).

৯৯ BOTANICA BORDER. French, 1909–20, block print. 4¹/₂" wide, 20¹/₄" repeat. Document at Musée des Arts Décoratifs. No.13437.06 (red on mauve).

below left
NOUVEAU FLEUR and border, 1910–30. Victorian Collectibles Limited.

৯৯ BOTANICA CORNER. French, 1909–20, block print. 13⁷/₈" wide each side. Document at Musée des Arts Décoratifs. No.13427.06 (red on mauve).

৯৯ MOTHER GOOSE BORDER ON VINYL. English, 1913, roller print. Designed by Mabel Lucy Attwell; originally printed by C. and J. G. Potter. Greysmith, fig. 131, p. 174; Oman and Hamilton, no. 753, p. 277. 8" wide, 18" repeat. Adaptation: document colors not reproduced

below right
URN and border, 1900–20. Victorian Collectibles Limited.

AURELIA BORDER, 1900–20. Brunschwig & Fils.

BOTANICA BORDER and corner, 1909. Brunschwig & Fils.

MOTHER GOOSE BORDER, 1913. Brunschwig & Fils.

below
LOTUS FRIEZE, 1900–10. Classic Revivals (St. James Collection).

and pattern reduced. Document in Brunschwig Archives. Period coloring: No.13630.06 (multi on white).

CLASSIC REVIVALS

Authentic Interiors Collection

&» BOBBIN BORDER. English, 1925–30, machine print. 8¼" wide, 1½" repeat. Archival Collection. No.B-196-8A (orange and yellow).

&» MAPLE LEAF BORDER. English, 1920–30, machine print. 4" wide, 18" repeat. Archival Collection. No.B-210-10A (red, black, and green).

&» ROSE TANA BORDER. English, 1925–30, machine print. 4" wide, 10½" repeat. No.F-177-8A (black and red).

Mauny Collection

&» CHAMPS ELYSEES. French, 1900–20, block print. 2⅞" wide. No.2612. Block print.

&» CORDE. French, 1920–30, block print. 1⅞" wide. No.5001 (series). Block print.

&» SAINT CYR. French, 1910–20, block print. 2¾" wide. No.5006B (blue on pink); No.5006E (orange on yellow). Block print.

&» SERPENTINE. French, 1920–30, block print. 1" wide. No.5000 (series). Block print.

St. James Collection

&» LOTUS FRIEZE. English, 1900–10, machine print. 10½" wide. No.LZ13 (turquoise).

top

RALAHYNE FRIEZE, 1900–10. Classic Revivals (St. James Collection).

above

ROSE AND RIBBON FRIEZE, 1900–10. Classic Revivals (St. James Collection).

მ♣ RALAHYNE FRIEZE. English, 1900–10, machine print. 18" wide. Adaptation: embossing not reproduced. No.HZ16 (drab olive).

მ♣ ROSE AND RIBBON FRIEZE. English, 1900–10, block print. 20" wide. No.RZ7 (pink).

CHRISTOPHER HYLAND INCORPORATED

მ♣ PARIS, 1930, BORDER. French, 1930, block print. 20¼" wide, 22" repeat, 11 yds. per s/r. No.AB157/1A (plum and pearl). Can be used as either a dado or a sidewall.

მ♣ PARIS, 1930, BORDER. English or French, 1920–30, machine print. 6¼" wide, 20½" repeat. No.AB146/4A (plum and pearl).

COWTAN & TOUT

მ♣ ROSEDALE BORDER. English, 1900–20, block print. 4" wide, 21" repeat. No.300 (multi on blue). Block print.

LEE JOFA

მ♣ ROSALIE BORDER. French, 1915–20, block print. 7" wide, 17¼" repeat. Adaptation: document color not reproduced. Period coloring: No.P902250 (multi on yellow).

RICHARD E. THIBAUT

მ♣ ACCOMACK BORDER. American, 1904–20, machine print. 9" wide, 13½" repeat. Historic Homes of America Collection, produced in collaboration with National Preservation Institute. Document at Harmonson House, Onancock, Va. No.839-T-790076 (rust and ochre on ivory).

ARTHUR SANDERSON & SONS

მ♣ VILLE DE LYONS FRIEZE. English, 1911, block print. 18" wide, 20¼" repeat. Adaptation. Document in Sanderson Archives. Period coloring: No.S/B WR 76043-1.

SCALAMANDRE

მ♣ STANROD LIBRARY STRIPE PANEL. American, 1900–20, machine print. 27" wide, 8' panel, 2 panels per s/r. Reproduced for Stanrod Mansion, Pocatello, Idaho. No.WP81073 (green on white). Special order.

მ♣ WISTERIA BORDER. English, 1900–25, block print. 21¼" wide, 26¾" repeat. Historic representation. Reproduced for Leixlip Castle, Kildare, Ireland, in cooperation with Irish Georgian Society. Document color, no. WB81313-99a, is a special order. Period coloring: No.WB81313-001 (coral and spruce on ivory).

SCHUMACHER

მ♣ STUPA BORDER. American, c. 1905, machine print. 13⅝" wide,

ROSEDALE BORDER, 1900–20. Cowtan & Tout.

Original document for "Rosalie Border," a paper of 1915–20 reproduced by Lee Jofa.

13⅞" repeat. Document in Schumacher Archive. No.513010 (document green).

WISTERIA BORDER, 1900–25. Scalamandré.

VICTORIAN COLLECTIBLES LIMITED

All documents are in the Brillion Collection. Samples from the same collection are at the Cooper-Hewitt Museum, and selected

TIFFANY BORDER,
1900–20.
Zina Studios.

samples are also at the Victoria and Albert Museum.

⊰❧ POPPY BORDER. American, 1900–20, machine print. Originally printed by William H. Mairs & Company. 18" wide, 16" repeat. No.32-051 (melon, terra cotta, and green on burgundy).

⊰❧ POPPY BORDER (narrow). American, 1900–20, machine print. 18" wide, 16" repeat. Half-scale adaptation of preceding pattern. No.32-061 (melon, terra cotta, and green on burgundy).

ZINA STUDIOS

Order by pattern name.

⊰❧ TIFFANY BORDER. American, 1900–20, machine print. 9¹/₄" wide, 5" repeat. Green and yellow on gray.

CEILING PAPERS

SCALAMANDRE

⊰❧ BARTON HOUSE RESTORATION BEDROOM CEILING. American, 1900–10, machine print. 48" wide, 12¹/₂" repeat, 3 yds. per s/r. Reproduced for Barton House, Lubbock, Tex. No.WP81136-001 (pinks, greens, white, and mica). Special order.

⊰❧ BARTON HOUSE RESTORATION HALL CEILING. American, 1890–1900, machine print. 48" wide, 1¹/₂" repeat, 3 yds. per s/r. Reproduced for Barton House, Lubbock, Tex. No.WP81110-1 (beige and gold). Special order.

⊰❧ HIRSHFELD HOUSE DOWNSTAIRS MAIN HALL CEILING. American, 1900–20, machine print. 20" wide, 6" repeat, 7 yds. per s/r. Reproduced for Hirshfeld House, Austin, Tex. No.WP81193-001 (metallic silver). Special order.

&» NATHANIEL ORR HOUSE PARLOR. American, 1900–20, machine print. 18" wide, 18⅝" repeat, 8 yds. per s/r. Reproduced for Steilacoom Historical Museum, Steilacoom, Wash. No.WP 81243-001 (ivory, pale greens, pearl, and apricot).

VICTORIAN COLLECTIBLES LIMITED

All documents are in the Brillion Collection. Samples from the same collection are at the Cooper-Hewitt Museum, and selected samples are at the Victoria and Albert Museum.

&» CRACKED ICE. American, 1900–30, machine print. Originally printed by Janeway & Company. 27" wide, 31½" repeat, 5 yds. per s/r. No.47-001 (white mica on white). Period coloring: No.47-005 (white mica on filigree cream).

Anaglypta comes in two weights: Anaglypta Supadurable is the thickness and weight of period Anaglypta, while Anaglypta Original is thinner and was invented in the 1960s to replace the thicker and heavier period product. All Anaglypta patterns listed below were embossed from period rollers. The products come unfinished and must be painted.	RELIEF DECORATIONS— ANAGLYPTA

CROWN DECORATIVE PRODUCTS

Crown Decorative Products are available through Bentley Brothers, Classic Ceilings, and Mile Hi Crown.

&» ANAGLYPTA SUPADURABLE. English, 1938, machine embossed. 20½" wide, 24" repeat, 11 yds. per roll. No.RD 108.

&» ANAGLYPTA SUPADURABLE. English, 1935, machine embossed. 20½" wide, 21" repeat, 11 yds. per roll. No.RD 117.

&» ANAGLYPTA ORIGINAL. English, 1900–20, machine embossed. 20½" wide, 3½" repeat, 11 yards per roll. No.RD 124.

&» ANAGLYPTA ORIGINAL. English, 1933, machine embossed. 20½" wide, 5½" repeat, 11 yards per roll. No.RD 125.

&» ANAGLYPTA SUPADURABLE. English, 1900–30, machine embossed. 20½" wide, 21" repeat, 11 yds. per roll. No.RD 137.

&» ANAGLYPTA SUPADURABLE. English, 1900–30, machine embossed. 20½" wide, 5¼" repeat, 11 yds. per roll. No.RD 148.

&» ANAGLYPTA SUPADURABLE. English, 1900–30, machine embossed. 20½" wide, 5¼" repeat, 11 yds. per roll. No.RD 151.

&» ANAGLYPTA SUPADURABLE. English, 1900–30, machine embossed. 20½" wide, 10½" repeat, 11 yds. per roll. No.RD 160.

&» ANAGLYPTA SUPADURABLE. English, 1900–20, machine embossed. 20½" wide, 10½" repeat, 11 yds. per roll. No.RD 648.

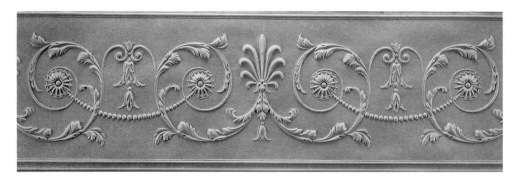

DIANA FRIEZE (top) and ADELPHI FRIEZE, 1900–30. Crown Decorative Products.

ప్ర ANAGLYPTA SUPADURABLE. English, 1920–30, machine embossed. 20$^1/_2$" wide, 10$^1/_2$" repeat, 11 yds. per roll. No.RD 650.

The following patterns were created in the 1960s but have a distinct period look.

ప్ర ANAGLYPTA ORIGINAL. English, machine embossed. 20$^1/_2$" wide, 10$^1/_2$" repeat, 11 yards per roll. No.RD 199.

ప్ర ANAGLYPTA ORIGINAL. English, machine embossed. 20$^1/_2$" wide, 7" repeat, 11 yards per roll. No.RD 326.

ప్ర ANAGLYPTA ORIGINAL. English, machine embossed. 20$^1/_2$" wide, 7" repeat, 11 yards per roll. No.RD 335.

RELIEF DECORATIONS— LINCRUSTA

CROWN DECORATIVE PRODUCTS

Crown Decorative Products are available through Bentley Brothers, Classic Ceilings, and Mile Hi Crown. The products come unfinished and must be painted.

ప్ర ADAM FRIEZE. English, 1900–30, impressed composition. 20$^7/_8$" wide, 21" repeat. No.RD 1955.

ప్ర ADELPHI FRIEZE. English, 1900–30, impressed composition. 10$^5/_8$" wide, 21$^1/_8$" repeat. No.RD 1949.

ప్ర ART NOUVEAU DADO. English, 1906–20, impressed composition. Panel size: 21$^1/_4$" wide, 36" high, 5 panels per box. No.RD 1951.

ప్ర CAMEO FRIEZE. English, 1900–30, impressed composition. 11" wide, 21$^1/_8$" repeat. No.RD 1948.

242

ART NOUVEAU DADO, 1906. Crown Decorative Products.

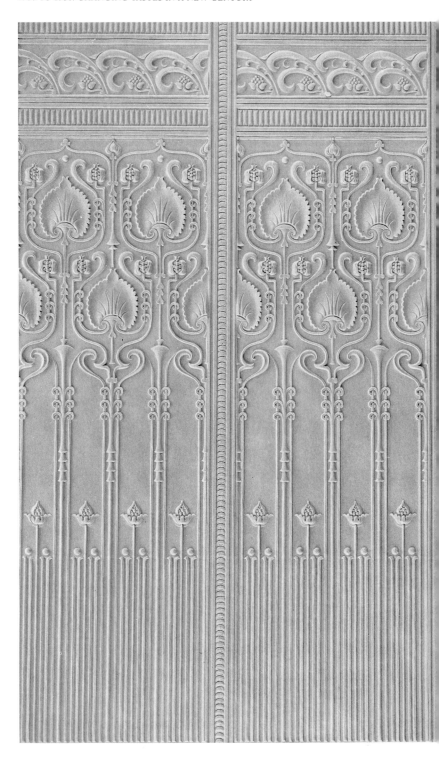

EDWARDIAN DADO,
1906. Crown
Decorative Products.

ᚼ DIANA FRIEZE. English, 1900–30, impressed composition. 11¹/₁₆"
wide, 20¹/₄" repeat. No.RD 1958.

ᚼ EDWARDIAN DADO. English, 1906–20, impressed composition.
Panel size: 24" wide, 40" high, 5 panels per box. No.RD 1950.

ZUBER

ᚼ LES COTES DE VILLEFRANCHE (THE COAST OF VILLEFRANCHE).
French, 1929, block print. Designed by Madame Ehney-Vogler. Total
width: 21' 7"; total height: 12' 10"; 18¹/₂" per panel; 14 panels per
set. Block printed in 8 shades of gray from 157 wood blocks or in 48
colors from 264 blocks.

ᚼ PAYSAGE ITALIAN (ITALIAN LANDSCAPE). French, 1912, block print.
Designed by Arnold Stutz in the style of Antoine Pierre Mongin. Total width: 15'5"; total height: 12' 10"; 18¹/₂" per panel; 10 panels per
set. Block printed in 10 colors from 240 wood blocks.

Zuber also prints a wide variety of wallpapers and borders. The company prefers that inquiries concerning these additional patterns be
made directly to its New York showroom.

BRADBURY & BRADBURY

ᚼ SWEET BRIAR. English, 1911, block print. Designed by J. H. Dearle.
Oman and Hamilton, no. 1076, p. 385. 27" wide, 13¹/₂" repeat, 5 yds.
per s/r. Document at Victoria and Albert Museum. Code SRW. Period
colorings: No.110 (ashes of roses); No.210 (terracotta); No.410 (aesthetic green); No.550 (eucalyptus).

ARTHUR SANDERSON & SONS

Morris & Company's wallpapers were originally printed by Jeffrey
& Company. The original wood blocks are now owned by Arthur
Sanderson & Sons, and the following patterns are printed from
them.

ᚼ ARBUTUS. English, 1903 or 1913, block print. Designed by Kathleen Kersey. Oman and Hamilton, no. 1076, p. 386. 21" wide, 15" repeat, 11 yds. per roll. Document in Sanderson Archives. No.493
(green). Block print.

ᚼ LILY BORDER AND CORNER. English, 1917, block print. Designer
unknown. Oman and Hamilton, no. 1076, p. 384. 3¹/₈" wide,
8³/₄" repeat. Document in Sanderson Archives. Border: No.533
(sage); No.535 (red); No.537 (blue); No.539 (light). Corner:
No.534 (sage); No.536 (red); No.538 (blue); No.540 (light).
Block print.

ORANGE BORDER AND CORNER. English, 1917, block print. Designer unknown. Oman and Hamilton, no. 1076, p. 385. 3¼" wide, 7½" repeat. Document in Sanderson Archives. Border: No.541 (green); No.543 (red); No.545 (bronze); No.547 (light). Corner: No.542 (green); No.544 (red); No.546 (bronze); No.548 (light). Block print.

SWEET BRIAR. English, 1911, block print. Designed by John Henry Dearle. Oman and Hamilton, no. 1076, p. 385. 21" wide, 10½" repeat, 11 yds. per roll. Document in Sanderson Archives. No.482 (green). Block print.

TULIP FRIEZE. English, 1903, block print. Designed by Kathleen Kersey. Oman and Hamilton, no. 1076, p. 388. Document in Sanderson Archives. No.385 (green). Block print.

The following designs by Morris & Company have been transferred to rollers and are printed by machine.

BLACKBERRY. English, 1903, block print. Designed by John Henry Dearle. Oman and Hamilton, no. 1076, p. 386. 21" wide, 18" repeat, 11 yds. per roll. Document in Sanderson Archives. Period coloring: No.WM 7425-1 (rose and green on ivory).

MICHAELMAS DAISY. English, 1912, block print. Designed by John Henry Dearle. Oman and Hamilton, no. 1076, p. 385. 21" wide, 21½" repeat, 11 yds. per roll. Document in Sanderson Archives. No.WM 7313 (series).

SWEET BRIAR. English, 1911, block print. Designed by John Henry Dearle. Oman and Hamilton, no. 1076, p. 385. 21" wide, 10½" repeat, 11 yds. per roll. Document in Sanderson Archives. Period coloring: No.WM 7421-3 (green and apricot on parchment).

CUSTOM PATTERNS FROM MUSEUMS

SOCIETY FOR THE PRESERVATION OF NEW ENGLAND ANTIQUITIES

HAMILTON HOUSE—RECEPTION ROOM. French, c. 1925, block print. 18½" wide, 22½" repeat, 7 yds. per roll. Reproduced for Hamilton House, South Berwick, Maine. Document at Society for Preservation of New England Antiquities. Green on gray.

HAMILTON HOUSE—TWIN ROOM. American, 1920–30, machine print. 18½" wide, 3¼" repeat, 7 yds. per roll. Reproduced for Hamilton House, South Berwick, Maine. Document at Society for the Preservation of New England Antiquities. Gray and white.

HAMILTON HOUSE—YELLOW ROOM. American, 1920–30, machine print. 19" wide, 2¼" repeat, 7 yds. per roll. Reproduced for Hamilton House, South Berwick, Maine. Document at Society for the Preservation of New England Antiquities. White on yellow.

SWEET BRIAR, 1911.
Arthur Sanderson &
Sons.

OTHER WALLCOVERINGS

Grasscloth became a popular wallcovering in the 20th century. Many firms, including Gracie and Scalamandré, can supply grasscloth in a variety of colors and weaves that are appropriate for restoration work.

GRASSCLOTH

Like grasscloth, metallic leaf and tea papers were used extensively in the early 20th century, especially in dining rooms. Most modern metallic papers are distressed or antiqued and therefore only approximate the appearance of the originals. Modern leaf papers are available from Louis W. Bowen, Gracie, Schumacher, and other specialty firms.

LEAF AND TEA PAPERS

Nonrepeating Chinese panels similar in style to those popular in the 18th through the early 20th centuries are available from the following companies: Louis W. Bowen, A. L. Diament & Company, Gracie, and Albert Van Luit and Company (Winterthur Museum Collection). Some of these panels are hand painted.

NONREPEATING CHINESE DESIGNS

Solid stripes were popular from the 1840s to the 1930s. Most firms carry a wide variety of striped wallpapers. Those listed below are only representative examples.

SOLID STRIPES

BRUNSCHWIG & FILS

❧ POMPEIAN STRIPE. English or French, 1850–1910. 27" wide, 5 yds. per s/r. No.13220.06 (series).

COWTAN & TOUT

❧ BALMORAL STRIPE. English, 1880–1900, block print. 21" wide, 2½" stripe, 11 yds. per roll. No.30390 (gray); No.30391 (aqua); No.30395 (blue). Block print.

❧ CLIVEDEN STRIPE. English, 1890–1920, block print. 21" wide, 3½" stripe, 11 yds. per roll. No.29081 (gold and aqua); No.29085 (gold and light rose). Block print.

Wallpaper printing machine at the Centennial Exhibition in Philadelphia, as illustrated in *Harper's Weekly,* December 23, 1876. (Society for the Preservation of New England Antiquities)

❧ MARLBOROUGH STRIPE. English, 1880–1900, machine print. 21" wide, 2¹/₂" stripe, 11 yds. per roll. Period colorings: No.29068 (green); No.29071 (red); No.29077 (dark yellow). Block print.

CHRISTOPHER HYLAND INCORPORATED

❧ CLARENDON. English, 1880–90, block print. 20¹/₂" wide, 11 yds. per roll. No.ZZBL01 (red); No.ZZBL02 (yellow); ZZBL04 (blue and white); ZZBL12 (gray and white).

❧ RAYURE. English, 1870–90. 21" wide, 11 yds. per s/r. No.ZZ2303 (magenta and red).

ARTHUR SANDERSON & SONS

❧ CUMBERLAND. English, 1850–1910, machine print. 20¹/₄" wide, 3¹/₄" stripe, 11 yds. per roll. Document in Sanderson Archives. Period colorings: No.WR 7511-1 (Chinese yellow); No.WR 7511-2 (claret); No.WR 7511-5 (bottle).

❧ MONTPELIER. English, 1840–60, block print. Originally printed by William Woollams & Company. 20¹/₄" wide, 1¹/₂" stripe, 11 yds. per roll. Document in Sanderson Archives. Period colorings: No.WH 7365-1 (blue and white); No.WH 7365-2 (red and white).

❧ SUSSEX. English, 1913–30, machine print. 20¹/₄" wide, 1" stripe, 11 yds. per roll. Document in Sanderson Archives. Period colorings: No.WR 7519-1 (regency red); No.WR 7519-2 (empire green).

THE TWIGS

❧ MRS. KEPPLE STRIPE. French, 1850–90, block print. 26³/₄" wide, alternating wide and narrow stripes, 5 yds. per s/r. No.97100/03 (light beige and dark gray); No.97100/005 (green and gray); No.97100/008 (maize and sage); No.97100/009 (bone and yellow).

WATERHOUSE WALLHANGINGS

❧ TOWNHOUSE STRIPE. Probably American, 1890–1910, machine print. 20¹/₂" wide, 2¹/₂" stripe, 7 yds. per s/r. Document in Waterhouse Archives. Period colorings: No.189518 (yellow and white); No.189488 (beige and white); No.189484 (light and dark blue); No.189635 (brown and white); No.189613 (gray and white); no. 189540 (maroon).

TOILES

In the late 19th and early 20th centuries, many wallpaper patterns were inspired by late 18th-century toiles or plate-printed fabrics. Specific patterns are not listed here because most of the toile patterns available today are direct copies of textiles. These patterns should be reviewed for consideration if a toile-patterned wallpaper is discovered in the course of a restoration project.

SUPPLIERS

Many of the firms listed are wholesale houses whose products are available to the trade only. This means that their wallpapers are sold only through interior designers, architects, and the decorating departments of fine retail and furniture stores. Some of these papers are also available through large wallpaper stores. In some cases, the firms will sell wallpapers directly to nonprofit institutions such as museums, historical societies, preservation organizations, and state-owned historic properties; in other cases, they may refer interested people to their local representative. Arrangements for custom reproductions should always be made through the manufacturer's main office.

LOUIS W. BOWEN. 200 Garden City Plaza, Garden City, NY 11530, (516) 741-9440

BRADBURY & BRADBURY ART WALLPAPERS. P.O. Box 155, Benicia, CA 94510, (707) 746-1900

BRUNSCHWIG & FILS. 979 Third Avenue, New York, NY 10022-1234, (212) 838-7878.

J. R. BURROWS & COMPANY. P.O. Box 522, Rockland, MA 02370, (617) 982-1812

CLARENCE HOUSE. 211 East 58th Street, New York, NY 10022, (212) 752-2890

CLASSIC REVIVALS INC. One Design Center Place, Boston, MA 02210, (617) 574-9030

COLE & SON LTD. P.O. Box 4 BU, 18 Mortimer Street, London W1A 4BU, England (available in the United States exclusively through Clarence House)

COLEFAX & FOWLER. Available through Cowtan & Tout

COWTAN & TOUT. 979 Third Avenue, New York, NY 10022, (212) 753-4488

CROWN DECORATIVE PRODUCTS

East Coast distributor: Bentley Brothers, 2709 South Park Road, Louisville, KY 40219, (800) 824-4777

West Coast distributor: Classic Ceilings, 902 East Commonwealth Avenue, Fullerton, CA 92631, (800) 922-8700

Mile Hi Crown. 1925 Blake Street, Suite 100, Denver, CO 80202

A. L. DIAMENT & COMPANY. P.O. Box 230, Exton, PA 19341, (215) 363-5660

GALACAR & COMPANY. 144 Main Street, Essex, MA 01929, (508) 768-6118

GRACIE. 979 Third Avenue, New York, NY 10022, (212) 753-5350

CHRISTOPHER HYLAND INCORPORATED. 979 Third Avenue, New York, NY 10022, (212) 688-6121

LEE JOFA INC. Headquarters: 800 Central Boulevard, Carlstadt, NJ 07072, (201) 438-8444. Showroom: 979 Third Avenue, New York, NY 10022

KATZENBACH & WARREN. 23645 Mercantile Road, Cleveland, OH 44122, (216) 464-3700

MT. DIABLO HANDPRINTS, INC. 473 E. Channel Road, Benicia, CA 94510, (707) 745-3388

ARTHUR SANDERSON & SONS. 979 Third Avenue, New York, NY 10022, (212) 319-7220

SCALAMANDRE. Showroom: 950 Third Avenue, New York, NY 10022, (212) 980-3888. Mill: Executive offices: 37-24 24th Street, Long Island City, NY 11101, (718) 361-8500

F. SCHUMACHER & COMPANY. Showroom: 939 Third Avenue, New York, NY 10022, (212) 415-3900. Main office: 79 Madison Avenue, New York, NY 10016, (212) 213-7900

RICHARD E. THIBAUT, INC. 706 South 21st Street, Irvington, NJ 07111, (201) 399-7888

THE TWIGS. 5700 Third Avenue, San Francisco, CA 94124-2609, (415) 822-1626

VICTORIAN COLLECTIBLES LIMITED. 845 East Glenbrook Road, Milwaukee, WI 53217, (414) 352-7290

ALBERT VAN LUIT & COMPANY. 23645 Mercantile Road, Cleveland, OH 44122, (216) 464-3700

WATERHOUSE WALLHANGINGS. 99 Paul Sullivan Way, Boston, MA 02118, (617) 423-7688

ZINA STUDIOS, INC. 85 Purdy Avenue, Port Chester, NY 10573, (914) 937-5661

ZUBER & CIE. 979 Third Avenue, New York, NY 10022, (212) 486-9226

CUSTOM ORDERS THROUGH MUSEUMS

ESSEX INSTITUTE. Museum Shop, Essex Institute, 132 Essex Street, Salem, MA 01970, (508) 744-3390

GUNSTON HALL. Gift Shop, Gunston Hall, Lorton, VA 22079, (703) 550-9220

HISTORIC DEERFIELD, INC. J. G. Pratt Museum Store, Historic Deerfield, Inc., Box 321, Deerfield, MA 01342, (413) 774-5581

POCUMTUCK VALLEY MEMORIAL ASSOCIATION. Curator, Memorial Hall Museum, Memorial Street, Deerfield, MA 01342, (413) 774-7476

SOCIETY FOR THE PRESERVATION OF NEW ENGLAND ANTIQUITIES. Reproductions Coordinator, Society for the Preservation of New England Antiquities, 141 Cambridge Street, Boston, MA 02114, (617) 227-3956

STRAWBERY BANKE MUSEUM. Museum Shop, Strawbery Banke Museum, P.O. Box 300, Portsmouth, NH 03802, (603) 433-1114

GLOSSARY

ADAPTATION. A modern wallpaper that retains the overall appearance of the original document although certain changes have been made in the design. The term may apply also to a modern wallpaper produced as a companion to a reproduction fabric.

ANAGLYPTA. A patented embossed wallcovering made from paper and cotton. The color is applied after the paper is hung.

BLOCK PRINTING. A process in which color is transferred to paper by means of a carved wood block.

BLOTCH. A term for a silk screen that prints a solid color. Blotch screens are often used to print the ground color of a reproduction wallpaper.

COLORWAY. A manufacturing term for identifying the predominant color or colors of a wallpaper design. Reproduction wallpapers are often available in several colorways. The document colorway copies the colors of the original wallpaper. The other colorways in which the reproduction design is available are created by the manufacturer to be compatible with modern decorating needs. Colorways that have a distinct period look are listed in this book as period colorings.

DADO. The lower portion of the wall of a room, between the baseboard and the chair rail, often decorated differently from the upper section.

DOCUMENT. The original wallpaper whose design and color are copied for a reproduction wallpaper.

DOCUMENT COLORWAY. See colorway.

FILL. An alternative name for a wallpaper when it is used in combination with a frieze or dado paper; also called a sidewall.

FRIEZE. An alternative name for a wide border.

FLOCKING. A textured surface created by adding chopped textile fibers that adhere to the paper.

GROUND. The background color of a wallpaper design.

HISTORIC REPRESENTATION. A term used by Scalamandré for a reproduction wallpaper in which the scale or composition has been altered slightly because of modern technological limitations.

INGRAIN PAPER. See oatmeal paper.

INTERPRETATION. A modern wallpaper in which one or more motifs from a document wallpaper are reworked into a new design.

LINCRUSTA. A patented composition in which the raised design is impressed with rollers. Color is applied after installation.

MACHINE PRINTING. See roller printing.

MULTI. A modern manufacturing term for a colorway containing many colors.

OATMEAL PAPER. A textured paper made from pulp consisting of colored cotton or wool rags.

PAINTED PAPER. An 18th-century term for wallpaper.

PIECE. An 18th-century term for a roll of wallpaper.

PLAIN PAPER. A wallpaper decorated only with the ground color.

REPEAT. The dimension of one complete design element in a wallpaper.

REPRODUCTION WALLPAPER. A modern wallpaper that faithfully copies the design, color, and scale of an original wallpaper document.

ROLLER PRINTING. A process in which color is transferred to a moving roll of paper by the raised surface of a metal cylinder.

ROOMSET. A modern term for a complete decorative wallpaper scheme that includes coordinated wall and ceiling patterns.

SANDWICH. Layers of wallpaper applied over a period of time. These are studied during historical research to determine the chronological sequence of application and the previous decorative styles of a historic building.

SCREEN PRINTING. A process, similar to stenciling, in which color is deposited on paper through a design cut into a fabric screen.

SERIES. A term for all the colorways of a particular pattern.

SIDEWALL. A term used to differentiate the wallpaper used on the wall from a border or dado paper; also called field or fill.

BIBLIOGRAPHY

This bibliography cites books and articles that will be useful for inquiry into the history and use of wallpapers as well as the history of interior decoration. Both Oman and Hamilton's *Wallpapers* and Lynn's *Wallpapers in America* include extensive bibliographies. *Wallpapers in Historic Preservation* contains an excellent list of 19th-century publications that discuss contemporary attitudes toward wallpaper. The first edition of *Wallpapers for Historic Buildings* contains photographs of many reproduction wallpapers that are not illustrated in this edition.

Ackerman, Phyllis. *Wallpaper: Its History, Design, and Use.* 2d ed. New York: Tudor Publishing Co., 1938.

Adams, Stephen. *The Arts and Crafts Movement.* London: Quintet Publishing, 1987.

Alswang, Hope, and Donald C. Pierce. *American Interiors: New England and the South: Period Rooms at the Brooklyn Museum.* Brooklyn, N.Y.: Brooklyn Museum, 1983.

Aslin, Elizabeth. *The Aesthetic Movement: Prelude to Art Nouveau.* New York: Frederick A. Praeger, 1969.

Ayers, James. *The Shell Book of the Home in Britain: Decoration, Design, and Construction of Vernacular Interiors, 1500–1850.* London: Faber and Faber, 1981.

Banham, Joanna, Sally Macdonald, and Julia Porter. *Victorian Interior Design.* New York: Crescent Books, 1991.

Barnes, Joanna. *A Decorative Art: 19th-Century Wallpapers in the Whitworth Art Gallery.* Manchester, England: The Whitworth Art Gallery, 1985.

Bulletin de la Société Industrielle de Mulhouse, Special issue, "Musée du Papier Peint," no. 793 (1984).

Clark, Fiona. *William Morris: Wallpapers and Chintzes.* London: Academy, 1973.

Clouzot, Henri, and Charles Follot. *Histoire du Papier Peint en France.* Paris: Editions D'Art Charles Moreau, 1935.

"Conservation of Historic Wallpaper," Special issue of the *Journal of the American Institute for Conservation of Historic and Artistic Works*, Spring 1981.

Cooke, Clarence. *The House Beautiful*. New York: Scribner, Armstrong, and Company, 1878.

Cooper-Hewitt Museum. *Wallpapers in the Collection of the Cooper-Hewitt Museum*. Washington, D.C.: Smithsonian Institution Press, 1981.

Cooper, Nicholas. *The Opulant Eye: Late Victorian and Edwardian Taste in Interior Design*. London: Architectural Press, 1976.

Cornforth, John. *English Interiors 1790–1848: The Quest for Comfort*. London: Barrie and Jenkins, 1978.

———. *The Inspiration of the Past: Country House Taste in the Twentieth Century*. New York: Viking, 1985.

———. *The Search for Style: Country Life and Architecture 1897–1935*. London: Andre Deutsch, 1988.

———. "Vitality and Variety: The Musée du Papier Peint at Rixheim, near Mulhouse, France," *Country Life*, April 9, 1987, pp. 138–42.

———. "The Vitality of Papier Peint," *Country Life*, July 11, 1985, pp. 103–6.

Davidson, Caroline. *Women's Worlds: The Art and Life of Mary Ellen Best 1809–1891*. New York: Crown Publishers, 1985.

Dornsife, Samuel A. "Wallpaper." In *The Encyclopaedia of Victoriana*, edited by Harriet Bridgeman and Elizabeth Drury. New York: Macmillan, 1975.

Downing, A. J. *The Architecture of Country Houses, with Remarks on Interiors, Furniture*. New York, 1850. Reprint. New York: Dover, 1969.

Dresser, Christopher. *Studies in Design*. London, 1876. Reprinted as *The Language of Ornament*. New York: Portland House, 1988.

Eastlake, Charles L. *Hints on Household Taste*. London, 1868. 4th ed., 1878. Reprint. New York: Dover, 1969.

Entwisle, Eric A. *The Book of Wallpaper*. London: Arthur Barker, 1954.

———. *French Scenic Wallpapers 1800–1860*. Leigh-on-Sea, England: F. Lewis, 1972.

———. *A Literary History of Wallpaper*. London: B. T. Batsford, 1960.

———. *Wallpapers of the Victorian Era*. Leigh-on-Sea, England: F. Lewis, 1964.

Forge, Suzanne. *Victorian Splendor: Australian Interior Decoration 1837–1901*. Melbourne: Oxford University Press, 1981.

Fowler, John, and John Cornforth. *English Decoration in the 18th Century*. Princeton, N.J.: Pyne Press, 1974.

Frangiamore, Catherine Lynn. *Wallpapers in Historic Preservation.* Washington, D.C.: National Park Service, U.S. Department of the Interior, 1977.

————. "Wallpaper: Technological Innovation and Changes in Design and Use." In *Technological Innovation and the Decorative Arts: Winterthur Conference Report 1973*, pp. 277–305. Charlottesville: University Press of Virginia, 1974.

————. "Wallpapers Used in Nineteenth Century America," *The Magazine Antiques*, December 1972, pp. 1042–51.

Garrett, Elisabeth Donaghy. *At Home: The American Family 1750–1870.* New York: Harry N. Abrams, 1990.

Gere, Charlotte. *Nineteenth-Century Interiors: The Art of the Interior.* New York: Harry N. Abrams, 1989.

Giouard, Mark. *Life in the English Country House: A Social and Architectural History.* New Haven: Yale University Press, 1978.

————. *Sweetness and Light: The "Queen Anne" Movement 1860–1900.* New Haven and London: Yale University Press, 1977.

————. *The Victorian Country House.* Rev. ed. New Haven and London: Yale University Press, 1979.

Gordon-Clark, Jane. *Paper Magic.* London: Frances Lincoln Limited, 1991.

Greysmith, Brenda. *Wallpaper.* New York: Macmillan, 1976.

Guibert, Mireille. *Papiers Peints, 1800–1875.* Paris: Société des Amis de la Bibliothèque Forney, 1980.

Halen, Wildar. "Christopher Dresser and the Aesthetic Interior," *The Magazine Antiques*, January 1991, pp. 256–67.

Hamilton, Jean. *An Introduction to Wallpaper.* London: Her Majesty's Stationary Office, 1983.

Hotchkiss, Horace. "Wallpaper Used in America, 1700–1850." In *The Concise Encyclopedia of American Antiques*, edited by Helen Comstock, vol. 2, pp. 488ff. New York: Hawthorne Books, 1958.

Hunter, George Leland. *Home Furnishing.* New York: John Lane Company, 1913.

In Pursuit of Beauty: Americans and the Aesthetic Movement. New York: The Metropolitan Museum of Art, 1986. See particularly Catherine Lynn, "Decorating Surfaces: Aesthetic Delight, Theoretical Dilemma" and "Surface Ornament: Wallpapers, Carpets, Textiles, and Embroidery."

Jackson-Stops, Gervase, and James Pipkin. *The English Country House: A Grand Tour.* Boston: Little, Brown, 1985.

Jacqué, Bernard, and Odile Nouvel-Kammerer. *Le Papier Peint Décor d'Illusion.* Schirmeck: Editions Jean-Pierre Gyss, 1986.

Jones, Chester. *Colefax & Fowler: The Best in English Decoration.* Boston: Little, Brown, 1989.

Jones, Owen. *The Grammar of Ornament*. 1856. Reprint. London: Bernard Quantritch, 1910.

Katzenbach, Lois, and William Katzenbach. *The Practical Book of American Wallpaper*. Philadelphia: J. B. Lippincott Company, 1951.

Kelly, Robert, ed. *Wallpaper Reproduction News*. Published four times a year. Lee, Mass.

Kaplan, Wendy. *"The Art That Is Life": The Arts and Crafts Movement in America, 1875–1920*. Boston: Museum of Fine Arts, 1987.

Lancaster, Clay, ed. *New York Interiors at the Turn of the Century*. New York: Dover, 1976.

Landsun, Susan. *Victorians at Home*. New York: Viking, 1981.

Leopold, Alison Kyle. *Victorian Splendor: Re-creating America's 19th Century Interiors*. New York: Stewart, Tabori, and Chang, 1986.

Loudon, J. C. *An Encyclopaedia of Cottage, Farm, and Villa Architecture and Furniture*. London: Longman, Brown, Green, and Longmans, 1833.

Lynn, Catherine. *Wallpaper in America from the Seventeenth Century to World War I*. New York: W. W. Norton & Co., 1980.

Mayhew, Edgar de N., and Minor Myers, Jr. *A Documentary History of American Interiors from the Colonial Era to 1915*. New York: Charles Scribner's Sons, 1980.

McClelland, Nancy V. *Historic Wall-Papers from Their Inception to the Introduction of Machinery*. Philadelphia and London: J. B. Lippincott, 1924.

———. *The Practical Book of Decorative Wall Treatments*. Philadelphia and London: J. B. Lippincott, 1926.

Murphy, Phyllis, comp. *The Decorated Wall: Eighty Years of Wallpaper in Australia, c. 1850–1930*. Elizabeth Bay: Historic Houses Trust of New South Wales, 1981.

Musée des Arts Décoratifs. *Trois Siècles de Papiers Peints*. Paris: Musée des Arts Décoratifs, 1967.

Naylor, Gillian, ed. *William Morris by Himself: Designs and Writings*. Boston: Little, Brown, and Company, 1988.

Nouvel, Odile. *Wallpapers of France 1800–1850*. New York: Rizzoli, 1981.

Nouvel-Kammerer, Odile, ed. *Papier Peints Panoramiques*. Paris: Flammarion, 1990.

Nylander, Richard C. "Elegant Late Nineteenth-Century Wallpapers," *The Magazine Antiques*, August 1982, pp. 284–87.

———. "English Wallpaper in New England," *Country Life*, April 26, 1979, pp. 1304–7.

———. "Wallpaper and the Historic House." Slide tape. Nashville, Tenn.: American Association for State and Local History, 1977.

———. "Wallpaper Before 1830," *Early American Life*, February 1980, pp. 40–43.

————. *Wallpapers for Historic Buildings: A Guide to Selecting Reproduction Wallpapers.* 1st ed. Washington, D. C.: Preservation Press, 1983.

Nylander, Richard C., Elizabeth Redmond, and Penny J. Sander. *Wallpaper in New England.* Boston: Society for the Preservation of New England Antiquities, 1986.

Olligs, Heinrich, ed. *Tapeten: Ihre Geschichte bix zur Gegenvart.* 3 vols. Brunswick: Klinkhardt & Breimaun, 1970.

Oman, Charles C. *Catalogue of Wallpapers, Victoria and Albert Museum.* London: 1929.

Oman, Charles C., and Jean Hamilton. *Wallpapers: An International History and Illustrated Survey from the Victoria and Albert Museum.* New York: Abrams, 1982.

Parry, Linda. *William Morris and The Arts and Crafts Movement: A Design Source Book.* New York: Portland House, 1989.

Peterson, Harold L. *Americans at Home.* New York: Scribner's, 1971. Reissued as *American Interiors: From Colonial Times to the Late Victorians.* New York: Scribner's, 1979.

Praz, Mario. *An Illustrated History of Furnishing from the Renaissance to the Twentieth Century.* New York: Braziller, 1964. Reissued as *An Illustrated History of Interior Decorating from Pompeii to Art Nouveau.* New York: Thames on Hudson, 1982.

Reichlin, Ellie, Jean Caslin, and Dan Younger. *A Photographic Intimacy: The Portraiture of Rooms, 1865–1900. Nineteenth-Century Photographs of Domestic Interiors from the Collections of the Society for the Preservation of New England Antiquities.* Boston: SPNEA and the Photographic Resource Center, 1984.

Sanborn, Kate. *Old Time Wall Papers.* Greenwich, Conn.: Literary Collector Press, 1905.

Saunders, Gil. *Ornate Wallpapers.* Exeter, England: Webb & Bower with the Victoria and Albert Museum, 1985.

Seale, William. *Recreating the Historic House Interior.* Nashville, Tenn.: American Association for State and Local History, 1979.

————. *The Tasteful Interlude: American Interiors Through the Camera's Eye, 1860–1917.* New York: Praeger, 1975. Nashville, Tenn.: American Association for State and Local History, 1981.

Stickley, Gustav. *Craftsman Homes.* New York: Craftsman Publishing Company, 1909.

Sugden, Alan V, and J. L. Edmondson. *A History of English Wallpaper, 1509–1914.* New York: Scribner's, 1925; London: B. T. Batsford, 1926.

Teynac, Françoise, Pierre Nolot, and Jean-Denis Vivian. *Wallpaper: A History.* New York: Rizzoli, 1982.

Thornton, Peter. *Authentic Decor. The Domestic Interior: 1620–1920.* New York: Viking Penguin, 1982.

Tunander, Ingemar. *Tapeter i Sverige.* Vasteras, Sweden: ICA Bokfor-log, 1984.

Watkins, Walter Kendell. "The Early Use and Manufacture of Paper-Hangings in Boston," *Old-Time New England*, January 1922, pp. 109–19.

Wells-Cole, Anthony. *Historic Paper Hangings from Temple Newsam Collection and from Other English Houses.* Leeds, England: Leeds City Art Galleries, 1983.

Wheeler, Candace. *Principles of Home Decoration.* New York: Double-day, Page, and Company, 1908.

Whitworth Art Gallery. *Historic Wallpapers in the Whitworth Art Gallery.* Manchester, England: Whitworth Art Gallery, 1972.

Winkler, Gail Caskey, and Roger W. Moss. *Victorian Interior Decoration: American Interiors 1830–1900.* New York: Henry Holt, 1987.

Woods, Christine, ed. *Sanderson, 1860–1985.* London: Arthur Sanderson & Sons, 1985.

SOURCES OF INFORMATION

AMERICAN SOCIETY OF INTERIOR DESIGNERS. 608 Massachusetts Avenue, N.E., Washington, D. C. 20002, (202) 546-3480

THE ANTIQUARIAN AND LANDMARKS SOCIETY, INC. 394 Main Street, Hartford, CT 06103, (203) 247-8996

COLONIAL WILLIAMSBURG FOUNDATION. P.O. Box C, Williamsburg, VA 23187, (804) 229-1000

COOPER-HEWITT MUSEUM. Smithsonian Institution, 2 East 91st Street, New York, NY 10028, (212) 860-6898

ESSEX INSTITUTE. 132 Essex Street, Salem, MA 01970, (508) 744-3390

HISTORIC CHARLESTON FOUNDATION. 51 Meeting Street, Charleston, SC 29401, (803) 723-1623

HISTORIC DEERFIELD. Deerfield, MA 01342, (413) 774-5581

HISTORIC SAVANNAH FOUNDATION. P.O. Box 1733, Savannah, GA 31402, (912) 233-7787

METROPOLITAN MUSEUM OF ART. 82nd Street and Fifth Avenue, New York, NY 10028, (212) 879-5500

MUSEE DES ARTS DECORATIFS. Palais du Louvre, Pavillon de Marsan, 107 rue de Rivoli, 75001 Paris, France

MUSEE DU PAPIER PEINT. 28 rue Zuber, 68170 Rixheim, France

MUSEUM OF ART, RHODE ISLAND SCHOOL OF DESIGN. 2 College Street, Providence, RI 02903, (401) 331-3511

MUSEUM OF EARLY SOUTHERN DECORATIVE ARTS. P.O. Box 10310, Winston-Salem, NC 27108, (919) 721-7360

NATIONAL PRESERVATION INSTITUTE. National Building Museum, Judiciary Square, N.W., Washington, DC 20001, (202) 272-3606

OLD STURBRIDGE VILLAGE. One Old Sturbridge Road, Sturbridge, MA 01566, (508) 347-3362

SOCIETY FOR THE PRESERVATION OF NEW ENGLAND ANTIQUITIES. 141 Cambridge Street, Boston, MA 02114, (617) 227-3956

STRAWBERY BANKE MUSEUM. P.O. Box 300, Portsmouth, NH 03802, (603) 433-1100

VICTORIA AND ALBERT MUSEUM. Exhibition and Cromwell Roads, London, England SW7 2RL

THE VICTORIAN SOCIETY IN AMERICA. 219 East Sixth Street, Philadelphia, PA 19106, (215) 627-4252

WHITWORTH ART GALLERY. Oxford Road, Manchester, England M15 6ER

WILLIAM MORRIS SOCIETY. 420 Riverside Drive, 7D, New York, NY 10025

WINTERTHUR MUSEUM AND GARDENS. Route 52, Kennett Pike, Winterthur, DE 19735, (302) 888-4600

AUTHOR

Richard C. Nylander is curator of collections for the Society for the Preservation of New England Antiquities in Boston, Massachusetts. Coauthor of *Wallpaper in New England*, he lectures extensively and has published numerous articles on historic wallpapers and period interiors in both popular and scholarly journals. He has served as a consultant for many historic house restorations and is a member of the Committee for the Preservation of the White House.